International Series on Public Policy

The International Series on Public Policy—the official series of International Public Policy Association, which organizes the International Conference on Public Policy—identifies major contributions to the field of public policy, dealing with analytical and substantive policy and governance issues across a variety of academic disciplines.

A comparative and interdisciplinary venture, it examines questions of policy process and analysis, policymaking and implementation, policy instruments, policy change & reforms, politics and policy, encompassing a range of approaches, theoretical, methodological, and/or empirical.

Relevant across the various fields of political science, sociology, anthropology, geography, history, and economics, this cutting edge series welcomes contributions from academics from across disciplines and career stages, and constitutes a unique resource for public policy scholars and those teaching public policy worldwide.

All books in the series are subject to Palgrave's rigorous peer review process: https://www.palgrave.com/gb/demystifying-peer-review/792492.

Anne Bellon

A Socio-History of Internet Policies

Weaving the Digital State in France

palgrave
macmillan

Anne Bellon
University of Technology
of Compiègne
Compiègne, France

ISSN 2524-7301 ISSN 2524-731X (electronic)
International Series on Public Policy
ISBN 978-3-031-69098-3 ISBN 978-3-031-69099-0 (eBook)
https://doi.org/10.1007/978-3-031-69099-0

"English translation of the original French edition published by Editions du Croquant, Vulaines-sur-Seine, 2022"

Translation from the French language edition: "L'Etat et la toile. Des politiques de l'internet à la numérisation de l'action publique" by Anne Bellon, © Editions du Croquant 2022. Published by Editions du Croquant. All Rights Reserved.

This Palgrave Macmillan imprint is published by the registered company Springer Nature Switzerland AG
The registered company address is: Gewerbestrasse 11, 6330 Cham, Switzerland

List of Interviews

1. Male, hacker activist, member of *La Quadrature du net*, 29/10/2013
2. Male, hacker activist, member of *La Quadrature du net*, 5/5/2014
3. Male, hacker activist, member of *La Quadrature du net*, 12/11/2014
4. Male, hacker activist*, 19/11/2014
5. Male, hacker activist, member of *La Quadrature du net*, 4/12/2014
6. Male, library curator and jurist, member of *La Quadrature du net*, 8/1/2015
7. Female, ecologist MP (2012–2017) in charge of digital issues, 10/02/2015
8. Male, digital advisor to N. Sarkozy's presidential campaign, General Secretary of the HADOPI, 17/3/2015
9. Male, digital advisor in the government (2012–2017), 12/8/2015
10. Male, hacker activist, 15/2/2016
11. Male, activist, coordinator of the campaign against the Hadopi law, 23/2/2016
12. Female, researcher and commons activist, 2/3/2016
13. Male, software engineer, digital advisor to the President (2017–2022), 4/3/2016

14. Male, Socialist MP (1997–2017) in charge of digital rights, 3/21/2016
15. Male, activist and permanent member of *La Quadrature du Net*, 22/3/2016*
16. Female, right-wing MP (2007–2021) in charge of digital issues, 23/3/16
17. Male, *Conseiller d'État*, former digital advisor to the French Ministry of Culture and the President (2007–2012), 29/3/2016
18. Male, Socialist MP (1988–2012), 27/4/2016
19. Male, digital entrepreneur and consultant, founder of FING, 6/5/2016
20. Male, former digital advisor for the Minister of Culture (2002–2005), 9/5/2016
21. Male, right-wing MP (2007–2017) in charge of IT and the digital Economy, 24/5/2016
22. Male, former digital advisor to the Prime Minister (2002–2005), 24/5/2016
23. Male, digital expert, Internet Forum, 27/5/2016
24. Male, digital expert, 28/5/2016
25. Female, *Vecam* association, former CNIL commissioner, 30/5/2016
26. Male, president of the X-Internet association, 1/6/2016
27. Female, researcher, founder of AUI and IRIS, 2/6/2016
28. Male, Communist MP (2002–2007), 8/6/2016
29. Male, hacker activist, 9/6/2016
30. Male, MTIC member, digital advisor to the Minister of Civil Service (2000–2002), 9/6/2016
31. Male, founding president of AFNet, 13/6/2016
32. Female, member of *Vecam*, 13/6/2016
33. Male, IT specialist, general delegate of APRIL, 14/6/2016
34. Male, jurist, intellectual property officer at the Ministry of Culture, 17/6/2016
35. Male, activist, digital expert, 20/6/2016
36. Female, former President of the Internet Forum, former President of the CNIL, 11/7/2016
37. Male, former digital advisor to the Prime Minister (1997–2002), 11 interviews between July 2016 and September 2017
38. Male, activist, director of institutional affairs at Google France, 22/7/2016

39. Male, digital consultant, former president of CNNum, 22/7/2016
40. Male, right-wing MP (1988–2017), 27/7/2016
41. Female, Socialist MP (2007–2017), 12/9/2016
42. Male, founder of *Admiroutes*, 12/9/2016
43. Male, former digital advisor to the French Ministry of Culture (2000–2002), 19/9/2016
44. Male, Law and Economics professor at Harvard University, 26/9/2016
45. Male, Law and Technology professor at Harvard University, 5/10/2016
46. Female, Law and Technology professor at Berkeley University, 2/11/2016
47. Male, Law and Technology professor at Stanford University, 8/11/2016
48. Female, Law and Technology professor at Berkeley University, 16/11/2016
49. Female, Law and Technology professor at George Washington University, 6/12/2016
50. 50. Male, digital expert, founder of *L'Atelier* and *Club de l'Arche*, 8/12/2016
51. Female, digital legal expert, member of AUI, 15/12/2016
52. Male, former digital advisor to the French Ministry of Culture (2000–2002), 27/12/2016
53. Male, scientific advisor to the Ministry of Culture, 3/1/2017
54. Male, director of IT services at the Ministry of Culture, 9/1/2017
55. Female, digital entrepreneur, 24/1/2017
56. Male, digital entrepreneur, 3/2/2017
57. Male, digital entrepreneur, 3/15/2017
58. Male, lawyer and digital activist, 10/7/2017
59. Male, former deputy director of cabinet at the Deputy Ministry of Digital Affairs (2014–2017), 9/14/17
60. Male, director of cabinet at the Ministry Delegate for the Digital Economy (2012–2014), 2/10/2017
61. Male, lawyer and activist, Head of the office of digital policy at the Ministry of Culture, 11/28/2017
62. Male, digital advisor of the Prime Minister (2014–2017), 1/12/2017
63. Male, digital advisor of the President (2009–2012), 7/2/2018

64. Male, director of cabinet Deputy Ministry of Digital Affairs (2014–2017), 8/10/2019
65. Male, former director of information services at IRD, *Vecam* activist, 5/26/2020
66. Male, *Vecam* activist, biblio-fr founder, 6/25/2020

Contents

List of Figures

Chapter 5

Chapter 6

Chapter 7

List of Tables

List of Boxes

CHAPTER 1

Introduction

Whether they seek to regulate platforms, fight online hate, protect personal data, provide broadband network coverage or resist cyber-attacks, national governments are caught up in an increasingly dense web of digital infrastructures and exchanges. For governments, the Internet has sometimes been considered as a space of opportunities to be conquered, sometimes as a territory "to be civilized".[1] Its development led to the emergence or the resurgence of public issues, such as the erosion of privacy or the proliferation of false information. Despite the omnipresence of digital issues in Western politics, Internet policies continue to raise questions and even generate contention. They are regularly called into question for being ineffective, intrusive or arbitrary. Witness, for example, recent debates on the powerlessness of the State when faced with Big Tech, the abusive surveillance of citizens carried out by national agencies, or widening inequalities in accessing digital public services. Internet policies—as a large set of public policies related to or based on the Internet—are a domain of public action with blurred contours, which embodies the numerous challenges to State intervention in our largely globalized and digitized societies.

With the widespread development of computer networks at the end of the 1990s, the State has come up against the Internet, a world presented

[1] Extract of French President Sarkozy's speech at the e-G8, May 24, 2011.

A. Bellon, *A Socio-History of Internet Policies*, International Series on Public Policy, https://doi.org/10.1007/978-3-031-69099-0_1

as an opposite, and a competitor: libertarian, decentralized, changing and borderless, the characteristics of the Internet contradict the very logic of bureaucracies and governmental intervention, which aim at defining sustainable, centralized tools for control, organization and coercion. Can national states make this complex world governable? How did they gain a foothold in the digital world? And what common features unite the disparate set of actions tied to the public handling of the Internet?

To answer these questions, this book offers to untangle the complex relationship between the State and the Internet, a relationship between a set of institutions in charge of public policies and services on the one hand and, on the other, a socio-technical infrastructure that now structures our economy, our public space and even our personal relationships. Yet, the State and the Internet should not be understood as two abstract entities that face each other. On the contrary, they have social and historical depth. The State and the Internet are complex social worlds made of individuals, with various cultures, resources and interests, who often navigate both worlds, and sometimes resemble each other more than they pretend to differ. Between moments of exacerbated opposition and the growing collaboration of public agencies with tech giants, the ties between the State and the Internet have been gradually created, undone and strengthened.

While the "digital revolution" seems frozen in an eternal recent past, this book explores the changing relationship between the State and the Internet as part of the long-term evolution of digital technologies and the reshaping of public action. If the digital changes that have taken place in public organizations are undeniable, this book offers a genealogical and historical investigation that questions the naturalization and immediacy of digital technologies within administrations. In other words, it refuses to take for granted the assumption of a State that has been reformed "from the outside" by digital technology or against it. Above all, it reveals the uncertainties met by political power as a result of rapid technological change. Far from an unequivocal path, the governments' handling of the Internet calls into question the ability of state agents to anticipate technological change and, above all, to accompany and adapt to it.

The resulting narrative begins at the origins of networked computing, in the 1960s, at the heart of America's military-industrial-scientific complex, where various interests, mindsets and ideals coexisted. Following the worldwide expansion of the Internet, it then moves on to Europe where the web was invented as the main application of the network enabling information browsing and content sharing. It delves into the 1990s, a period of enthusiasm and experimentation sparked by the digital imagination. It then explores the beginning of the twenty-first century as a time of disillusionment, with the bursting of the Internet bubble, copyright battles and the development of State surveillance on the Internet. It ends with the advent of a "Government as a Platform" promoted by Western leaders, along with new policies using digital technologies as an answer to various social issues.

Along the way, this book tackles several well-established myths—the birth of the Internet as a sole military or cyberlibertarian project, for example—and sheds light on forgotten aspects of Internet history—such as the fierce opposition of French telecoms to Internet development in the mid-1990s. While the history of the network and its policies has often taken the United States as a main case study, this book bridges the gap between the two sides of the Atlantic, studying national variations of Internet policies in Europe. The extension of the Internet to the old continent was not simply a transposition of US digital culture to European countries. It was accompanied by specific resistances, new appropriations and hybridizations and relied on sometimes long-standing support for open communications networks. In this respect, France is a particularly interesting example. First it is the home of the "Internet that could have been" and a country where the development of alternative networks to the Internet has been pushed the furthest. Often presented as an emblematic model of centralized management of technological innovation, the French case allows us to describe the slow dilution of techno-scientific policies in a generalized neo-liberalization of State's technological action.

In a single historical movement, the story told by this book thus reveals how the State has come to terms with the Internet and has contributed to its shape and its development. Doing so, it demonstrates the gradual domestication, by technocratic agents, of a technological infrastructure, which, in many respects, seemed designed to resist them. At a time of widespread digitization, it discusses the new forms of political power in the digital era.

In the end, this book takes a fresh look at this history, not just by *looking at* the State but rather by adopting *the point of view of* the State, paying close attention to the power relations that run through it and the properties of those who embody it. Doing so, it responds to and completes a now abundant literature which, while presenting the progressive hold of governments on digital space, has excessively reified the properties of national states, to the point of ignoring the profound upheavals induced by the Internet.

1 Between the "Digital Revolution" and the State's "Counter-Revolution"

Since the development of the Internet, a great deal of research—not only in political science, but also in law or information and communication sciences—has sought to describe the relationship between the State and the Internet.

This vast literature initially comprised a series of works discussing the weakening of state bureaucracy in the face of the digital revolution : the political properties of the Internet, an open, borderless and decentralized network, were contrasted with those of the State, which appeared excessively centralized and rigid. In 1997, communication sociologist Manuel Castells announced in his best-selling book on the *Information Age* that, with the Internet, "computer-mediated communication is escaping the control of nation-state, ushering in a new era of extra-territorial communication" (Castells, 1996, p. 312). In the field of law, scholars of the 1990s were discussing whether state regulation would be made obsolete, in favor of a "cyberspace law" that would consider the specific properties of digital spaces (e.g. Johnson & Post, 1996; Kahin & Nesson, 1997). As a consequence, specific modes of regulation—by code (Lessig, 1999)—or of governance—decentralized and multipartite (e.g. Bygrave & Bing, 2009; Johnson et al., 2004)—became the subject of scholarly attention, to the detriment of traditional public policies. These new forms of political power distribution were as much studied as promoted, as they were deemed to foster better regulation, efficiency and democratic governance in the information age (Johnson et al., 2004). The digital revolution was considered to hold great promise, translated into political experiments in political parties or public administrations. The development of Wikipedia and free software communities (Benkler, 2006), the first world summits on the information society (Klein, 2002), or the Arab Spring (Snider & Faris, 2011) are only some examples of the transformation of power relations made possible by the Internet, bypassing the central role of the State in the organization and control of societies.

Yet this enthusiastic literature was soon met by a rapidly growing bulk of research on the everlasting power of States after the digital revolution. As early as 1997, James Boyle (1997) was warning "digital libertarians" about the many ways in which nation states could use privatized enforcement and technologies to keep their grip on societies. He notably drew on Foucault's conception of power and its challenge to the acception of power as mere sovereignty, showing how governmental control can also be exercise through "surveillance" and "discipline" (1979, 1999). Foucault also introduced the concept "governmentality" to describe logics of power that aim at directing, constraining and framing behaviors—a conception particularly fit to technological infrastructures that provide instruments of control beyond the law, through the mediation of technical resources, such as software, algorithms and operating systems (Badouard et al., 2016; Lessig, 1999). Following this idea, many works have asserted the permanence of traditional forms of state violence in the digital society: surveillance, censorship and the repression of protest movements did not end with the development of the Internet—quite the contrary. At first, these academics focused on authoritarian governments, such as Russia (Morozov, 2012), China or Iran (Deibert et al., 2008)—emblematic examples, if any were needed, of the limits of Internet-mediated emancipation. But these critical accounts also concerned Western democracies, notably after September 11. The field of "surveillance studies" (Lyons, 2007) in particular has played a major role in highlighting the State's stranglehold on networks, enrolling private actors in the control of digital communication (Birnhack & Elkin-Koren, 2003; Cartwright, 2020). Attentive to the infrastructure of surveillance, these studies describe the advent of a new technological governmentality, which confines rather than liberates individuals. The Internet scandals of the twenty-first century—and notably the Snowden's revelations of NSA surveillance in 2013—have confirmed as much as reinforced these critical analyses (Bauman et al., 2014; Lyon, 2015). In the field of political participation as well, many scholars have demonstrated the limits of democratization and emancipation through information technologies. They study how power structures have resisted the cyberspace revolution and annihilated the political aspirations of activists, and even favor conservative movements (e.g. Margolis & Resnick, 2000; Schradie, 2019; Tüfekçi, 2017). Closer to our case study, Felix Tréguer (2019) has described the decline of the "Internet utopia" in France, or the failure of an emancipatory project in the face of constantly renewed control strategies developed by economic and governmental powers.

By opposing the State and the Internet as two antagonistic worlds, these works conclude on the victory of the former over the latter, extending the empire of its control over the web of digital exchanges. In the end, they have contributed to a "counter-revolutionary" rhetoric in response to the early enthusiasts of the digital revolution. In a pioneering book on *Networks and the State*, Milton Mueller (2010) drew the following unambiguous conclusion: "Yes, there has been a counter-revolution, as States and other incumbent powers have fought back against these disruptions and innovations, asserting their sovereignty and coming up with new ways to border or regulate the Internet" (p. 11). The resistance of bureaucratic structures, the hijacking of participatory mechanisms and the alliances between political and capitalist elites would have contributed to the collapse of the revolutionary project promoted by the digital pioneers. The titles of famous books in this vein speak for themselves: *Politics as Usual* (Margolis & Resnick, 2000), *The Revolution that wasn't* (Schradie, 2019), *The Net Delusion* (Morozov, 2012) …as if the advent of digital technology had changed nothing.

2 Digital Technologies, Bureaucratic Politics and Policy Change

Yet, this conclusion tends to overlook the undeniable changes that have taken place over the past twenty years in public organizations and modes of government. They miss the omnipresence of digital technology within national states, the rhetoric of the digital revolution in the mouths of our leaders and the institutionalization of its models and representative forms in public action. They also seem to ignore the ever-present contestation of new Internet laws in Western countries, the difficulty governments have in regulating a digital space fortified by the presence of major transnational players and the permanence and ever-increasing sophistication of tools for resisting or circumventing public control. In fact, both the "cyber enthusiast" and "counter-revolutionary" discourses have reified the State and the Internet as antagonistic entities. They pitted an unchanging utopia that Internet pioneers defined nearly forty years ago against a homogeneous State, reduced to its most coercive institutions.

Indeed, these various works have often stayed out of the State, studying it from the outside, ignoring the debates that the development of the Internet has sparked within it, and the power relations it has transformed. Far from being unified entities, national states, particularly in the face of the Internet, have been divided between competing agencies, ministry departments and institutions. Digital technologies have been unevenly distributed and endorsed, and in many public administrations, the use of algorithms goes along with the persistence of paper files, and smartphones coexist with leather-bound binders. It is high time that political sociology opens up the black box of the State and understands what has really been going on in public administrations since the digital revolution.

This book thus offers to re-inscribe the study of State-Internet relationships in the perspective of bureaucratic politics and historical institutionalism. The first tradition argues that public policies are the result of an increasingly complex decision-making process, characterized by conflict, coordination, bargaining, and compromise, inside and between bureaucratic organizations, which are more or less autonomous from the government (e.g. Allison, 1969; Bach & Wegrich, 2019; Hart & Wille, 2012). Recent development along these lines have enhanced, in a comparative perspective, the specific features of these processes shaped by bureaucracies' relations to their government and other external actors, as well as the principles and rationales that guide their action (Brierley et al., 2023; Dahlström & Lapuente, 2022). Adopting this perspective means taking into account the different preferences, resources and cultures that coexist and sometimes collide within the State. In this book, we consider that Internet policies reveal specific configurations of organizations that may vary along space and time. Regarding the historical institutionalism perspective, its sociological approach has mostly been interested in the emergence and persistence of institutions, as the formal and informal foundations of political behaviors and public policies (DiMaggio & Powell, 1983; Hall, 1986; Thelen & Steimo, 1992). It emphasizes how changes in the political and socioeconomic context can bring new actors into the game, or reconfigure coalitions pushing for new institutional arrangements (Emmenegger, 2021; Mahoney & Thelen, 2009; Pierson, 1993). It has also put forward the role of ideas in fostering or preventing institutional changes (Blyth, 2002; Culpepper, 2008). In the case of the Internet, it invites us to discuss how organizational cultures and beliefs clash over technological policies, and how unprecedented coalitions between Internet and administrative players can bring changes within public administration.

We argue that the approach provided by these two scholarly traditions can reconcile the paradoxical assessment of a State that has been both challenged and reinforced in the digital age. More generally, the book is nourished by the strong conviction that the Internet, as an element destabilizing bureaucratic routines, constitutes a strategic observation point to grasp the transformation of modes of government in Western countries. The sustained pace of technological innovation, the globalization of trade, the growing power of transnational players, the spread of liberalism and the mutations of capitalism are all challenges studied by political sociology to explain recent transformations in public action, particularly in the fields of finance and the environment. Interestingly enough, these different phenomena also converge around the arrival and international development of the Internet, characterized by the questioning of borders, the succession of innovations and the emergence of new economic giants such as Google, Amazon and Facebook. Between the disappearance of the State, the reduction of its social action and the privatization of public intervention, the book helps to contest the timeless "myth of the powerless State" (Weiss, 1998) showing the many ways in which public agents preserve their capacity for action in the digital society.

Our stance goes even further to defend the idea that the development of the Internet has gone along with a "bureaucratic revolution", which concerns both the use of information technologies by the administration and the ways in which digital markets are governed. Against the idea that bureaucracies are only vectors of conservatism or immobilism, Max Weber already considered that they could produce social change, through the operation of technical devices (Weber, 1978). In this vein, the concept of "bureaucratic revolution" has been mobilized by various traditions in French political sociology to account for changing housing policies brought about by newcomers in the administrative elites (Bourdieu & Christin, 1990) or, for the part played by State in the liberal transformation of society (Le Galès & Scott, 2008).

However, the aim of this book is not to assert the indestructible power of the State, as the proponents of the State's counter-revolution have done. Rather, it is a study of the debates and transformations that the Internet has brought about and made possible within public administrations and governments. It highlights the dynamics of Internet policies and how they can nurture the understanding of state transformation, more specifically contributing to three domains of bureaucratic politics and policy change: the sociology of state reform, the institutionalization of policy domains and the transformation of the power elite.

2.1 *Internet as a New Policy Domain?*

Bureaucratic politics organize public action through the differentiation of various policy domains to which different ministerial portfolios are associated (Browne, 1995; Burstein, 1991; Laumann & Knoke, 1987; Muller, 1985). Yet even after 40 years of existence, the Internet does not refer to a stabilized category of state intervention. In many countries, there is no "ministry of the Internet" on which to focus our attention, but rather ephemeral institutions. The public handling of the Internet is also characterized by changing administrative terminology. At the end of the 1990s, policymakers spoke of "information society" or "multimedia" policies, "e-commerce" and "NICT", and more recently the "digital" word is ubiquitous, which refers to algorithms, platforms, big data and even the development of artificial intelligence. This semantic vagueness comes on top of a certain institutional precariousness. Combined with it, it reflects the lasting illegitimacy of the State in the digital world.

The Internet is an elusive political object: to grasp it, we need to hold together a patchwork of policies and organizations.

For while the administrative boundaries of the Internet remain blurred, they nonetheless refer to tangible realities for those in charge within the State: an economic sector, made up of start-ups, access providers and online service companies, a set of principles and ideas, such as the protection of online rights or the defense of net neutrality; and finally, an arsenal of technological instruments, from applications to platforms. The case of Internet policies thus sheds light on new forms of institutionalization, articulating "*sector*", "*causes*" and "*instruments*" as the main features of new policy domains. These hybrid institutionalizations are linked to recomposed public bureaucracies, diversifying their institutional forms and modes of action. In this regard, the Internet is not so different from environmental or gender policies, policy domains with cross-cutting ramifications that break from historically established bureaucratic boundaries. In fact, just like the Internet, these new policies invite us to examine the cross-sectoral and multilayered aspect of State governance in the twenty-first century.

More than that, the Internet appears as a laboratory for a new organization of public policies, as a project for reconfiguring the very logics of public action. Indeed, the multiple issues linked to the development of the Internet have not given rise to lasting institutions and norms, but rather to a plurality of public policies that cut across all ministries—economy, education, culture and defense. In each of these domains, the digital revolution has transformed and challenged established procedures and routines. The domestication of the Internet across the State shows the paradoxical effects of this transversal and rapid institutionalization. We observe the erosion of Internet's original culture and causes on the one hand, and the widespread adoption of digital logics and models in public action on the other. As our story unfolds, we will see the category of "Internet" disappearing from public discourse and programs in favor of the vague notion of "digital" action. The latter holds together various policies which, while addressing issues as diverse as the fight against online hate or data protection, claim to share the same conception of the Internet and public action, inspired by the political forms, players and instrument of the digital world. The book is thus at the same time a socio-history of Internet policy and of the transformation of all public policies through technological development. It investigates the gradual shift from the Internet as a field of intervention with impossible boundaries to digital technologies a core instruments for the reinvention of public action.

2.2 *Internet and the Reinvention of the State*

One of the challenges of this book is to reintegrate the process of Internet domestication by the State into the long history of administrative reform. From the 1980s to the beginning of the twenty-first century, nation states have indeed changed profoundly, both in terms of governance and administrative organization. A rich literature has studied these changes through two major trends: first, the spread of economic rationality and managerial tools as central instruments of a "New Public Management" or NPM (e.g. Hood, 1991; Pollitt et al., 2007), second, a shift toward the use of legal authority and regulation over tools of stabilization and redistribution characterizing the advent of a "Regulatory State" in Europe (e.g. Majone, 1994; Loughlin and Scott 1997; Moran 2002). Yet, these major diagnoses have often overlooked the place and role of digital technologies in these recent changes, nor have they discussed how these transformations relate to the almost concomitant advent of the information society.

One needs to borrow from the history of science and technology to find a rich conceptualization of how information devices, from paper to screen, have played a part in the elaboration of complex bureaucracies throughout the twentieth century (Agar, 2003; Gardey, 2008). Bridging the gap between these two literatures, the book offers new insight into the ways in wich Internet development contributed to the continuation, deepening or adaptation of the managerial and regulatory State in Europe. From "e-government" programs (Tolbert et al., 2008; West, 2000) to the "Government as a Platform" (O'Reilly, 2011) new policies have indeed tried to use digital technologies to reinvent public administration. Although echoing NPM and governance reforms, they differ regarding both the instruments they promote and the intellectual tradition they draw on (Dunleavy et al., 2006). In this book, we do not separate reform programs according to the successive technologies they use, from computer software to artificial intelligence (Jeffares, 2021): we rather discuss what holds together a global project for transforming the State in the information age, inspired by the Internet, as an infrastructure, as a culture and a mode of organization. Drawing on the Net pioneers' critique of bureaucracy, reform policies have indeed defended a more open, efficient, simplified and participatory government that would learn from hackers' experimentation, digital firms' innovation and peer-to-peer production. Yet the digital reinvention of the State should not be understood as a mere reduction of public intervention. It has rather been defended as an opportunity to redeploy the State's modes of existence and action in the digital society. Following Bezes' idea that public reforms can be understood as moments of neo-bureaucratization or re-bureaucratization of the administration (Bezes, 2009), this book analyzes how digital technologies have indeed become new means of bureaucratic control in a neoliberal society. To do so, it examines the translation from the Internet culture to digital public reform programs. It studies the exchanges and interaction between the Internet world and the bureaucratic field, the policies they have built together or opposed about, and the changes they provoked within the State.

2.3 *The Internet and the State Elite*

The State does not act homogeneously in front of the digital revolution. In the spirit of bureaucratic politics, one needs to deconstruct this artificial unity and put back at the center of the analysis the various agents who embody the State and act on its behalf, agents whose role has been largely neglected by the literature on Internet policies. More specifically, the book offers an analysis "from the top", focusing mainly on the specific resources and trajectories of members of the executive government, in keeping with the political sociology dedicated to the "power elites" (Mills, 1956; Scott, 2008; Wedel, 2017) or more recently to "policy elites" (Saunders, 2022; Smyrl & Genieys, 2016). Members of the elite debated over the proper role of the State in steering technological innovation and the way it should adapt to the Internet revolution. From claims of modernity to accusations of incompetence, from "technophobia" to the "geek" stigma, digital technologies have been part and parcel of local strategies and struggles for defining and implementing a new set of public policies for innovation and communication. The advent of the Internet, for example, saw a relative erosion of the power of civil engineers within the State and of their hold on the conduct of technological innovation. Conversely, it has brought new players at the top of the government, whose careers move between public administration and private firms. The latter showcase their proximity to the Internet culture and digital organizations as a resource for transforming the State and reinventing its modes of action. More generally, through their knowledge and atypical careers, they actively participated in the reshaping of public–private interdependencies, particularly around Internet's regulation.

The book thus contributes to analyzing the figure of the "digital" civil servant, and the ways in which he has imported into the administration the instruments and culture associated with the Internet. Over the period under study, digital civil servants have indeed promoted the use of the digital technologies as much in the name of preserving their capacity for action in the information society as in the service of the global transformation of the State. They have advocated and created new organizations and institutions that came to symbolize the advent of a digital governmentality. Studying this group also provides an opportunity to renew our understanding of "institutional" or "policy entrepreneurs" (DiMaggio, 1988; Hardy & Maguire, 2008, Petridou & Mintrom, 2021), "state modernizers" or "bureaucratic revolutionaries" (Bourdieu, 2018) and exhibit new models that inform institutional change as well as the trivialization of reform policies.

In the current context, painting the portrait of this new elite is also of particular importance for political history, insofar as they have helped to define and deploy the agenda of neoliberal governments in Europe, rallying representatives of the digital economy around the banner concepts of "Government as a Platform" or the "Start-up Nation". The study of these actors is part of a broader project to develop a social anatomy of neoliberal reforms, combining the privatization of State intervention with the widespread digitization of public action. Understanding these intersecting issues is among the main challenges currently facing public policy analysis and the studies of public administration, the ramifications of which—for democracy, governance and economic development—are tentacular.

3 Investigating a Split Fieldwork

To analyze these developments, the book is based on a four-year investigation that offers fieldwork insight on Internet policies, the study of which has until now often been reduced to oppositions between a priori ideologies or rationalities. Confronting major players' narratives, this fieldwork is first and foremost based on 66 extensive interviews with key figures in the construction of Internet policies in France.[2] They enabled us to grasp the variety of practices, discourses and interactions through which the government of the Internet has been organized. By multiplying points of view on the making of Internet policies, the survey obeys a principle of constant displacement which, by diversifying the places of observation, reveals links, circulations or oppositions between them.

The book takes the reader from the computer labs of the Silicon Valley to the discreet salons of French government ministries. It follows the threads of the web winding in and around the State, bringing to light hitherto little-documented exchanges between public administrations and Internet communities. The chapters bring to life the French Internet meetings that took place in a small mountain town in the 1990s, as well as "geeky" gatherings in the basements of the BNP bank in Paris, high places of digital sociability largely forgotten today, where senior civil servants, hackers and activists crossed paths in the days of a nascent Internet.

Although digital technologies have been the occasion for fertile exchanges between tech-savvy people, the development of the Internet and its regulation have also given rise to strong oppositions between public officials and Internet activists. Navigating on either side of this

[2] See list of interviewees in appendix. Authorization to quote the interviews was granted by all the interviewees and the use of real names was consented to in most cases. As many of the interviewees can be identified by the position they held at the French government, full anonymization was not possible, which was also agreed by concerned interviewees. Some digital activists asked not to be recognized, in which case their names were changed, along with any identifying details.

"split fieldwork" (Ollion, 2017), the book questions this allegedly impassable boundary between the State and the Internet by going back to emblematic debates such as copyright battles or online surveillance. It confronts the rationalities of those who elaborated Internet policies with those who challenged them. Doing so, the book sheds light on worlds little known to the public, illuminated here by prolonged immersions: ministerial cabinets, places where public policies are formalized, on the one hand, but also hacker conventions, where resistance to the incursions of central powers into the digital space is organized. Studying these venues, which are organized by highly codified practices and languages, allows us to put into perspective opposing visions of the Internet and the challenges of its regulation. But by moving from one to the other, the fieldwork also nuances the strength of these divisions and bring to light points of transition and even hybridization between entrepreneurial, activist and bureaucratic practices.

Betting on extensive sociological fieldwork entails strong methodological choices. Although interested in the global spread of the Internet and its encounter with a new European regulatory State, the book focuses essentially on France as its main case of study. This national case was chosen for two reasons: firstly, France is often seen as an emblematic example of strong economic interventionism and a vast public bureaucracy (Trumbull, 2004); secondly, the country has distinguished itself in recent years by numerous initiatives at national and European level to reinforce Internet regulation.[3] The book challenges these common understandings, showing how French elites have taken up the digital revolution, while changing the forms of—and preserving—their bureaucratic domination. Drawing on historical comparisons with Germany and England, we discuss the specific features of the French case that appears as a paradigmatic example rather than an exception in the global transformation of the European State.

Investigating the Internet as a socio-technical and political object is a methodological challenge (Schneider & Foot, 2004). While it has given rise to new methods in the social sciences, from "online ethnography" (Hine, 2015) to the analysis of massive data (Bastin & Tubaro, 2018; Marres, 2017), the Internet presents itself as an elusive object whose

[3] For example, it is no coincidence that Thierry Breton, the French Commissioner for the Digital Market, was in charge of preparing the Digital Services Act and the Digital Market Act at the European Union.

historical and material contours are not always easy to grasp. In addition to the instability of institutional structures mentioned above, the changing nature of technologies and uses also contributes to blurring the evolution of Internet policies. Under the permanent banner of institutional innovation, progress in this policy field has been more chaotic than it might seem, with many repetitions and steps backward. The relative absence of socio-historical work on the public handling of the Internet, particularly in Europe, calls for great caution in the conduct and interpretation of interviews, especially as the rehabilitation of roles played by successive policymakers has become both an issue and a resource in recent political competition.

To meet these challenges, the book draws on a wide range of written sources—public reports, scientific documentation, ministerial minutes and memos—to compare the often "heroic" account of interviewees with traces of their past actions. Above all, the investigation mobilizes numerous web archives, both public and private, most of them accessible through the Internet Archive. The "Wayback Machine" made it possible to find early French government sites, French activists' discussions and e-government programs. However, the reproduction of these sites is often incomplete: as with paper documents, web archives provide only a fragmented, timeworn vision of the history of the net.

At a time when the use of social media platform and smartphones is widespread in political life, the book finally documents the changing uses of technologies within the State. From the days when "only secretaries knew how to type" as described by an interviewee, to the development of AI algorithms to perform public policies, it shows the gradual and unequal distribution of technological uses within public administrations, the stigmatization or opportunity effects they create as well as the power relations in which they are caught.

* * *

Undoubtedly, the digital transformation of public administration is not exactly how it was imagined by Internet pioneers who championed a reinvention of the State through technologies. If genuine innovations have been introduced—open data repository, participatory platforms and online communication—we are far from the democratized networked State, which had been prophesied by some pioneers. Yet, less visible, but more profound, new ways of conceiving public action and its relation to private actors and digital markets largely inspired by the Internet world have taken hold within the State. Algorithmic governmentality, collaboration with major platforms and data-driven regulation now mark the unexpected combination of digital transformation and neoliberal governance. How did this convergence come about? And how did the Internet and the State finally align in the development of these new forms of government?

To answer these questions, the book unpacks an untold socio-history of how the State took over the Internet and was changed by it. The first two following chapters discuss and qualify the alleged antagonism between the State and the Internet. Chapter 2 goes back to the origins of computer networks, and explains how the Internet project gradually gained autonomy from national bureaucracies. The involvement of an international community of researchers and early web users helped create what was later homogenized as the "cyberspace utopia", claiming independence from governments. Chapter 3 relocates the opposition between the State and the Internet in France, the country of the Minitel. At a time when public administrations were planning the development of "information superhighways", the arrival of a "U.S." network was regarded with concern by French public officials. The challenges of the ICT sector prompted lasting reforms regarding innovation policies and the role of the technical elite within the French State.

The book then analyzes the development of Internet policies in France. Chapter 4 describes the key role of Internet "evangelists" who promoted public policy reform in France at the end of the 1990s. At the intersection of private and public fields, these players favored the exchange of ideas and practices between Internet communities and major government departments. Chapter 5 examines a "revolutionary moment" in Internet policies, characterized by numerous experiments and innovations in online public intervention. It shows the use of Internet technologies as a central tool in administrative reforms. The chapter also questions the resistance of the bureaucracy and the limited diffusion of Internet principles within public organizations.

The final two chapters document the gradual bureaucratization of Internet policies; which should not so much be understood as a step back in the use of digital technologies in the administration as their adjustment to bureaucratic rules and divisions. In Chapter 6, we use the example of anti-piracy policies to demonstrate the sectoral division of Internet-related issues within the State and the development of dedicated expertise within ministry departments. Chapter 7 examines the present and future of Internet principles within the State, in a context where digital technology use is widespread. Based on a few quintessential programs of the 2010s—support for the start-up economy, regulation of Internet firms and government-as-a-platform programs—it describes the conditions under which Internet policies are now produced, in an increasingly competitive field of policymaking, where Internet activism fades behind the global digitization of public action.

In the end, this book should nurture our understanding of how the State has gradually gained a foothold in the digital space, and how this development has come with a neo-liberalization of government, largely based on the use of digital technologies and the delegation of public services to digital markets. It suggests important milestones for a political history of Internet policies, a history that is diverse and complex and to which this book only contributes. Yet the study that follows is intended to provide a number of avenues and perspectives for considering current and future developments in the everchanging relations between public players and digital organizations.

References

Agar, J. (2003). *The government machine: A revolutionary history of the computer*. Cambridge: The MIT press.

Allison, G. T. (1969). Conceptual models and the Cuban missile crisis. *American Political Science Review, 63*(3), 689–718.

Bach, T., & Wegrich, K. (Eds.). (2019). *The blind spots of public bureaucracy and the politics of non-coordination*. Palgrave Macmillan.

Badouard, R., Mabi, C., & Sire, G. (2016). Beyond" Points of Control": Logics of digital governmentality. *Internet Policy Review, 5*(3), 1–13.

Bastin, G., & Tubaro, P. (2018). Le moment big data des sciences sociales. *Revue française de sociologie, 59*(3), 375–394.

Bauman, Z., Bigo, D., Esteves, P., Guild, E., Jabri, V., Lyon, D., & Walker, R. B. (2014). After Snowden: Rethinking the impact of surveillance. *International Political Sociology, 8*(2), 121–144.

Benkler, Y. (2006). *The wealth of networks: How social production transforms markets and freedom*. Yale University Press.

Bezes, P. (2009). *Réinventer l'État: les réformes de l'administration française (1962–2008)*. Presses Universitaires de France.

Birnhack, M. D., & Elkin-Koren, N. (2003). The invisible handshake: The reemergence of the state in the digital environment. *Virginia Journal of Law and Technology, 8*, 1.

Blyth, M. (2002). *Great transformations: Economic ideas and institutional change in the twentieth century*. Cambridge University Press.

Bourdieu, P., & Christin, R. (1990). La construction du marché. *Actes de la recherche en sciences sociales, 81*(1), 65–85.

Bourdieu, P. (2018). *On the State: Lectures at the Collège de France, 1989–1992*. John Wiley & Sons.

Boyle, J. (1997). Foucault in cyberspace: Surveillance, sovereignty, and hardwired censors. *University of Cincinnati Law Review, 66*, 177.

Brierley, S., Lowande, K., Potter, R. A., & Toral, G. (2023). Bureaucratic politics: Blind spots and opportunities in political science. *Annual Review of Political Science, 26*, 271–290.

Browne, William P. (1995). *Cultivating congress: Constituents, issues, and interests in agricultural policy-making*. University Press of Kansas.

Burstein, P. (1991). Policy domains: Organization, culture, and policy outcomes. *Annual review of Sociology, 17*(1), 327–350.

Bygrave, L. A., & Bing, J. (Eds.). (2009). *Internet governance: Infrastructure and institutions*. OUP Oxford.

Cartwright, M. (2020). Internationalising state power through the internet: Google, Huawei and geopolitical struggle. *Internet Policy Review, 9*(3), 1–18.

Castells, M. (1996). *The Rise of the network society, the information age: Economy, society and culture* (Vol. I). Blackwell.

Culpepper, P. D. (2008). The politics of common knowledge: Ideas and institutional change in wage bargaining. *International Organization, 62*(1), 1–33.

Dahlström, C., & Lapuente, V. (2022). Comparative bureaucratic politics. *Annual Review of Political Science, 25*, 43–63.

Deibert, R., Palfrey, J., Rohozinski, R., & Zittrain, J. (2008). *Access denied: The practice and policy of global internet filtering* (p. 472). The MIT Press.

DiMaggio, P. (1988). Interest and agency in institutional theory. *Institutional Patterns and Organizations. Culture and Environment, 1*, 3–22.

DiMaggio, P. J., & Powell, W. W. (1983). The iron cage revisited: Institutional isomorphism and collective rationality in organizational fields. *American Sociological Review, 48*(2), 147–160.

Dunleavy, P., Margetts, H., Bastow, S., & Tinkler, J. (2006). *Digital era governance: IT corporations, the state, and e-government*. Oxford University Press.

Emmenegger, P. (2021). Agency in historical institutionalism: Coalitional work in the creation, maintenance, and change of institutions. *Theory and Society, 50*(4), 607–626.

Foucault, M. (Alan Sheridan ed. & trans., 1979). *Discipline and punish: The birth of the prison*. Vintage Books.
Foucault, M. (1999). 'Governmentality' (Lecture at the Collège de France, Feb. 1, 1978). In: G. Burchell, C. Gordon, & P. Miller (Eds.), *The Foucault effect: Studies in governmentality* (pp. 87–104). Harvester Wheatsheaf.
Gardey, D. (2008). *Écrire, calculer, classer. Comment une révolution de papier a transformé les sociétés contemporaines (1800–1940)*. La Découverte.
Hall, R. E. (1986). The role of consumption in economic fluctuations. In *The American business cycle: Continuity and change* (pp. 237–266). University of Chicago Press.
Hardy, C., & Maguire, S. (2008). Institutional entrepreneurship. The Sage handbook of organizational institutionalism, 198–217.
Hart, P., & Wille, A. C. (2012). Bureaucratic politics: Opening the black box of executive government. In B. Guy Peters, & J. Pierre (Eds.), *The SAGE handbook of public administration* (2 ed., pp. 369–379). SAGE Publications Ltd.
Hine, C. (2015). *Ethnography for the internet: Embedded, embodied and everyday*. Routledge.
Hood, C. (1991). A public management for all seasons? *Public Administration, 69*(1), 3–19.
Jeffares S. (2021). *The virtual public servant. Artificial intelligence and frontline work*. Palgrave Macmillan.
Johnson, D. R., & Post, D. (1996). Law and borders: The rise of law in cyberspace. *Stanford Law Review*, 1367–1402.
Johnson, D. R., Crawford, S. P., & Palfrey, J. G., Jr. (2004). The accountable Internet: Peer production of Internet governance. *Virginia Journal of Law and Technology, 9*, 1.
Kahin, B., & Nesson, C. R. (Eds.). (1997). *Borders in cyberspace: Information policy and the global information infrastructure*. MIT Press.
Klein, H. (2002). ICANN and internet governance: Leveraging technical coordination to realize global public policy. *The Information Society, 18*(3), 193–207.
Laumann, Edward O., & Knoke, David. (1987). *The organizational state: Social change in national policy domains*. University of Wisconsin Press.
Le Galès, P. & Scott, A. (2008). Une révolution bureaucratique britannique? Autonomie sans contrôle ou «freer markets, more rules». *Revue française de sociologie, 49*(2), 301–330.
Lessig, L. (1999). *Code: And other laws of cyberspace*. Basic Books.
Loughlin, M., & Scott, C. (1997). The regulatory state. *Developments in British Politics, 5*, 205–219.
Lyon, D. (2007). *Surveillance studies: An overview*. Polity Press.
Lyon, D. (2015). *Surveillance after snowden*. John Wiley & Sons.

Mahoney, J., & Thelen, K. (Eds.). (2009). *Explaining institutional change: Ambiguity, agency, and power*. Cambridge University Press.

Majone, G. (1994). The rise of the regulatory state in Europe. *West European Politics, 17*(3), 77–101.

Margolis, M., & Resnick, D. (2000). *Politics as usual. The Cyberspace "Revolution"*. Sage Publications.

Marres, N. (2017). *Digital sociology: The reinvention of social research*. John Wiley & Sons.

Mills, C. W. (1956). *The power elite*. Oxford University Press.

Moran, M. (2002). Understanding the regulatory state. *British Journal of Political Science, 32*(2), 391–413.

Morozov, E. (2012). *The net delusion: The dark side of Internet freedom*. PublicAffairs.

Mueller, M. L. (2010). *Networks and states: The global politics of Internet governance*. MIT Press.

Muller, P. (1985). Un schéma d'analyse des politiques sectorielles. *Revue française de science politique, 35*(2), 165–189.

Ollion, É. (2017). *Raison d'État: histoire de la lutte contre les sectes en France*. La Découverte.

O'Reilly, T. (2011). Government as a Platform. *Innovations: Technology, Governance, Globalization*, *6*(1), 13–40.

Petridou, E., & Mintrom, M. (2021). A research agenda for the study of policy entrepreneurs. *Policy Studies Journal, 49*(4), 943–967.

Pierson, P. (1993). When effect becomes cause: Policy feedback and political change. *World Politics, 45*(4), 595–628.

Pollitt, C., Van Thiel, S., & Homburg, V. (Eds.). (2007). *New public management in Europe*. Palgrave Macmillan.

Saunders, E. N. (2022). Elites in the making and breaking of foreign policy. *Annual Review of Political Science, 25*, 219–240.

Schneider, S. M., & Foot, K. A. (2004). The web as an object of study. *New Media and Society, 6*(1), 114–122.

Schradie, J. (2019). *The revolution that wasn't: How digital activism favors conservatives*. Harvard University Press.

Scott, J. (2008). Modes of power and the re-conceptualization of elites. *The Sociological Review*, *56*(1_suppl), 25–43.

Smyrl, M., & Genieys, W. (2016). *Elites, ideas, and the evolution of public policy*. Springer.

Snider, E. A., & Faris, D. M. (2011). The Arab spring: US democracy promotion in Egypt. *Middle East Policy, 18*(3), 49–62.

Thelen, K. and Steinmo, S. (1992). 'Historical institutionalism in comparative politics'. In S. Steinmo, K. Thelen, and F. Longstreth (Eds.), *Structuring politics: Historical institutionalism in comparative analysis*. Cambridge University Press (Cambridge Studies in Comparative Politics), 1–32.

Tolbert, C. J., Mossberger, K., & McNeal, R. (2008). Institutions, policy innovation, and E-Government in the American States. *Public Administration Review*, *68*(3), 549–563.

Tréguer, F. (2019). *L'utopie déchue. Une contre-histoire d'internet XVe-XXIe siècle*. Fayard.

Trumbull, G. (2004). Silicon and the state: French innovation policy in the Internet age. Rowman & Littlefield.

Tüfekçi, Z. (2017). *Twitter and tear gas: The power and fragility of networked protest*. Yale University Press.

Weber, M. (1978, 1st Ed. 1922). *Economy and society*. University of California Press.

Wedel, J. R. (2017). From power elites to influence elites: Resetting elite studies for the 21st century. *Theory, Culture & Society, 34*(5–6), 153–178.

Weiss, L. (1998). *The myth of the powerless state*. Cornell University Press.

West, D. M. (2000). *Assessing E-government: The internet, democracy, and service delivery by state and federal government*. The Genesis Institute.

CHAPTER 2

The Origins of Networks: From Research Policies to Internet Politics

> Collectively, they form what their inhabitants call the Net. It extends across that immense region of electron states, microwaves, magnetic fields, light pulses and thought which sci-fi writer William Gibson named Cyberspace. Cyberspace, in its present condition, has a lot in common with the 19th Century West. It is vast, unmapped, culturally and legally ambiguous, verbally terse (unless you happen to be a court stenographer), hard to get around in, and up for grabs. Large institutions already claim to own the place, but most of the actual natives are solitary and independent, sometimes to the point of sociopathy. It is, of course, a perfect breeding ground for both outlaws and new ideas about liberty.
> John Perry Barlow, "Crime and Puzzlement", 1990

Much has been written about the Internet utopia, the promise of emancipation and social transformation offered by the emergence of a decentralized and free communication network, spanning national borders and escaping the eye and the grip of national states. To grasp the unconventional spirit of the early years of the Internet, we are left with the texts of pioneers who visited this "electronic frontier" in the 1990s. No one described it better than John Perry Barlow, a former hippie turned gentleman farmer who connected to the virtual communities from a personal computer at the Wyoming family ranch. In a language as lyrical as it was colorful, he contributed to forge the image of the Internet as "the

A. Bellon, *A Socio-History of Internet Policies*, International Series on Public Policy, https://doi.org/10.1007/978-3-031-69099-0_2

perfect breeding ground for both outlaws and new ideas about liberty" (Barlow, 1990).

And so, began the history of Internet utopianism, under the pen of those who were inventing and promoting, rather than faithfully describing, a new social space for communication and exchange. In this field also emerged, in the mid-1990s, what came to be known as the "Internet Politics", a set of principles for network governance. It planted the seeds of an antagonistic relationship with the bureaucratic state in the name of the new freedoms of cyberspace. The opposition between the Internet and the state is therefore a social construct of cyber-utopianism, the enigmatic product of a history that yet goes back to the Cold War, at a time when computer research and innovation were heavily supervised by the US administration. How did scientific policies designed to promote US sovereignty against soviet technology turn into this political project for the autonomy of the cyberspace? How did the Cold War military-industrial complex, in which the Internet was born, become the breeding ground for a radical critique of the technical bureaucracy?

To answer these questions, one needs to go back to the origins of computer networks, to reassess the social conditions of their emergence, as well as the successive configurations in which they have developed. This historical detour is both essential and challenging. For the history of the Internet is marked by the logic of the "great tale", burdened by the weight of so many heroic accounts of the "wizards" (Hafner & Lyon, 1996) and early geniuses of computer science at its beginnings. The "invention" of the Internet is thus sometimes attributed to the US army, to the first IT companies or to the most prominent computer scientists of American laboratories. It continues to be the subject of conflicting appropriations, underlining the ever-present gratifications linked to claiming authorship on the creation of computer networks.

Far from a mythical story, the version proposed in this chapter aims to move away from the "false question" of "who" invented the Internet (Schafer & Thierry, 2012), and from the assumption of a pre-existing political project shaping its development. It draws on the work of historians who, following Janet Abbate, have shown that the Internet "is *not* a *story* of a *few heroic inventors*; it is a *tale* of *collaboration* and *conflict among* a remarkable *variety* of actors" (Abbate, 1999a; see also Ceruzzi, 2008). The emergence of computer networks, as well as their ongoing development in the 1980s and 1990s, were indeed the result of complex social relations between researchers, industries, governments, businesses and early users, debating over the management of computer resources and the definition of the network's use and conditions (Pelkey et al., 2022). Who should finance the infrastructure? What form should it take? Who could connect to the Internet? Who should be responsible for the information exchanged on the network? These were just some of the many questions that gave rise to battles over network design and conditions of use.

One should also bear in mind that the study of any technology should not insolate technical properties from the discourses and social practices through which they are produced (Akrich, 1992; Seaver, 2017; Winner, 1980). In the case of the Internet, the features of the network—borderless and distributed—were often considered as obstacles to state intervention. These political features were less the realization of a clear political intention than the result of a long development during which professional ethos and organizational norms of various players clashed, coexisted or converged. More broadly, the Internet politics, as the self-preservation of the network through ethics and robust technical standards, mirrored the more general politicization of scientific programs, a process in which not only researchers are involved, but also administrations, politicians and users.

The development of the Internet politics can be described in three stages. First, the creation of a large decentralized computer network in the US stemmed from ad hoc alliances between scientific, economic and governmental players, at the heart of the Cold War military-industrial-academic complex (1). In a second phase, the international development of the network of networks involved a growing number of computer scientists who set up original organizations and instruments for the management of their project. The emerging "technical governance" (DeNardis, 2009) of the Internet referred then specifically to the handling of critical resources—the addresses that identify connected devices—and to the creation of communication standards, an operation necessary to ensure the smooth running of the network. These processes favored the empowerment of an international IT community who claimed responsibility over Internet development (2). Finally, the convergence of the academic Internet and the first "virtual communities" (Rheingold, 1993) contributed to consolidation of the cyberculture (Turner, 2006) with new discourses on the independence of the cyberspace. At a time when the international expansion of the Internet once again aroused the interest of national governments, a new movement to defend online freedoms emerged, in order to protect the cyberspace from state intervention (3).

1 The Emergence of the Internet: Between Science, Industry and Government

The development of the Internet was rooted in a military-industrial-academic organization of science that characterized the US in the 1960s (Leslie, 1993). This Cold War period was also marked by scientific competition between the two blocks (Wolfe, 2013). In 1958, a year after the launch of Sputnik into orbit, the US Department of Defense set up the Advanced Research Projects Agency (ARPA) to make up for what was then perceived as a technological lead by the Soviet Union. Among the many projects funded by the new agency, machine-to-machine communication and the networking of university supercomputers appeared as key scientific avenues. ARPANET, the forerunner of the Internet and the first network of computers, was created in 1969. But the project reflected only partly the political context and the strong influence of US administration on computer science research. Networked computing was not a simple transposition of US defense and geopolitical imperatives into science. The architecture of the ARPANET was as much the result of technical arbitration as it was of economic or security concerns, which revealed the close interweaving of scientific, commercial and political motives in the development of computer science (Ceruzzi, 1998; Pelkey et al., 2022). Then, in the 1970s and 1980s, the Internet project grew independent from the defense agency, as its development brought together numerous computer labs collaborating around the definition of new communication protocols.

1.1 A Defense Network?

From the 1950s onward, computer science in the United States was characterized by government investment and the military supervision of scientific programs. Mainly funded by the ARPA, computer research involved numerous university laboratories (MIT, Stanford, Harvard, UCLA, etc.), private research institutes (such as the Rand Corporation, based in California) and emerging computer companies (such as Palo Alto-based Xerox). Bound by contract to the agency, these various organizations formed a porous ecosystem and a playing field for computer scientists. The career of Vinton Cerf (Box 1), recognized as one of the main "fathers of the Internet", is paradigmatic of the hybrid career of computer scientists in the US: he navigated between government agencies, universities and private companies. These circulations cemented social relationships between institutions and enabled researchers to accumulate hybrid resources (economic, political and social capital) to claim responsibility over the management of computer network projects.

Box 1 Vinton Cerf, portrait of one the "founding fathers" of the Internet

Born in 1943 in New Haven, Vinton Cerf grew up in Los Angeles, California. Both his parents graduated with Bachelor degrees. His father worked as an engineer for a company under contract to the U.S. Department of Defense. As a teenager, Vinton Cerf attended Van Nuys High School in Los Angeles—a prestigious high school with a strong math and science program—along with two other future Internet researchers, Steve Crocker and Jon Postel. In 1965, he graduated from Stanford University with a bachelor's degree in mathematics. He then worked for two years as a system engineer at IBM, America's leading computer firm at the time. In 1967, he returned to UCLA, where he obtained a master's degree and then a doctorate in computer science, under the supervision of Leonard Kleinrock and Gerald Estrin, two specialists in networked computing and packet switching. At the time, UCLA was home to a central laboratory of the ARPA-led computer science research ecosystem. Between 1968 and 1969, as a doctoral student, Vinton Cerf contributed to the establishment of the ARPANET, of which UCLA was one of the first nodes. In 1972, he was appointed assistant professor at the Stanford Research Institute. In 1976, he joined the DARPA (the new name for ARPA), still in charge of the Internet project. In 1982, he left the US agency for the telecommunications company MCI, heading a team that developed one of the first Internet messaging applications. In 1986, he joined the CNRI (Corporation for National Research Initiatives), an independent research institute for the development of information technologies and the Internet, which had just been founded by Robert Kahn, another founding father of US computer networks. In 1992, he also helped found the Internet Society and became its first president. As the Internet's "public representative", he was a frequent speaker at conferences, as well as appearing before international organizations and governments (both American and European). He also served in the board of several Internet governance organization such as the ICANN between 1999 and 2007. He finally joined Google in 2005 as Chief Internet Evangelist. This honorary title, which sanctioned a career dedicated to the development of the Internet, revealed his hybrid position within the company, between institutional representation and direction of research on the network. At this position, he testified before the US Senate to defend net neutrality, as a core principle of the Internet.

Within this vast research ecosystem, data transmission and machine communication were key issues. In the 1960s, several teams started working independently on "packet switching" communication: this transmission method divides information into packets of data forwarded asynchronously through the network by intermediate nodes. Paul Baran explored this concept at the Rand Corporation, at the same time as Leonard Kleinrock at UCLA. In 1968, the latter convinced the ARPA to pursue research on data transmission using an experimental network of computers, the ARPANET, which would link the central processing units of four Western university labs (UCLA, Stanford, Santa Barbara and Utah). At the time, Robert Taylor, the new director of ARPA's IT department—the Information Processing Techniques Office (IPTO)—was also pushing for the networking of the agency's computer labs, partly for economic reasons. BBN (Bolt, Beranek, Newman), a consulting firm founded in 1948 by two MIT professors, was awarded the public contract to build the ARPANET and to foster the development of communications between East Coast universities and the Boston area. Hence, the ARPANET network was born in 1969, linking major computer science university laboratories, as well as the BBN and the Rand Corporation research centers, all under contract with the ARPA (Fig. 1).

Because it depended almost exclusively on subsidies from the U.S. Department of Defense, the ARPANET has sometimes been seen as the product of strictly military interests, instrumentalizing computer science research for strategic purposes. However, while the construction of the network was indeed the result of a government contract to develop a reliable, secure and sophisticated communication system for the army, the project also involved many other considerations: favor exchanges between researchers working on similar issues, test hypotheses on data transmission or increase the computing power of machines. At the time, networking supercomputers was also seen as a way of rationalizing the organization of research, and even potentially reducing its costs by sharing tasks between machines. One should indeed remember that in the 1960s a

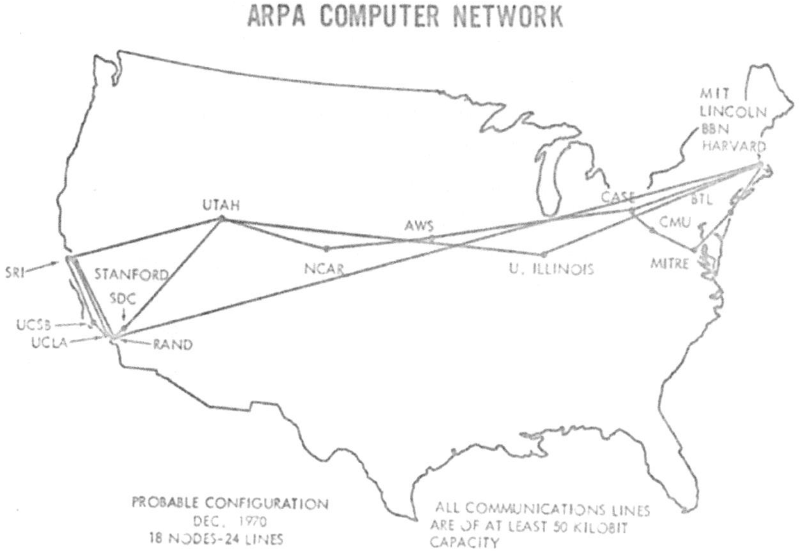

Fig. 1 The fifteen nodes of ARPANET in 1971

"computer machine" took up the space of an entire room (Fig. 2) and that the execution of programs could last several days.

In this context of dependence on government investment and race to innovation, military issues were put forward by researchers to obtain funding or to promote one project against another. For example, Paul Baran was able to advocate for packet-switching transmission and distributed network architecture against the advice of telecommunications companies by presenting the features of the "centerless" network as a strategic way to resist a targeted attack on the communication infrastructure. The fortuitous alliance of military and scientific interests around this technical option overcame the reluctance of US telecommunications, notably the powerful AT&T (Abbate, 1999b). On the contrary, at the same time in France, telecommunications engineers won out over computer scientists: they developed a more centralized network against the packet-switching solution advocated by computer scientists (see next chapter).

To sum up, in the United States, large-scale public investment and the positions enjoyed by computer scientists in various public and private

Fig. 2 Two BBN Computers connected to the ARPANET at the end of the 1970s

institutions enabled the emergence of the first distributed computer network. It was mainly dedicated to advancing research into data transmission between machines. A few years later, it was again the convergence of military interests—ensuring the exchange of information between heterogeneous systems such as a radio and a satellite—and scientific concerns—developing communication between networks—that led to the extension of the ARPANET into the Internet project.

1.2 The Gradual Autonomy of the Internet

In the early 1970s, the ARPANET became an inspiration for a number of experiments in packet-switched transmission, giving rise to new networks developed by university or corporate computer labs. ARPANET, Telnet, BITNET (CUNY), or Csnet, coexisted side-by-side on the US territory. In 1972, the now DARPA launched a new research program on communication between heterogeneous networks, led by Robert Kahn, formerly researcher at BBN. The exact same year, American and British researchers set up an International Network Working Group (INWG) to study and develop standards for inter-networking. The interconnection of computer networks was indeed far from being just a military issue: it presented a major scientific challenge for computer science research. The two research programs converged and in 1974, Robert Kahn and Vinton Cerf, as heads of the INWG, published a landmark article outlining the principle of a protocol for inter-network communication, the Transmission Control Protocol (TCP). The first brick of the future Internet was laid.

Gradually, inter-networking research emancipated from DARPA's control to involve foreign laboratories, such as the INRIA in France or Karlsruhe University in Germany. The development of the Internet was indeed part and parcel of the internationalization of science (Gingras, 2002; Skolnikoff, 1993). It became one of its main vehicles, offering new means of communication and exchanges between researchers scattered around the globe. International discussions and symposia organized around the definition of compatible standards also favored the mobility of IT scholars. As for financing, the heavy cost of computer networks projects often required complex arrangements that brought together private and public institutes from several countries. In 1983, the cooperation of several hundred of researchers, far from all US based, enabled the deployment of the "TCP/IP" protocols. They connected the ARPANET to other computer networks, forming a vast inter-network that came to be known as the "Internet".

One year later, to protect the security of military communications, the DARPA created an independent military network MILNET and the National Science Foundation (NSF) took over overall management of the Internet. The NSF notably financed the Internet backbone, a set of university supercomputers linked by high-speed connections. They formed the heart of the Internet infrastructure, to which a myriad of machines and regional networks got connected. The NSF also established "terms and conditions of use" for the Internet.[1] It reassessed the scientific and educational vocation of the network, access to which was still completely free. After all, the Internet was first and foremost a medium for scientific exchanges and joint projects in computer science or other academic fields. Further cooperation on communication protocols led to the development of the main Internet applications: e-mail, file exchange (FTP standard) and above all the "World Wide Web", an information system developed at the CERN (European Organization for Nuclear

[1] The «Acceptable Use Policies» were published by the NCSA (National Center for Supercomputing Applications). See for example the handbook written by NCSA's director Ed Krol "*The Whole Internet User's Guide and Catalog*", Sebastopol, CA, 1992, Annexe C.

Research) in 1989. At this point, Internet development was no longer confined to DARPA contractors, but involved researchers from all over the world.

2 A New "Republic" for IT Researchers

Throughout the 1980s, the Internet was first and foremost a university network. Computer scientists used it as a working tool and a platform for a wide range of cooperative projects. But getting hundreds of laboratories around the world to work together was a challenge. So, they developed original instruments for coordination and governance of the network. The publications and representative organizations built up as part of the Internet project displayed efforts to legitimize technical choices and to define a "network policy", underpinned by scientific rationale. Against administrative or political tutelage, computer scientists asserted their independence by defending a set of specific standards and modes of organization. Above all, they imported their idiosyncratic practices, professional ethos (Zarca, 2009) and shared imaginary into the infrastructure and management of the Internet. For sociologist Patrice Flichy (2007), the Internet then reflected the aspirations of an "ideal scientific community" that, for a decade or so, governed by itself the development of computers networks.

2.1 *"A Swath Cut Through Miles of Red Tape and Pedantic Process"*[2]

The expansion of the Internet was based on the ongoing specification and production of technical standards to determine how machines should communicate and how information should be routed on the network. The Internet was thus not the invention of a handful of pioneers but the result of a collective enterprise for which a growing number of computer scientists collaborated. To enable the coordination of researchers scattered across several universities and institutions, the IT community relied on an original medium of communication: the "Requests for comments", a series of documents shared online, halfway between scientific publications, institutional memos and informal correspondence. Despite their hybrid

[2] RFC 2555 « 30 years of RFC» published in April 1999.

nature, the RFCs were, and still are, the Internet's official documentation, specifying the technical and organizational standards that ensured the smooth running of the network. Published and exchanged from the very beginnings of the ARPANET, the "RFCs" are also a formidable material for studying the development of the Internet "in action". They form, at the time of writing, an ever-growing database of 9,170 documents, accessible on the web.[3] Although obscure technical specifications are dominant in this series of publications, the RFCs enable the reader to grasp the interweaving of scientific discussion and ethical norms, as well as the growing importance of governance issues in the development of the Internet. They convey the working atmosphere of a research collective that saw itself as an "ideal community", rejecting the model of scientific bureaucracy.

The publication conventions defined by Steve Crocker as early as 1969 in "RFC 3" broke with classic academic production:

> The content of a NWG note may be any thought, suggestion, etc. related to the HOST software or other aspect of the network. Notes are encouraged to be timely rather than polished. Philosophical positions without examples or other specifics, specific suggestions or implementation techniques without introductory or background explication, and explicit questions without any attempted answers are all acceptable. The minimum length for a NWG note is one sentence. These standards (or lack of them) are stated explicitly for two reasons.
>
> First, there is a tendency to view a written statement as ipso facto authoritative, and we hope to promote the exchange and discussion of considerably less than authoritative ideas. Second, there is a natural hesitancy to publish something unpolished, and we hope to ease this inhibition.

The RFCs give us an idea of the work culture and ethos that developed in computer labs and IT companies after the Student and Civil Rights Movements (Turner, 2006): disdain for bureaucratic red tape, appreciation of tinkering and stroke of genius, cooperation rather than competition between researchers. For example, the RFCs do not indicate the status of their authors, who were more often young researchers than tenured professors: in 1969, Steve Crocker was only 25 and did not yet hold a

[3] https://www.rfc-editor.org.

doctorate. Academic "jargon" was abandoned in favor of informal discussion, often punctuated by puns, jokes[4] and even satirical poems that are not without recalling the ethics and aesthetics of the hacker community (Coleman, 2013). In the words of computer scientist Jake Feinler in a 1999 review of "30 years of RFCs", the aim of this original medium was really to "cut a swath cut through miles of red tape and pedantic process".

The hybridization of scientific, political and ethical language also echoed the growing importance of governance issues in the Internet project management. During the 1980s, the Internet indeed faced a series of problems—traffic congestion, viruses, hacking—linked to the increasing number of participants. In 1988, for example, a worm damaged several thousand computers connected to the Internet. At a time when only few citizens were aware of the Internet's existence, the episode of the "Morris worm", named after the student who distributed it, contributed to associating the name "Internet" to new social threats in the collective imagination.[5] It even led to the creation of an ephemeral government committee to examine the possibility for the administration to take back control over the Internet. As a consequence, the IT departments of several universities embarked on a hunt for the "Morris worm" in order to "save the Internet": they finally succeeded in identifying the flawed program and its origin and putting a stop to the spread of the virus. In RFC 1135, "The Helminthiasis of the Internet" (December 1989), University of Southern California researcher Joyce Reynolds looked back at this episode and its significance for the Internet community. She euphemistically described the worm as a mere technical challenge that pitted teams of researchers against each other to determine the source version of the program. She concluded:

> In the short term, the worm program did heighten the computer community's awareness of security flaws. Also, the "old boy network" proved it

[4] See for example the 1st of April RFCs: RFC 1149 « A Standard for the Transmission of IP Datagrams on Avian Carriers» (April 1st, 1990), RFC 1217 « Memo from the Consortium for Slow Commotion Research» (April 1st, 1992), and RFC 1438 "Statements of Boredom SOBs», April 1st, 1993.

[5] In the *New York Times*, the « Morris worm» was presented as the "most dangerous computer attack" known so far in the history of the US. The article introduced at the same time the Internet as "an international computer communication network" to an audience that probably read this name for the first time. John Markoff, "Author of Computer 'virus' is son of N.S.A expert on data security", *New York Times*, Nov. 5, 1988.

> was still alive and well! While networking and computers as a whole have grown by leaps and bounds in the last twenty years, the Internet community still has the "old boys" who trust and communicate well with each other in the face of adversity.

For Reynolds, the worm had the merit of exposing failures that computer scientists, forming an "old boys club", were quick to repair. In her opinion, the event only confirmed the resilience of the Internet and the effectiveness of its community-based governance. The episode led the IT community to establish collective principles and ethical rules to ensure that the network functioned properly. RFC 1087, for example, defined an "Internet ethic" that essentially called on the individual responsibility of researchers. Earlier in the development of the Internet, Jon Postel, a pioneer member of the Internet project, formulated in RFC 761 (January 1980) a maxim considered to be one of the first "laws" of the Internet: "be conservative in what you send, liberal in what you accept". Hence, user self-restraint was hailed as the main guarantee for the free flow of information, and a cardinal principle of the network.

Against access restrictions or increased control by the US federal government, professional ethics and the collective intelligence of the IT community were thus asserted as the only valid principles of governance for the Internet. They were articulated with the establishment of governance bodies to steer Internet development and manage resources on the network.

2.2 *The Technical Governance of the Internet*

In 1979, the Internet Configuration Control Board was set up as the first steering body for the Internet project, with Vinton Cerf at its head. In a 2001 interview, he said he had wanted to set up a "thing with the most boring name possible", in order to keep out unwelcome guests and preserve the direction of the project by the researchers of the international group.[6] As the network grew and the DARPA gradually withdrew, the ICCB became an independent board (Internet Advisory Board), part of a larger Internet governance body, the IETF (Internet Engineering Task Force), founded in 1986 (see Fig. 3). Scott Bradner (Harvard University),

[6] Interview for the ComputerWorld Honor Program, available thanks to the Wayback Machine of the Internet Archive at: http://www.cwhonors.org/archives/histories.htm.

who had been a leading member of the IETF, described it as a "membership organization without members" (Bradner, 1999), where the only thing that counted was participation and collective discussions. Indeed, the IETF relied, and still relies, on a series of "working groups" open to all: any individual can, in principle, join a team or propose a new research project. In 1993, a special RFC was published to serve as a "welcome guide" for newcomers. Written in a light-hearted style with plenty of jokes, the "Tao of the IETF" detailed the history of the organization, the way in which working groups operated, and the informal rules that structured the "Internet community" (the general rule was "dress for the weather"). In line with meritocratic values adopted for the RFCs, the quality of contributions had to always take precedence over the position of their authors in the validation process.

More generally, the organization reflected a strong anti-bureaucratic culture running through the IT community: the latter rejected both rigid sets of rules and hierarchies, as well as federal government meddling in the organization of research. In a presentation to the IETF in 1992, David Clark, Vinton Cerf's successor at the head of the IAB, proposed the following motto, widely endorsed by the computer science community: "We reject: kings, presidents and voting. We believe in: rough consensus and running code". Against the stranglehold of administration and politics, the phrase asserted the principle of a governance of the Internet by

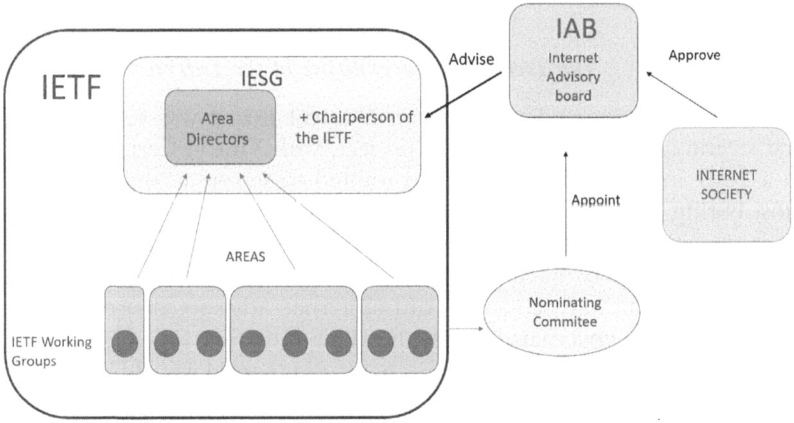

Fig. 3 Institutions for the technical governance of the Internet

technical standards only. As masters of code, computer scientists were thus bound to reign over the Internet. At the end of the 1980s, the network appeared indeed as the main medium for and an example of ideal scientific community, offering new opportunities of intellectual exchange between peers across state borders.

2.3 *The Invention of the Web, an Old Scientific Dream Come True*

The aspirations of the IT "Republic" found an ideal–typical translation with the creation of the web in 1989. Following the internationalization of computer network research, the web was not a US invention: it was developed at the European Center for Nuclear Research (CERN) by a team of computer scientists led by British researcher Tim Berners-Lee. The web consisted in the development of a series of protocols (HTTP and URL) and a dedicated language (HTML) that enabled users to identify relevant information and navigate from one document to another via hypertext links. Linked to Internet protocols, the "World Wide Web" was bound to offer access to thousands of documents located on connected devices all around the world.

The invention of the web prolonged a long-held dream of the scientific community regarding access to universal knowledge. As early as the end of the Second World War, the hypothesis of a global encyclopedia hosted on computer machines was imagined by Vannevar Bush, former scientific advisor to Roosevelt and director of research at the National Defense Research Committee. In 1945, he published a bound-to-be classic article in the *Atlantic Monthly*, entitled "As we may think" (Fig. 4), in which he pondered the future of science and of computing. Faced with the continuing specialization of disciplines, scientific progress, according to V. Bush's vision, would be based on the pooling of an ever-growing stock of knowledge, organized, preserved and, above all, consulted thanks to a new type of computer, the "memex". Vannevar Bush imagined that "wholly new forms of encyclopedias would appear, ready made with a mesh of associative trails running through them, ready to be dropped into the memex and there amplified". Sometimes hermetic, the article was nevertheless regarded by researchers as a visionary description of the new generations of computers, the Internet and above all the Web. For many years, it had influenced research and the development of human–machine interactions.

Fig. 4 Vannevar Bush's article in the Atlantic monthly (1945)

For the fiftieth anniversary of the publication of "As we may think", computer scientists from all over the world gathered at a symposium co-organized by the MIT and Brown University. There, Tim Berners-Lee gave the keynote address in tribute to Vannevar Bush, describing the creation of the Internet and the Web as a direct extension of the engineer's 1945 visions:

> I had (and still have) a dream that the web could be less of a television channel and more of an interactive sea of shared knowledge. I imagine it immersing us as a warm, friendly environment made of the things we and our friends have seen, heard, believe or have figured out. I would like it to bring our friends and colleagues closer, in that by working on this knowledge together we can come to better understandings.[7]

Echoing Martin Luther King's emblematic speech, Tim Berners-Lee described a networked scientific community, in which the sharing of knowledge could bring people together and foster mutual understanding.

[7] Tim Berners-Lee, « Hypertext and our collective destiny», Colloque pour les 50 ans de l'article de Vannevar Bush, MIT, 12 octobre 1995. The text is available at https://www.w3.org/Talks/9510_Bush/Talk.html.

For him, the web was not just about the advancement of knowledge, but of society as a whole. This shift from science to politics—i.e. what concerns the city (polis) as a whole—was even more marked in the rest of his speech, which dealt with the organization of research and its relationship to power:

> The Internet grew as a decentralized system. Its design was tasked by the US military, a centrally controlled system, but the Internet Protocols, being decentralized, outgrew that space. The Internet has bred in its engineers a respect for decentralized systems which has in some cases led to anarchic political views. Just as IP packets have no single point of control, nor do Internet news groups. A feeling grows in the community that the whole Internet design process should be able to exist on its own account in a vacuum. It is not clear that this model has survived increase of scale, or impact with the commercial world, which happened at the same time. The lessons, though, have been well learned. The web, like IP, grew because it was decentralized. There was no central authority for web sites, so they could grow at will, appearing spontaneously. Bush's vision is of a decentralized academic society, in which no central figure or library is essential to the process.

The Internet and the Web's decentralized organization are held up as a model for research and innovation, an infrastructure to free them from bureaucratic tutelage. Tim Berners-Lee's comments draw a parallel between the technical architecture of the Internet and the organization of the scientific community that designed it: in fact, defending the former means protecting the latter, against the temptation of national states and businesses to "centralize" the management of the network and, more broadly, the material and immaterial resources of knowledge production. The decentralized nature of the Internet became, in the words of Berners-Lee, a safeguard to protect the new freedoms it has brought about. This excerpt thus shows the political appropriation of the Internet by the IT community and the claims it entails. The network, a space for scientific cooperation beyond state control, was hailed as a symbol as well as an instrument for autonomous and internationalized research. Furthermore, its transformative ambition became a universal project, extending far beyond the borders of the academic world.

In line with this idea, the IT community sought to promote the spread of their invention. Two years before the symposium, the CERN had agreed to place the protocols of the World Wide Web in the public domain. In a document signed by the management on April 30, 1993, the research center officially declared that the web code would be made available to all:

> CERN's intention in this is to further compatibility, common practices and standards in networking and computer supported collaboration. This does not constitute any precedent to be applied to any CERN copyright content.
>
> CERN relinquishes all intellectual property rights to this code both source and binary form, and permission is granted for anyone to use, duplicate, modify and reproduce it.[8]

Contrary to the widespread tendency of patenting software, illustrated by the nuance introduced in the first paragraph above, this emblematic gesture clearly marked the utopian dimension of the "web" project and the penetration of free and open software ideas into the IT community. While most computer scientists had been trained at a time when programs were still freely exchanged (Kelty, 2008; Turner, 2006) and while the Free Software Foundation had just been created by Richard Stallman in 1984, IT scientists imprinted these principles on the development of networks and information systems that required the collaboration of various research teams around the world. By making their codes available, the Internet and the Web thus expanded far beyond the scientific sphere—a distinctive features of these two innovations, compared to other proprietary networks of the time. In a 1996 interview, Jon Postel hence recalled that "*It is very unusual in the research world, that something done as a research project actually gets out there into the world to that extent*".[9]

As a final step in the construction of the Internet utopia, the connection between the IT community and pioneering users of personal computing contributed to the universalization of these principles into a political manifesto for the cyberspace.

[8] Documentation on the arrival of the Internet at the Cern, the invention and licensing of the web are available at https://home.cern/fr/science/computing/birth-web.

[9] Jon Postel, interviewed for OntheInternet in 1996, quoted in Hilary W. Pool (ed.), *Internet: a historical encyclopedia*, volume 2, MTM Publishing, 2005, p. 1999.

3 From Research Network to Cyberspace: The Birth of the Internet Utopia

Alongside the academic development of the Internet, the spread of personal computing enabled the emergence of new electronic communication services in Western societies. By the 1980s, entrepreneurs, journalists, engineers, hackers and even computer-savvy artists could meet online via mailing lists, discussion fora and bulletin board systems (BBS). These exchanges led to the rise of "virtual communities", described by writer Howard Rheingold in a pioneering work on the "electronic frontier" (1993). His work focused notably on the Whole Earth "Lectronick Link" (WELL), a BBS created in 1984 and a popular reference for technology enthusiasts. By the early 1990s, it had around 3,000 subscribers. On its online forums, they discussed freely about politics, culture and sexuality, subject to minimal moderation that encouraged impertinence and heated debate. The WELL heralded the emergence of a new online public space, cemented by shared references and the same ideals of freedom (Turner, 2006).

With the commercial opening of the Internet in the 1990s, these discussions migrated to the new network. The "virtual" and academic communities thus got more intertwined, along with the ethical principles and practices they each defended. Likewise, the scientific utopia truly became a social one. Above the defense of the Internet's project autonomy, the independence of cyberspace evolved into a central political issue around which activists gathered and exchanged online.

3.1 The Privatization of the Internet

In 1990, the NSF was still managing the Internet backbone. Commercial use of the network was prohibited, and private companies were only allowed to connect if they were contributing to a scientific or educational project. The expansion of the Internet, however, challenged the financing of the network by public research. The connection of private institutes and, above all, of an ever-increasing number of personal computers, led to traffic congestion and increased the risk of online viruses. Furthermore, the end of the Cold War, as well as the State's withdrawal initiated by Reagan presidency, entailed a cut in public funding for technological programs. The burden and responsibility of a now global network started to weigh heavily on American research.

Among other founding members of the Internet and the IETF, Vinton Cerf recommended to open up the network to private for-profit companies. In his view, the Internet was to be transformed into a "business machine" to ensure its self-sufficiency.[10] In other words, it was high time people charged for Internet access. The solution also enabled to cut the link to the government purse once and for all, by introducing private contribution for the maintenance of the network. In 1992, Vinton Cerf created the Internet Society (ISOC), a non-profit organization whose main objective was to raise fund and awareness in order to ensure the financial autonomy of the Internet project and of its technical governance bodies, such as the IETF. Faced with increasing external and internal pressure, the NSF gradually relaxed the conditions of use for Internet access and, in 1993, handed over the operation of the "backbone" to private companies (Kelsan & Shah, 2001). Internet access providers emerged, with big telecommunications companies such as AT&T standing alongside local and/or militant players. A few years later, the management of domain names, until then the sole responsibility of the computer science department headed by Jon Postel at the University of Southern California, was also entrusted to a private organization, the Internet Corporation for Assigned Names and Numbers (ICANN) (Klein, 2002).

The privatization of the Internet signaled the end of the IT "Republic". A greater number of private-sector representatives joined the boards of its key organizations (IETF and ICANN), gradually placing researchers from public non-for-profit institutes in a minority. The opening up of the Internet also contributed to the emergence of new political issues, marking the return of national governments, particularly the United States, in the technical governance of networks (Weinberg, 2000). Far from favoring a global society of scientific equals, the network's expansion brought to light new inequalities and issues, such as a digital divide between Western countries and the Global South, as well as the geopolitical stakes pertaining a global dissemination of information. In a 2001 interview, Vinton Cerf recalled the challenges faced by the ISOC at the time, as follows:

> There were all kinds of questions that were economic, social and educational. There were policy questions about what would get in the way of propagating Internet everywhere. There were countries that did not have

[10] Interview from the ComputerWorld Honor Program, *ref. cit.*

> telecommunications infrastructure that could support it. There were countries that had weak economies. There were countries that had no one trained who could actually run a piece of the Internet. There were countries whose governments were agitating against the Internet because they didn't like the free flow of information that it could produce. So, there were just a blizzard of reasons why a societal task force should work on those questions to try to make them more visible, and to try to make at least constructive recommendations for how to spread the Internet and why it was an important thing to do.[11]

At a time when the network was still largely unknown outside specialized circles, the ISOC evolved into an organization to promote the Internet. It was no longer simply a matter of coordinating the international definition of standards among scientists, but of educating, studying and democratizing the development of computer networks and electronic exchanges around the globe. To do so, the ISOC organized international conferences, published reports and recommendations to governments. In this way, the association aimed to defend the interests of the IT community that is to say to preserve the technological architecture of the network and its specific mode of governance, in a context of increasing intervention by governments and private companies.

Paradoxically enough, the end of the IT Republic's golden age also marked the global success of the Internet over national and regional networks. The releasing of the web code to the public domain and the multiplication of access providers enabled the Internet to gain new uses and users all around the world. Yet, the network remained durably permeated by its academic origins and imbued with the scientific imaginaries and collaborative practices that had characterized its development. In this new era of network expansion, the ethics of Internet pioneers was even more asserted, as a set of principles to cherish and preserve in the face of new political and economic players. This challenge was no longer endorsed by researchers alone, but benefited from the mobilization of new activists from the "electronic frontier".

[11] Interview from the ComputerWorld Honor Program, *ref. cit.*

3.2 *Defending Cyberspace: The Birth of the Electronic Frontier Foundation*

In the early 1990s, Internet users formed a small, relatively homogeneous population of passionate technophiles. Although not all of them were academics, they shared with computer researchers a rejection of bureaucratic authority, a fierce attachment to freedom of expression and an appreciation of technical achievements and know-how (Turner, 2006). They populated a virtual territory that was still largely unregulated. As a result, hacker practices flourished on the electronic frontier: they consisted in computer operations involving infiltration, playing with or remote modification of programs that elicited more comment online on their technical virtuosity than on their legality. Yet, with the development of the information economy and the patenting of software, the US federal government grew more and more concerned about these practices deemed as a new form of "computer crime". It launched several operations to put an end to it. Hackers, often very young, were arrested, their homes searched and their computer equipment confiscated. More broadly, many members of online communities suspected of owning or sharing copies of pirated software were interrogated during this period.

The "hacker crackdown" (Sterling, 1992) targeted the very heart of the freedoms and experimentations of cyberspace. In reaction, it cemented virtual communities around a defense of the emblematic values of the early Internet. Of course, data piracy and computer attacks were not unreservedly embraced by all connected users at the time. The definition of an "ethic" that all hackers would respect and endorse was even the subject of much discussion on online forums. But the FBI's intrusion into what had been a relatively protected space, and the confusion between "hackers" and "dangerous outlaws", brought together previously scattered positions to safeguard the emblematic principles and practices of cyberspace.

In 1990, John Perry Barlow was a prominent figure of the cyberspace. An active member of online communities, he took part in several hacker conferences. He was visited by FBI investigators at his ranch during the "hacker crackdown". He recounted his experience in a text entitled "Crime and Puzzlement" that widely circulated on the network. The account is a virulent pamphlet against the government's "despotism tempered with incompetence", and the ignorance of FBI agents, unable to distinguish "a ROM chip from a Vise-grip". John Perry Barlow called for the establishment of a political organization to defend online communities, stating that "it [was] becoming urgent to define the conceptual and legal map of Cyberspace before the ambiguophobes do it for us (with punitive over-precision)". His proposal met with the approval of other Internet pioneers, including Mitch Kapor and John Gilmore, two IT entrepreneurs with whom he founded the Electronic Frontier Foundation, the first advocacy association for the cyberspace.

The organization was officially created in July 1990 "to help civilize the electronic frontier, to make it truly useful and beneficial to everyone, not just an elite, and to do this in a way that is in keeping with our society's highest traditions of the free and open flow of information and communication".[12] It quickly gained the support of other IT entrepreneurs, journalists, civil rights lawyers and other pioneering Internet users. The creation of *Wired* magazine in 1992, "the flagship of Internet culture", whose founder Louis Rossetto joined the EFF, provided a media outlet for the association's members: in the columns of the new magazine, they defended their ideas on the obsolescence of intellectual property[13] or the "open platform" as a mode of regulation.[14]

Early members of the EFF constituted a relatively homogeneous group: with the notable exception of Esther Dyson, a former Wall Street analyst and director of an investment fund specializing in IT, most were men born in the 1950s, self-taught programmers whose recent social ascent relied on the development of the information economy. They formed an early-connected elite, standing out for their intensive, sometimes on the edge of legality, use of new technologies. As Fred Turner demonstrated in his classic work on the countercultural origins of the "cyberculture" (2006), EFF members were heirs to the social movements of the 1960s. This heritage was evident in their social trajectories as much as in their "creative" and "individual" relationship with technology. Perry Barlow, for instance, was the former lyricist of the psychedelic group The Grateful Dead, and a former member of the Students for a Democratic Society in the 1960s. Mitch Kapor had been a teacher of transcendental meditation before founding the company Lotus in 1982, becoming a millionaire at just 35 years old.

[12] *EFFector Online*, Issue 0, December 1990.

[13] "The Economy of Idea", by John Perry Barlow, *Wired*, March 1994.

[14] "Where is the Digital Highway really heading" Mitch Kapor, *Wired*, March 1993.

The EFF is thus paradigmatic of the dissolution of countercultural heritage in the new information economy, as highlighted by Turner. Through their defense of cyberspace, the organization promoted not only the protection of civil liberties online but also the principle of individual emancipation through technology and the advent of more creative relationships to work, freed from bureaucratic rigidities. This evolution echoes the post-68 transformation of capitalism analyzed by Luc Boltanski and Eve Chiapello in France, which they described as an absorption of the "artistic critique" by the networked economy (Chiapello & Boltanski, 2018). This evolution was sometimes met with resistance, even among Internet pioneers and media activists, especially coming from Europe. In 1996, English media scholars Richard Barbrook and Andy Cameron denounced the rise of a new "Californian ideology" marked by the fusion of "the independent spirit of hippies and the entrepreneurial zeal of yuppies" (1996).

Yet the EFF actually brought together a heterogeneous mix of political inclinations: while some members drew closer to the ultra-liberal "New Right" (Esther Dyson) or the libertarian movement (John Gilmore), others, such as Mitch Kapor or Jerry Berman, a former member of the ACLU and first lobbyist for the organization, defended a more positive vision of the role of the State, within the framework of a more or less institutionalized cooperation with the Clinton administration. Between technophile evangelism and lobbying at the Congress, the EFF maintained, during its first years of existence, an opportunistic relationship with public authorities.[15] The organization indeed took an active part in the government's "information superhighway" program, launched by Vice-President Al Gore. It took the tentative intervention of the US government, notably in the context of the telecommunication regulation reform, to push the EFF toward a more oppositional stance. In 1994, the association gave up its Washington office and moved to San Francisco: it marked a clear break with the federal institutions of the East Coast, supported by a virulent discourse on the independence of cyberspace.

[15] "The Merry Pranksters go to Washingon" by Joshua Quittner, *Wired*, June 1994.

3.3 A Declaration of Independence of the Cyberspace

In February 1996, CEOs, politicians and intellectuals gathered in Davos for the 25th World Economic Forum. The mood was one of commercial enthusiasm: the development of the information and communication economy seemed to promise an acceleration of growth and innovation in the industrial world. EFF founder John Perry Barlow was among the guests, invited as an expert on cyberspace. Far from sharing the enthusiasm of many of the leaders present, he deplored the new interest of governments and industries in taming the virtual world, in which practices on the bangs of the market and political institution had flourished. To address the attempt of businesses and nation states to claim back the network, he published an online Declaration of Independence for Cyberspace, widely shared on mailing lists. It began as follows:

> Governments of the Industrial World, you weary giants of flesh and steel, I come from Cyberspace, the new home of Mind. On behalf of the future, I ask you of the past to leave us alone. You are not welcome among us. You have no sovereignty where we gather.
> We have no elected government, nor are we likely to have one, so I address you with no greater authority than that with which liberty itself always speaks. I declare the global social space we are building to be naturally independent of the tyrannies you seek to impose on us. You have no moral right to rule us nor do you possess any methods of enforcement we have true reason to fear.[16]

John Perry Barlow's declaration of independence epitomized the establishment of the Internet as a political utopia in the 1990s. The cyberspace was there described as a "non-place" (the literal Greek translation of "u-topia"), a negation of the real or the "meat" space within the virtual. Perry Barlow further emphasized the fundamental distinction between these two territories: for him, physical constraints, borders and even social identities were purportedly abolished in cyberspace. Through the elimination of prejudices and power relations, the Internet marked the advent of a "civilization of the mind", "more humane and fair", a new society breaking from the physical world and the order of the past represented by governments' bureaucracies. The declaration drew on the imaginary of

[16] Message posted on February 9, 1996. The full text is available on the website of the EFF at: https://www.eff.org/fr/cyberspace-independence.

science fiction, contributing to the ambivalence of this description. The text evoked simultaneously a vanishing world—perhaps one that never truly existed—and an ideal to be brought forth. More than the political project it embodied, it was the poetic strength of Barlow's text that really made it a founding and unifying reference for online activism and cyberspace organizations.

This text was all the more so utopian that it described cyberspace as a world apart, at a time when this separation was being called into question by the expansion of the e-commerce and the development of new regulations. John Perry Barlow indeed wrote on the very day after the adoption of a major telecommunications reform in the United States. As part of the Telecommunication Act, the Communication Decency Act attempted to set up greater control over online communications. Since the bill's introduction in Congress in 1995, the EFF had played a leading role in preventing its adoption. The legislative proposal mainly aimed at fighting online child pornography but the EFF denounced the vagueness of the law, its inapplicability and, above all, the risk of a "major and disproportionate censorship" of the Internet it entailed. They organized the first online campaign to fight the legislation, notably an operation called "Turn the web black", during which a thousand websites displayed an all-black homepage to protest against the introduction of "internet censorship".

In the Declaration of Independence, the illegitimacy of government intervention in cyberspace was particularly emphasized. For Barlow, government had "no rights" in a de-territorialized cyberspace and their action was bound to ineffectiveness ("no means"). On the other hand, Barlow's pamphlet contributed to the "naturalization" of self-regulatory practices that had developed early-on in cyberspace, engaging the sole responsibility of users:

> We believe that from ethics, enlightened self-interest, and the commonweal, our governance will emerge. Our identities may be distributed across many of your jurisdictions. The only law that all our constituent cultures would generally recognize is the Golden Rule. We hope we will be able to build our particular solutions on that basis. But we cannot accept the solutions you are attempting to impose.

The "Golden Rule" or "netiquette" referred to the informal code of conduct claimed by hackers. Not without recalling the answer of the IT community to the "Morris Worm", it was here considered as the only legitimate and effective governance principle for the network. The text could thus be read as another fundamental stance against government intervention, at a time when nation states were attempting to regain control of a virtual space whose development has largely escaped them.

As much a eulogy for a world of freedoms that was disappearing without ever really having existed as a political project for online activism in the years to come, the Declaration of Independence of Cyberspace marked a final stage in the construction of a utopian Internet. In fact, it formulated a political project that would be adopted by several pioneering Internet organization in Western countries: preserving the cyberculture and Internet freedoms against the attempt of nation states to control the network. Written during the World Economic Forum of Davos, the declaration indeed circulated outside the US, contributing to the internationalization of the Internet culture as a cause to defend. In 1996, new associations inspired by the EFF appeared around the world to protect the "laws" of cyberspace and the free flow of information and communication. « Citadel-EFF»[17] was created in France, as well as the Electronic Frontier Finland and the Electronic Frontier Norway. On the French organization's website, the presentation referred directly to the US movement: Citadel-EFF, "like the EFF in the United States, aims to ensure that the exercise of citizens' rights, recognized by the French Constitution and the Declaration of Human Rights, is properly enforced in the realm of communication technologies". Citadel-EFF became part of a network of "partner" associations fighting against government control of the Internet: it relayed actions taken against Internet censorship in the United States, Germany and Singapore.[18] At the time, these affiliations were only supported by rare contacts and cooperation between activists scattered around the globe. Yet, their development enabled the emergence of bridging points for transnational campaigns and mobilizations. It marked a new stage in the globalization of Internet activism, with the dissemination of principles and motives of protest against State intervention on virtual networks.

[17] Citadel stands for «Citizens and Internet users association for the defense of liberties» Citoyens et internautes tous associés pour une défense des libertés.

[18] Information and documents are to be found on the archived website, accessible via the Wayback Machine of the Internet Archive. https://web.archive.org/web/19991007083618/http://www.citadeleff.org.

* * *

John Perry Barlow's "home of the mind" in the Declaration of Independence of Cyberspace is reminiscent of Berners-Lee's "ocean of shared knowledge". Likewise, the professional ethic claimed by the IT community during the "Morris worm" episode echoes the "Golden Rule" that the Internet pioneers opposed to US government laws. The utopia of the Internet and the antagonism between the Internet and the State is based on the convergence of these scientific and social mobilizations for the network's independence. These struggles defined a genuine network "politics", that is to say a set of principles and objectives that should govern the development of the Internet. The aim was to protect the collaborative production and exchange of information, embedded in a decentralized communication infrastructure. These principles characterized new forms of governance through ethics and technical standards that had a lasting impact on the ways in which Internet and digital policies would be conceived.

This conception of networked governance, or Internet constitutionalism, has never been better formulated than by Lawrence Lessig's sentence that "code is law" in cyberspace (1999). The phrase was rapidly endorsed by Internet pioneers and activists; it is still used nowadays to protest against laws that are insufficiently attentive to technological constraints or may damage the core values embedded in the decentralized architecture of the Internet. The sentence helped establish the programmers of code as the legitimate actors to manage the Internet and its core resources, while largely eluding national administrations and traditional bureaucratic agents. Even today, and despite the transformations in the technical governance of the Internet, the institutions created by 1980s computer scientists are still standing, promoting coordination between the various technical communities connected to the Internet.

This chapter has thus shown that, far from a coherent political project, the Internet utopia was the product of ad hoc political claims against government intervention, throughout the 1980s and 1990s. It draws on a patchwork of discourses whose various intellectual origins, between liberal influence and libertarian culture, scientific ideal and countercultural heritage, have retrospectively been forgotten. Consequently, this utopia has grown into a myth, a reference and almost a fetish for digital activism and internet companies. From the 1990s onward, it has constantly been reclaimed or reinvented, embroidered around a canvas sewn from the threads of independence, free knowledge and distributed powers; a banner never so much brandished as when these principles seemed under threat. The combined charisma of its founding fathers and the evocative power of their emblematic manifestos have given this specific politics an undeniable social force, substantiating the antagonism between the Internet and the State.

References

Abbate, J. (1999a). *Inventing the internet*. MIT Press.

Abbate, J. (1999b). Cold war and white heat: The origins and meanings of packet switching. In: D. Mackenzie, & J. Wajcman (Eds.), *The social shaping of technology* (pp. 351–371). Open University Press.

Akrich, M. (1992). The description of technical objects. *Shaping technology/building society. Studies in sociotechnical change* (pp. 205–224).

Barbrook, R., & Cameron, A. (1996). The californian ideology. *Science as culture*, *6*(1), 44–72.

Barlow, J. P. (1990). *Crime & Puzzlement*. Electronic Frontier Foundation. https://www.eff.org/pages/crime-andpuzzlement

Bradner, S. (1999). The internet engineering task force. In: DiBona, C., Okman, S. Stone, M. (Eds.), *Open Sources: voices from the open source revolution* (pp. 47–52). Sebatopol, O'Reilly.

Ceruzzi, P. E. (1998). *A history of modern computing*. MIT Press.

Ceruzzi, P. E. (2008). *Internet alley: High technology in Tysons Corner, 1945–2005*. MIT Press.

Chiapello, E., & Boltanski, L. (2018). *The new spirit of capitalism*. Verso Books.

Coleman, E. G. (2013). *Coding freedom: The ethics and aesthetics of hacking*. Princeton University Press.

DeNardis, L. (2009). *Protocol politics: The globalization of Internet governance*. MIT Press.

Gingras, Y. (2002). Les formes spécifiques de l'internationalité du champ scientifique. *Actes de la recherche en sciences sociales, 141*(2), 31–45.

Flichy, P. (2007). *The internet imaginaire*. MIT Press.

Hafner, K., & Lyon, M. (1996). *Where wizards stay up late: The origins of the Internet*. Simon and Schuster.

Kelsan, J., & Shah, R. C. (2001). Fool us once shame on you—Fool us twice shame on us: What we can learn from the Internet privatizations of the Internet backbone network and the domain name systems. *Washington University Law Quaterly, 1*(79), 89–220.

Kelty, C. (2008). *Two bits. The cultural significance of free software*. Duke University Press.

Klein, H. (2002). ICANN and Internet governance: Leveraging technical coordination to realize global public policy. *The Information Society, 18*(3), 193–207.

Leslie, S. W. (1993). *The Cold War and American science: The military-industrial-academic complex at MIT and Stanford.* Columbia University Press.

Lessig, L. (1999). *Code and other laws of cyberspace.* Basic Books.

Pelkey et al. (2022). *Circuits, Packets, and Protocols.* ACM.

Pool, H. W. (Ed.). (2005). *Internet: A historical encyclopedia* (Vol. 2). MTM Publishing.

Rheingold, H. (1993). *The virtual community: Finding commection in a computerized world.* Addison-Wesley Longman Publishing Co., Inc.

Schafer, V., & Thierry, B. (2012). *Le Minitel. L'enfance numérique de la France.* Nuvis.

Seaver, N. (2017). Algorithms as culture: Some tactics for the ethnography of algorithmic systems. *Big Data and Society, 4*(2).

Skolnikoff, E. B. (1993). Knowledge without borders? Internationalization of the Research Universities. *Daedalus, 122*(4), 225–252.

Sterling, B. (1992). *The hacker crackdown: Law and disorder on the electronic frontier.* Penguin Books.

Turner, F. (2006). *From counterculture to cyberculture: Stewart Brand, the Whole Earth Network, and the rise of digital utopianism.* University of Chicago Press.

Weinberg, J. (2000). ICANN and the problem of legitimacy. *Duke LJ, 50*, 187.

Winner, L. (1980). Do artifacts have politics? *Daedalus, 109*(1), 121–136.

Wolfe, A. J. (2013). *Competing with the Soviets: Science, technology, and the state in Cold War America.* JHU Press.

Zarca, B. (2009). L'ethos professionnel des mathématiciens. *Revue française de sociologie, 50*(2), 351–384.

CHAPTER 3

The State Against the Internet: Bureaucratic Resistance to the Network in France

> The limits of the Internet demonstrate that the infrastructure cannot, in the long term, become the world's network for information superhighways.
> Civil Engineer Gerard Théry, Public Report to the Prime Minister, France, 1994

In the mid-1990s, advances in information and communication technologies sparked enthusiasm in Western countries, which embarked on the development of new "information superhighways". Popularized by the Clinton administration and its National Network Infrastructure Plan, the expression points to economic power and modernity. Yet, enthusiasm for virtual communication networks should not be confused with unanimous support for the Internet. In many countries, the Internet competed with proprietary networks, more or less sponsored by national governments. France, home of the Minitel, epitomized this national resistance to the Internet.

In 1994, French Prime Minister Edouard Balladur commissioned Gérard Théry, General Civil Engineer in Telecommunications, to write a strategic report on the development of networks in France. In a few terse lines, Gérard Théry discarded the Internet. He advocated instead in favor of a "faster Minitel" that would lead France toward an "Eldorado of video-phoning". The report's conclusion was unambiguous: future

A. Bellon, *A Socio-History of Internet Policies*, International Series on Public Policy, https://doi.org/10.1007/978-3-031-69099-0_3

networks should be based on a centralized infrastructure, rather than on the Internet, a "limited" network with a bad reputation.

More than twenty-five years later, now that the Internet has spun its web around the world and that the Minitel has been definitively abandoned, reading the Théry report would undoubtedly make you smile. Its erroneous predictions about the future of the Internet, its gargantuan budget proposals—11 billion of francs of annual investment, i.e. 2.3 billion euros for ten years—have become in France the symbol of a worn-out *colbertism*.[1] The episode displayed technocrats unable of anticipating, triggering or even supporting a key innovation. With the benefit of hindsight, the report's recommendations seem "absurd" as they kept France on an outdated technological rut, carved out by civil engineers of the 1980s. During the 1990s, France indeed lagged behind in terms of Internet spread, compared to similar countries such as Germany (Fig. 1). Thery report also reinforced the illegitimacy of state intervention in the realm of technology, an idea supported not only by the Internet communities, but also, increasingly, by a fringe of the elite within the public administration itself.

How can we understand the French government's reluctance toward the Internet? Was Théry's project really so "absurd" in the light of state sovereignty issues? And is the suggested program for France really so far removed from others that proliferated at the same time in other developed countries? To answer these questions, this chapter invites the reader to forget, just for a moment, the "end of the story". It is a prerequisite to investigate the reasons why whole sections of the French administration held back the development of the Internet in the 1990s. Rather than establishing in retrospect the inanity of public policies designed decades ago, one should endorse Pierre Bourdieu's "postulate of intelligibility" as constitutive of the social science epistemology (2018). According to him "state institutions work properly, they have a reason, in the sense of the reason of a series which means that once understood, it is no longer random, it is no longer just any old way. (…) And sometimes, reason

[1] *Colbertism* is a political economic doctrine that refers to Jean-Baptiste Colbert, General Controller of Finances under Louis XIV, King of France during the seventeenth century. Its central principle is that the economy and the industry of France should serve the state, and that state intervention was needed to secure and to organize limited resources. ***Industrial colbertism*** is an expression commonly used in France to describe strong state interventionism as opposed to market-driven innovation.

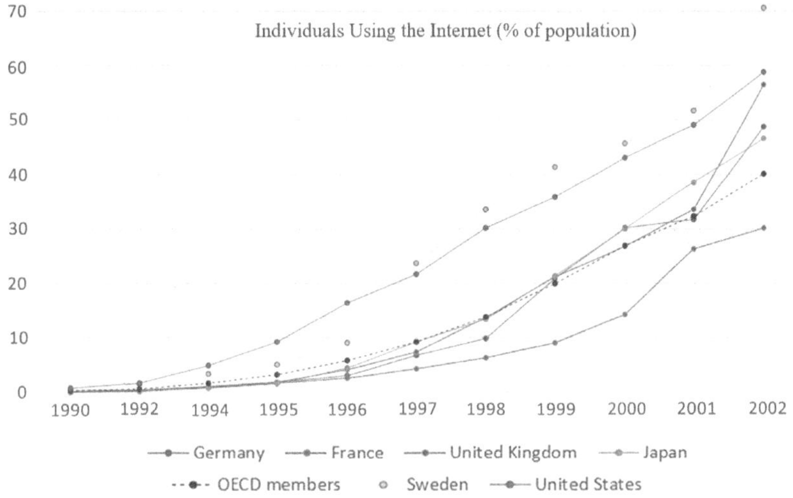

Fig. 1 France lags behind in Internet adoption

has not only scientific but also political virtues: it pulls things out of absurdity" (ibid., p. 238). Hence, finding the political and bureaucratic rationales of French government toward the Internet is the aim of the following chapter.

The sociology of decision has already looked beyond the confines of the State to examine the logic behind "radical errors", showing that the absurd dimension of a decision cannot be reduced to "bad foresight" or "poor judgement". Rather, the uncertain, collective and interactionist nature of the decision-making process helps explain how individuals tradeoff between different options, to the point of preferring a solution that may seem aberrant in retrospect (Ermakoff, 2008; Morel, 2004). Similarly, attention to the social and economic context help us understand the technological choices made during the 1990s. At the time, the coexistence of multiple information networks, the uncertain future of technologies and their social acceptance did not secure a self-evident "victory" for the Internet.

This chapter intends to show that the logics of political decision-making produces lasting "framing effects" (Goffman, 1974) on the conduct of innovation policies, especially in the case of information network policy. It contributes to the discussion of the role of expertise as a disputed attribute of political decision, claimed by competing groups of players and asserted in specific contexts. Indeed, the respective merits of each technology were debated in a bureaucratic field that was deeply divided between sectors and professions. Far from being a unanimous point of view within the French State, distrust of the Internet aroused mainly from the technical elite and sovereign ministry departments—such as the ministries of Interior, Defense, Foreign Affairs and Justice—relegating to the margins the engineers who dared to defend the "US" network. The battle over networks that happened within the state reveals the existence of an internal critique of the bureaucracy in France, that used the Internet, its political forms and its rhetorical motives, to reject the excessive power of the *grand corps*. More generally, this case study sheds light on the reform of technological policies in Europe, in a context of economic liberalization promoted by the European Union.

This chapter relies on the testimonies of civil engineers and senior civil servants that served in the 1990s. Their accounts enabled us to reconstruct oppositions toward the Internet and the concrete conditions of access to information networks within the French administration at the time. These testimonies were complemented by a careful study of administrative reports, professional literature and online archives, which, even better than a posteriori accounts, provide a context for the rationale behind bureaucratic opposition to the Internet. By comparing these different sources, we can capture the atmosphere of the time, and the conditions under which the French government favored a Minitel-like solution.

The chapter first delves into the production of a government stance against the Internet, the result of an exercise in administrative prophesying that seeks to make sense of technological disruptions and guide public decision-making (1). It then demonstrates the integration of this decision into an administrative space that was less uniform than the analysis of reports alone might suggest, undoing the artificial homogeneity of the French State and the irreducibility of the "bureaucracy" versus "Internet" antagonism (2). Another, more comprehensive story emerges, outlined at the end of the chapter—one of a general reform of innovation policies, with the administrative battles surrounding the Internet serving as its foundation (3).

1 Administrative Expertise Versus Technological Uncertainty

Théry's report describes the "information revolution" as an ongoing process from which new public issues have emerged. Like the industrial revolution before it, the information revolution relies on a series of technological disruptions that modify economic structures, work organizations, and social relationships. These simultaneous and convergent upheavals contribute to the blurring of traditional references for government intervention. They confront public decision-makers with a situation of "sociotechnical uncertainty" (Callon et al., 2011) resulting from the rapid evolution of technologies, as well as correlated social, economic, and political developments that condition the adoption and dissemination of these new technologies in society. In this uncertain context, administrative expert commissions serve as the primary support for political decision-making, and the one coordinated by Gérard Théry has a particular impact, due to its popularity as a prominent figure in the French telecommunication industry.

In 1994, Gérard Théry was indeed a true public figure in France: the former Managing Director of the Telecommunications administration (from 1974 to 1981), "he was one of the few high-ranking civil servants to grace magazine covers" (Cohen, 1992, p. 74, *our translation*). He enjoyed rare prestige and legitimacy within the upper echelons of civil service and in economic circles. He embodied a generation of modernizing civil engineers whose commitment within the State had contributed to the industrial successes of Arianespace, Airbus, and the Minitel. In the tradition of these large state-supported programs, the Théry report put into play the proclaimed ability of the technical elite to position themselves as "prophets" of public action, both experts and decision-makers in the field of new technologies. The style of the report is characterized by a blend of technical popularization and literary descriptions designed to captivate the reader's imagination. Indeed, the main challenge was not so much to predict the future as it was to project technological development and mobilize national economic actors around a shared future. The approach taken by Théry thus mimicked previous state-led innovation plans: technological developments were discussed in regard of the social transformations they enabled and the forms of public policies they required. Far from being a neutral comment on current technological evolutions, the report must be analyzed "as a product and as a producer of bureaucratic rationality" (Gayon, 2016). Its content and reception reveal a particular technocratic rationale that had lasting symbolic effects on the perception of the Internet within the upper administration.

The conclusions of the Théry report should therefore be read as an emblematic performance of technocratic expertise: they reveal how the technical elite address socio-technical uncertainty, the symbolic weight of the Minitel as a major industrial success and innovation management conceived as a prerogative of civil servants, in the name of national sovereignty.

1.1 Information and Technology Networks in Europe

At the start of the 1990s, communications networks represented a wide range of infrastructures, equipment, protocols and services (Table 1). In Europe, Germany had the Bildschirmtext (Box 1), the UK Prestel and France the Minitel; these services coexisted with Usenet and CompuServe messaging systems; academics were rather using specific research network, such as EUnet or the Internet. In an unstable technological landscape, these options competed and often overlapped: in 1991, for example, a young French entrepreneur created an access to the Internet via the Minitel. While more and more services were gradually being connected to the Internet, the landscape was still dominated by so-called closed networks, which formed multiple virtual communities developing under the shelter of proprietary protocols.

Table 1 Describing a network environment and the various technical layers of communication networks

Network technical element	*Examples*
Infrastructures: the physical material used to carry communications. Connections between countries are usually made via undersea cable or satellite. Conversely, the "local loop"—the part of the network between the service provider center and the subscriber—was based on the copper wires of the landline phone system	Fiber optic cable, coaxial cable, copper phone lines, satellite

(continued)

Table 1 (continued)

Network technical element	*Examples*
Devices: All the machines connected to a network. They could be terminals (endpoints) or servers and routers, that store and route information	Computers, Minitel Box, TV sets, telephones and cell phones
Protocols: IT standards that specify how information is transmitted or displayed. Some standards are "open", i.e. they are in the public domain and can be used by anyone. This is the case for Internet protocols. Others are "proprietary", belonging to one or more telecoms operators	TCP/IP, http (open protocols) X.25, Vidéotex (Minitel proprietary protocol), X.400 (research networks protocol)
Services: the various applications based on a network. We also speak of "proprietary" services when access is configured and restricted to subscribers only. They include mailing services, forums, chat, etc.	*Compuserve* or *Microsoft Network*, for example, were network e-mail services: initially "proprietary systems", they migrated to the Web in 1996, becoming freely accessible from any browser

Box 1 Communication Networks in Germany

As in many other countries, the Internet entered Germany through the global community of computer research: in 1984, a first Internet mail was sent to Karlsruhe University.[2] Germany was thus the third country to join the research network, after the US and Israel, a few months before. This early connection was largely the result of the involvement of the Karlsruhe informatics computer center, headed by Werner Zorn, computer scientist in interconnection research. If Germany was thus the first European country connected to

[2] Early history of Internet in Germany and the local battles between TCP/IP and OSI protocols was found at https://www.internethalloffame.org/2013/07/29/historic-first-email-us-germany-arrives-1984/

the Internet, the development of the network was also confronted with competing networks and protocols supported by the State (Röhr, 2021). In Germany, the Bildschirmtext or Btx, run by the German Post Office, offered a Minitel-like service between 1983 and 2001. The Btx was an interactive online service, combining telephone and television functions into one means of communication. Much like the Minitel, it originally used the English videotext standard and was heavily centralized in terms of content and communication control. It allowed the development of business services (especially in banking) as well as erotic messaging. Yet the Btx did not enjoy the same success as the Minitel, mainly due to its restrictive policy and high usage fees. Service providers had first to contract with the Bundespost, then purchase separately, and at high prices, a special hardware approved by the postal service. This was one of the main differences with the Minitel, based on a relatively cheap hardware, often rented by the Telecom administration in France. Although less successful than other systems, the Btx experience reveals the intertwining of industrial and innovation policies, as well as the stranglehold that administrations had on telecommunications in Europe. Yet the postal monopoly on these end devices, modems and telephones, fell with the liberalization of telecommunication in Germany on July 1989. From that date on, private mailbox networks such as FidoNet or MausNet became widespread and were able to offer some of the services available via Btx. Gradually, these new services migrated on the Internet. In 1993, Btx became part of the newly created Datex-J service in order to separate the network infrastructure from the information service. As soon as 1995, Datex-J was not pursued further and was replaced by the T-Online service in 1995. Contrary to France, the lesser success of Btx solution and the early liberalization of the sector in Germany undoubtedly favored the adoption of Internet solutions by businesses and individuals alike in the 1990s.

In the 1990s, the various components of information networks were affected by a series of innovations: the invention of new communication protocols and softwares, the creation of more efficient and cost-effective machines, the development of optical fiber technology, etc. These innovations constantly modified the ways in which information was exchanged and processed. They gave rise to a state of radical uncertainty regarding the future of technology. Will the progress of optical fiber make the transmission of information through copper wire obsolete? Will new microcomputers favor the adoption of the Internet by French households (Fig. 2)? Will the new protocols developed by telecommunications companies be adopted as widely as Internet standards? To these open questions, experts could only respond with speculations, based on incomplete information and prejudiced visions, deeply tied to the professional environments in which they were elaborated.

The propensity of networks to incorporate recent innovations was a decisive issue in the technological battles of the time. In reports and specialized journals, the advent of one large-encompassing network providing access to a multitude of services, as the Internet would later become, was hailed as the most likely option, but also the most profitable. The term "information superhighways" referred to this idea of a network that will encompass all others, capable of transporting both voice and image and likely to contribute to the development of various economic sectors such as education, culture, finance or health. However, the physical (infrastructures) and software (protocols) features of this "super-network" were still a subject of debate. While some experts, especially among computer scientists, championed the generativity of the Internet, it was largely dismissed by French companies and online service

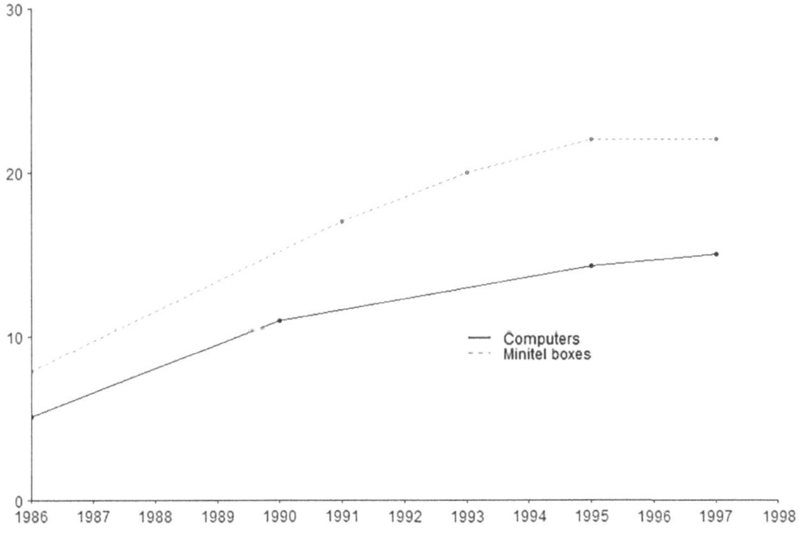

Fig. 2 Electronic equipment in French households (in %)

providers who viewed the US network as a tool reserved for research, not compatible with the development of new businesses. In 1994, the annual report of the French Association of Multimedia Telematics (AFTEL), a professional union of online content publishers, considered that the Internet was not reliable enough to host French-language messaging services.

Technological uncertainty increased the risk associated with any decision. Indeed, any option came with high investment costs: choosing a network meant investing in a new IT system, staff training and maintenance contracts. To ensure the profitability of such investments, the ability of economic players to anticipate socio-technical developments, to avoid falling behind and to secure their position was crucial. A service provider had to ensure the compatibility of its software with the network(s) used and preferred by its clients. A telecommunications operator had to be able to recover investment in the infrastructure through market expansion. Both private and public entities primarily sought to avoid being locked into "irreversible" technological environments. It was all the more true for large state-led programs: while the French government was still pondering the mixed results of the "Cable Plan"—an investment program to connect every household with optic fiber cables—public decision-makers remained cautious. They delayed decision through the organization of expert missions, including the one entrusted to Gérard Théry. The latter suggested a relaunching of the Cable Plan to boost the multimedia industry and to favor the development of new video services, such as virtual museum tours or video conferencing. This integration of telecommunications and audiovisual industries echoed the success of the Minitel, an industrial project in which Théry had been largely involved.

1.2 The Heyday of the "Little Black Box"

The Minitel was developed in France by the General Department of Telecommunications (DGT) in the late 1970s, as both a technological and a social project. It relied on a series of innovations developed by the DGT's research centers: the Minitel combined an easy-to-use device with limited specifications—the "little black box" (Fig. 3)—based on innovative data transmission and screen display protocols—Videotex—running on a centralized communication network—Transpac. The launch of the Minitel in French took place in 1982, but its success owed much to an original business model invented in 1984. The Minitel indeed worked on a per-minute pricing structure based on premium-rate numbers operated by the state-owned telecommunication company (3614, 3615 and 3616). The revenue was then distributed between the telecommunication operator and various service providers. In a few years, this system made the whole program profitable. At first reluctant media companies rapidly got on board when they discovered that Minitel services, especially erotic messaging services, were very lucrative and a good way to pay for the paper press. In the second half of the 1980s, tele-services mushroomed in private as well as public organizations: state administrations created Minitel services to get exam results, to read official reports or to find assistance for administrative procedures.

Not without a certain pride, the Théry report emphasized in 1994 that "the Minitel had allowed the development of a unique dynamic in the world" (p. 61, *our translation*), providing businesses, administrations and a large portion of the population with an early experience of interactive media and electronic commerce. For historians of technology and science, the Minitel indeed facilitated the emergence of online conversation and virtual practices, sowing in French society the seeds of an upcoming "digital revolution " (Schafer & Thierry, 2012).

And in 1994, the Minitel was far from being on its deathbed. It generated over 7 billion francs that year (equivalent to 670 million euros), shared between France Télécom and numerous service providers. The number of devices and services also reached their peak in 1994, with over

Fig. 3 A Minitel in 1980

20% of households owning a Minitel box. Yet, the success of the Minitel remained confined to France. Despite the praise from many commentators abroad (William & Towsik, 1994), including Clinton's technology advisor (Lytel, 1989), despite France Telecom's attempts to conquer foreign markets (Mailland, 2015), the French technology did not export well, leading French researcher Benjamin Thierry to playfully say that "the whole world envied us, but no one bought it from us". Unlike Internet protocols that were in the public domain, French telematic services relied on proprietary software that France Télécom sold at a high price.

1.3 Who Is Afraid of the Internet?

In view of the national success of the Minitel, mistrust toward the Internet in France primarily stemmed from its US origin. The Internet was indeed conceived as a rival technology at a time when the liberalization in telecommunications markets had intensified competition between large companies in the OECD. The Théry report was also haunted by the fear of France "lagging behind" in the new economy of information. This fear was a recurring theme in the "industrialist rhetoric" of the French technocracy, justifying the support of national champions on the dread of decline and loss of economic power (Cohen, 1992). The strategy outlined in the Théry report aimed to preserve the position that the French industries have gained with the Minitel. Gérard Théry did not properly advocate for the Minitel as it was, but rather for a "modernized" version of the Minitel, incorporating the latest innovations.

> My ambition is to create a multimedia Minitel. We're preparing a new project based on high-speed fiber-optic ATM, a network that will be better than the Internet. An industrial call for tenders is underway. The Internet does not work well with multimedia services because it doesn't offer sufficient bandwidth for interactive video. Even in the United States, there is resistance to the Internet, because it is still too expensive and not accessible to everyone. (...) Of course, the Internet is nothing to sneeze at. But when you miss an express train, you don't run like crazy to catch it up. Especially if there's a faster train behind it. This train's about to leave and we're taking it.[3]

[3] Interview of Gérard Théry, in the French economic newspaper *La Tribune,* on November 25, 1996. [our translation].

His vision was shared by many professionals involved in the Minitel industrial ecosystem. The information superhighway project indeed embraced three industrial sectors marked by state-led monopoly and state-owned companies: audiovisual, IT and telecommunications. At a time when the Internet did not have a stable business model, the Minitel system with its centralized pricing made it possible to envision new markets for online multimedia services. Besides, the rapid development of the Internet in the 1990s was causing traffic jams, slowing down the network. On the contrary, the French telecommunications research center had developed a new scalable communication standard, the "ATM" (Asynchronous transfer mode), to ensure the transmission of audiovisual data on electronic networks. This protocol, compatible with packets of data of varying sizes, was at the heart of the strategy developed in the Théry report:

> The [ATM] enables connections with variable speeds according to demand and ensures the continuous flow of information with an acceptable delay for audiovisual communications. An enormous advantage is that it allows for processing voice, text, and audiovisual connections indifferently, efficiently switching signals at very high speeds, particularly for multimedia. ATM will therefore be the key technology of the information superhighway. (Théry Report, p. 26, our translation)

Finally, as the Internet gradually spread its web in Europe, security concerns added to industrial sovereignty issue in building a national reluctance toward the Internet. One must not forget that the 1980s were marked by the "ECHELON" affair in Europe, a surveillance program operated by the US and its partner (Australia, Canada, New Zealand and the UK). Not unlike the Snowden revelations thirteen years later, a series of disclosures and investigations showed that the system was being misused for industrial espionage and surveillance of US's Western allies (Keefe, 2006).[4] In France, the Ministry of Defense thus feared a new "breach in the national security systems" [Interview 22, male, advisor to the Ministry of IT and Research (1994–1996), May 2016]. General Desvignes, head of the department dealing with Security and Information Systems (SCSSI), declared a war on the Internet, which he considered as

[4] See also Franco Piodi and Iolanda Mombelli, "The Echelon Affair, The EP and the global Interception System (1998–2000)", Study of the European Parliamentary Research Service, November 2014.
https://www.europarl.europa.eu/EPRS/EPRS-Study-538877-Echelon.pdf

"structurally unsafe". He managed to make it compulsory for any administrative agent connecting to the Internet to use an electronic security box, a device that greatly complicated (and slowed down) the access to the network. One interviewee ironically described this complex process:

> The IT security department, led by the formidable General Desvignes, a subdivision of the General Secretariat for National Defense, was managing various matters such as arms export authorizations, security interceptions, and a few other highly sensitive issues. He imposed on us the installation of this manual communication box. The principle was very simple (smiling). For anyone wishing to use the internet, one must first turn off their computer, manually switch on the box, wait a minute, then restart the computer, and then, finally, connect to the Internet. [Interview 37, technology expert for the General Planning Commission (1994–1997) then Information Society Advisor to the Prime Minister (1997–2002), July 2017].

Although reading these precautions make us smile nowadays, security concerns about the Internet were not entirely unjustified at the time. Let us recall for example, the damages provoked by the uncontrolled spread of computer viruses such as the "Morris worm" (see Chapter 1). For the civil engineers writing the report with Gérard Théry, the fundamentally "open" nature of the Internet was regarded as its main political pitfall. The technological features of the Internet contrasted with the one chosen for the Minitel, a "reliable" and "closed" network system that allowed for the control of access and communication, and organized exchanges between economic players. The centralized architecture of the Minitel network had been designed to enable technocratic management of communications and innovations. It facilitated the implementation of public policies on the network and the regulation of online practices. With Minitel, the State had many levers for public intervention: as one engineer interviewed recalled, it was possible to "cut off" communications, increase the price of a service or withdraw a publisher's authorization to transmit—all types of action that the open protocols of the Internet would soon make inoperative [Interview 54, male, Head of IT at the Ministry of Culture, January 2017].

Eventually, the bureaucratic defense of the Minitel over the Internet was not so much a matter of technological superiority but a ponderation on the respective political properties of the two networks. With the Minitel, the French State was able to organize an industrial ecosystem and enjoyed various levers of action on online communication. Théry's emphasis on the Internet's technical "limitation" must therefore be understood in the light of the bureaucratic rationality he embodied as a career civil engineer: economic—safeguarding a lucrative business model—industrial—supporting a national multimedia industry—as well as security and political interests—preserving national sovereignty over communications, explain his stance on the Internet. Taking these interests into account more generally help us understand why many Minitel players, including telecommunications services and content providers, favored at first the national option. This logic encouraged a distrust toward the Internet that spread across the public administration in the 1990s. Yet a few agents were still favoring the Internet: and like their opponents, they did so, not so much in the name of its technological superiority, but against a vision of State's economic intervention that they considered archaic. In the course of the 1990s, the Internet thus became the focus point of struggles between technical experts within the French bureaucracy. By fighting over the Minitel and the Internet, they promoted in fact opposing conceptions of innovation management and the role of the government.

2 Technological Battles Across the State

After the recommendations of the Théry report, the investments of the newly established "Interministerial Committee on Information Highways", were, in fact, relatively cautious: only "experiments" for the deployment of optic fiber cables were launched, as well as calls for projects for new multimedia services. Their amount did not exceed 50 million francs, far from the 11 billion advocated by Gérard Théry. In fact, the French government rather seemed unwilling to make a decisive choice among different technological options, while criticisms of the Théry report aroused in the industrial and administrative fields. In some public organizations, Internet services were even created, contrary to the Committee's recommendations. Often ignored, sometimes fought against by their hierarchies, these initiatives slowly contributed to the penetration of the Internet into the administration. After having studied the rationale of Minitel supporters, this section is devoted to their opponent's narratives, demonstrating that, far from a homogenous reluctance of the State toward the Internet, the US network also had ardent supporters within the French administration.

1990s technology and innovation policies are indeed a strategic observation point for the study of intrastate power relationships. The Internet notably crystallized oppositions between sectors and administrations, bringing into play the hierarchies, beliefs and skills that structured the distribution of power in the administrative field. Old quarrels were resumed, with the Internet network as a new point of contention. Even among the major administrative bodies—the so-called *grand corps*—the Internet was a divisive issue, sparking the support of a handful of mavericks, scattered across ministries and whose incursions online were sometimes roundly condemned. From the margins of central government, Internet promoters used the network to criticize the technical bureaucracy, holding back the need for the State to evolve at the dawn of a new information age. Experts on both sides debated technological options and the choice for or against the Internet *in the best interest of the State*, revealing competing visions on what this *interest* should be.

2.1 *Revenge of the Computer Scientists*

In France, the development of the Internet was part of a long-standing conflict between computer scientists and telecommunications engineers. While in the United States, the former enjoyed a central position in innovation programs, notably due to their presence within the Defense agency, their status regarding the government was less advantageous in France. In 1978, for example, the launch of the Minitel took place at the expense of a competing project—the *Cyclades* network—developed by the French National Institute for Research in Applied Computer Science (INRIA in French) (see Box 2). The difference between the two networks reflected the antagonistic logics, cultures and professional interests of computer scientists and telecommunications engineers. While the former developed a flexible communication protocol mainly designed for information sharing, the latter preferred the control and reliability of centralized electronic communications in order to develop new services. After the end of the *Cyclades* project, the interconnection of computer laboratories nonetheless progressed and research communication networks appeared in Europe, mostly based on the Internet protocols (see Chapter 1). In 1988, the INRIA's research center in Sophia Antipolis was the first entry point of the Internet in France.

Box 2 When France Almost Invented the Internet

As in many other countries, the development of Information and Communication Technologies in France interweaved scientific, industrial and political interests. In 1967, the creation of INRIA (National Institute for Research in Applied Computer Science) was part of a vast governmental program, the "Plan Calcul", adopted in 1966 to develop the computer industry of France. INRIA was installed in the former NATO premises – at Rocquencourt on the outskirts of Paris. At the time, General de Gaulle's France had just left the transatlantic organization, and the situation of INRIA demonstrated the role that computer science was supposed to play in the global strategy for national sovereignty.

In the early 1970s, two research projects on electronic communication networks were launched in parallel by the government: one was hosted at the CNET (Telecommunication Research Center), under the supervision of the Ministry of Industry, the other at the INRIA. The parallel command exacerbated competition between the two institutes, resulting in solutions with opposing rationales. At INRIA, the project led by Louis Pouzin favored a packet switching system, relatively similar to that adopted by the ARPANET. The *Cyclades* network was based on a datagram system that allowed packets to be routed autonomously on the network. CNET, on the other hand, provided a system based on "virtual circuits", which offered greater control over the flow of information. This last solution was better suited to the implementation of a national communication service controlled by the government. These divergent rationalities displayed social and statutory difference between Telecom engineers, an established *grand corps*, and INRIA members, closer to the scientific community.

The administrative and professional recognition enjoyed by the former led to the adoption of the "telecom" solution, which foreshadowed the development of the Minitel and the longstanding influence of Telecommunications engineers over French network policy. On the other hand, the *Cyclades* project was abandoned in 1978 for lack of resources. The team led by Louis Pouzin nonetheless pursued a close dialogue with the US working group on the Internet. In public communications, Vinton Cerf often credits Louis Pouzin's work on datagrams with important influence on the design of TCP/IP.

In the 1990s, INRIA took a leading role in the expansion of the Internet and the Web. Christian Huitema, research director at INRIA, even became the first non-US chairman of the Internet Architecture

Board in 1993. Two years later, INRIA was chosen to host, after the MIT, the second World Wide Web Consortium, an organization created by Tim Berners-Lee to manage the evolution of the Web protocols. While telecommunications engineers refused to encourage Internet expansion in France, computer scientists—who were also pioneer users of the Net—tenaciously supported its development. The network's international expansion strengthened their position in political controversies about networks and favored their visibility in the public sphere.

Christian Huitema, for example, was described by journalists as the French "Pope of the Internet" or its "best French specialist". In 1995, he published *Et Dieu créa l'Internet* (*And God created the Internet*),[5] a work of popularization and an enthusiastic petition for the Internet. For Huitema, Internet was destined to dethrone all other networks, especially those based on hybrid protocols such as ATM, launched by the telecommunications administration. Despite the glowing description of the Théry Report, ATM was indeed a complex communication protocol, more suited to telephone networks than computer networks, and many network applications would rather adopt TCP/IP, an open and easier-to-use protocol.

In his book, Huitema constantly disparaged the Telecommunication *grand corps*:

> Right now, France is under the thumb of the Telecommunications administration, a state monopoly. Of course, this administration has tried to disguise itself as a normal company, by rebranding itself *France télécom*. But it's a bizarre company in which most of the employees are civil servants. As for their managers, they all belong to one of those republican feudalities that France is famous for, the *corps des Télécoms*, which recruits right out of the *École Polytechnique*. Technical skills count for something, but not too much, as it is said that an engineer who locks himself up in technical expertise will never become a great leader. *Esprit de corps*, or even allegiance to factions within the *corps*, counts a greater deal if you want to make a career of it. This Napoleonic system may have had its advantages when France needed to be equipped as quickly as possible, and industry could be managed like the arsenal of a country at war. But those days are gone. [our translation]

[5] The title of the book is a direct reference to the 1965 romantic drama film *And God Created Women*, starring Brigitte Bardot. With its depiction of a woman's sexuality and desires, the movie was a huge success abroad, notably in the United States.

The archaism of the *grand corps* was vividly denounced throughout the book. The description above specifically calls into question the alleged modernity of telecommunications engineers, as their technical expertise and sense of innovation has been lost with recent managerial transformation. Implicitly, Huitema pitted INRIA computer scientists against these "X-Telecom"[6] officials. Unlike the latter, Huitema and his peers chose a career path distant from the French bureaucracy, from governmental cabinets and administrative directions. As computer scientists, they contended that the technical superiority of the Internet should prevail over corporate interests and national preferences. Huitema also condemned the short-sightedness of telecommunications engineers, whose obsession with the Minitel's business model and control system prevented them from seeing the potential of more generative networks, such as the Internet. In retrospect, the book also developed a counter-narrative of French network history by demonstrating the visionary position of INRIA computer researchers, as a revenge on the historical domination of telecommunications engineers.

While Huitema's book brought this feud into the public sphere, building on the reputation he had acquired on the international scientific scene, conflicts and criticisms were even stronger within the closed door of the French government. During his interview, Bruno Mannoni, a former member of INRIA and head of IT systems at the French Ministry of Culture accounted for the many disputes and arguments that took place over this issue during government meetings:

> There was this former head of *France Télécom*, Général Théry, his favorite phrase was "I looked up Proust on the Internet and I found nothing" (smiling). I remember attending a debate at the CNIT-La Défense in 1993 or 94, I can't remember the exact date. Sarkozy was there [*future President Sarkozy was then in charge of Budget and Communication at the government*], and so was Gérard Théry. Because Théry was explaining to government members that the Internet was a catastrophe, we came out in force with INRIA. And INRIA started to display top-rank scientific papers, peer-reviewed articles and so on, showing that X.25 *[the communication protocol on which the Minitel was based*] couldn't go faster than... I don't remember, but let's say no more than 200 Megabits per second. And

[6] The expression referred to graduates from the Ecole Polytechnique (the "X") that became telecommunication civil engineers.

> Théry started "Oh, you're aware of these studies... but they're wrong", or at least he got a bit confused. I stood up and said "Mr. Théry, you are a liar". And then Sarkozy took the floor to say, 'Politicians are criticized for having a lot of chapels, but I see it's even worse among technical experts'. [Interview 54, January 2017].

The extract outlines two opposing camps: on one side, INRIA computer scientists, "in numbers", defending the Internet; on the other, General engineer Théry, single-handedly embodying the entire Telecommunications *grand corps*. For the latter, the Internet raised political issues, such as the question of national sovereignty—the presence of emblematic works of French literature in opposition to US cultural hegemony—while INRIA members developped scientific arguments. But the Internet appears merely as an excuse for a larger struggle, a competition for the recognition of legitimate technical competence. In opposition to resources accumulated by Gérard Théry (career, prestige of the *grand corps*, bureaucratic capital), computer scientists resort to the weapons of scientific legitimacy: "top-rank" articles, peer-review, empirical data, etc. They saw themselves as the guarantors of an objective and neutral expertise at the service of public decision-making.

Of course, these written and oral accounts are reinterpretations of a larger administrative and technical history that meets the individual history of those who told them during the interviews. Nevertheless, they can be considered as part of a reconstruction process that gives historical consistency to the opposition between telecommunication engineers and computer scientists, as well as, between the State and the Internet. This opposition reached its climax, and the beginning of its decline, with the arrival of the Internet in France. For, away from these top-level meetings, the Internet was silently spreading throughout the administration, supported by local, sometimes clandestine, initiatives that directly challenged bureaucratic hierarchies.

2.2 Fighting the Internet from the Inside: The Official Bulletin Affair

The technological battle over the Internet was not just an abstract conflict for expert legitimacy, involving reports, demonstrations of knowledge, and administrative prophecies. It also fitted into everyday bureaucratic practices, with some administrative agents prematurely migrating their services to the new network. From indifference to sanction, the reaction of their hierarchies allows us to grasp the concrete modalities of the opposition to the Internet. Among several episodes, the "affair" of the Official Bulletin was often cited as a paradigmatic example[7] of the challenges the Internet presented to the State bureaucracy.

As shown in the previous section, the Minitel allowed for great control over online communication and the dissemination of official documents. With its billing system, Minitel services even provided a significant income for some public organizations. This was the case with the Official Bulletin, which contains laws, decrees and nominations as well as parliamentary debates, and whose distribution through Minitel was subject to an exclusive deal with the company ORTélématique, that operated various administrative services. Marginally, though with vigor, this deal was yet criticized by some public officials who favored the free and open dissemination of public information. At the time open, the opening of public information was indeed becoming a global trend, promoted by international organizations and the European Union as a way to foster the transparency and accountability of government institutions. In order to protest these exclusive deals with private companies, Christian Scherer, a public executive at the Ministry of Industry, decided to develop one of the first websites for free administrative information, *admi.net*.

Born in 1947, Christian Scherer was the son of a schoolteacher that later became a telecommunication engineer. With an early passion for electronics, he developed its first bulletin board system (BBS) at the age of 17. After just one year of preparatory class (instead of two), he entered the École Polytechnique in 1966, and then join the *Corps des Mines*, one of the most prestigious *grand corps* in the administration. With the exception of a brief leave of absence to launch an educational software company (between 1983 and 1986), Christian Scherer spent most of his career in the public administration, working on IT development for several ministry department. In 1994, he opened Admi.net, as the first unofficial platform for French administrative information. The website was hosted on a server at the *École des Mines*, without any official authorization or specific mandate. Scherer disclaimed on the home page that "Adminet [was] is not an official government service". Nevertheless, the website provided an impressive amount of information from

[7] This affair was used as an example in no less than 5 interviews with bureaucratic agents (Interviews 26, 37, 42, 50, 54).

official documentation to government agenda, including a digital copy of the Official Bulletin. As a free website, *admi.net* was thus competing with the paid Minitel service 3617 JOEL, which arouse huge concerns in the administration. Worried about the terms of the deal made with the company ORTélématique, the General Secretary of the Government sent a letter to the Ministry of Industry requesting that C. Scherer ceased his Internet activity. The letter was accompanied by an official request from the French Parliament to the *École des Mines*, calling for the closure of *admi.net*, effective March 1, 1996. A few days before closing, the website displayed this explanation, denouncing the pressures faced by the webmaster: "Christian Scherer is reproached for using his affiliation at the Ministry of Industry and also, it seems, for using some technical means at its disposal, to put on the Internet, available to the public for free, information that is itself in the public domain" (Fig. 4).

Fig. 4 Christian Scherer, front page of an article entitled "The Ugly Duckling of Administration" (*Planète Internet*, 1995)

Eventually, *admi.net* reopened a few days later, without mention of the Official Bulletin. At the same time, an exhaustive copy of the former website (with the OB) was hosted "clandestinely" on another server at the University of Saarbrücken, Germany, and appeared on the web at the new address *adminet.org*. Mirror websites were already a well-known trick among Internet communities to circumvent government censorship. It was nonetheless uncanny to see this trick used by a top official, showing that hacking shrewdness already circulated within the administration as a means to bypass, but also to delegitimize, the bureaucratic reluctance to the Internet. The displacement of the server to Germany also reveals similar initiatives across Europe, with cross-sectorial mobilizations for free and open information at the intersection of the administrative and the academic fields. The bureaucratic decision to forbid the online spreading of the French Official Bulletin collided with the network's transnational and decentralized features, which enabled to circumvent restrictions by hosting the same documents outside of France, while making them accessible from any French-connected computer.

If the Official Bulletin affair left such a mark on the memory of French Internet pioneers, it was also because it symbolized for them the difference between bureaucratic secrecy and an "Internet culture" characterized by openness and the free flow of information. In their narratives, the Minitel became the symbol of excessive state control over information and communication. According to Jean-Michel Yolin, another member of the *Ecole des Mines* and a strong supporter of Christian Scherer's initiative, "The Minitel culture was in fact a state culture that went back to Louis XI, at the time of the dark cabinet. The idea was to prevent anyone to communicate without the king knowing what they were saying" (Interview 26, June 2016). A little later in the interview, he even asserted that "the Minitel was the State itself", an equivalence also established by another Internet pioneer, Bruno Mannoni, introduced earlier: "[With the Minitel], they had a toll highway, built by the State, administered by the State, maintained by the State, and generating taxes for the State. So, you see, it was really an absolutely brilliant thing in terms of bureaucracy". The defiant and informal tone used by these Internet pioneers in interviews emphasized the transgressive dimension of their position as Internet promoters within a reluctant bureaucracy. In retrospect, they presented themselves as mavericks who did not hesitate to challenge official rules and to use "hacking" in order to develop web services in the administration. The case of the Official Bulletin enabled them to demonstrate the obstacles they faced, as well as to valorize what they considered a "heroism" of pioneers. Their position, however, was paradoxical. While presenting themselves opposed to the State—seen as an illegitimate power apparatus confiscating public resources such as information—they also declared to work "*for the State*"—considered this time as the guardian of the general interest—by defending values of "*selfless dedication to the public good*" (Interview 26).

Hence Internet pioneers in France should not be seen as mere libertarian or anti-State. In their eyes, *admi.net* was merely enabling the realization of the rule of law and could legitimize state intervention through the free flow of administrative information. It becomes evident, therefore, that the conflict between the Minitel and the Internet was also a conflict for the power to define what the State should do, insofar as it prohibits or justifies technological practices in the name of the general interest. Indeed, they were mostly expressing, from within, a criticism toward the "bureaucratic mindset" that impeded the State's efficiency in the information society.

2.3 *Admiroutes or the Internal Critique of Bureaucracy*

While the administrative doxa advocated a national strategy to curb the expansion of the Internet, resistance was organized at the heart of the administration. In 1996, Jean-Michel Baquiast, secretary of the Interministerial Committee for IT, created the organization Admiroutes, with an associated website, to promote the use of the Internet in the administration. A graduate of the *Ecole Nationale d'Administration*, this left-wing politician and IT expert had been contributing to the computerization of the French administration since the late 1960s. The organization he founded in 1996 brought together a heterogeneous group of senior civil servants, IT specialists, researchers, and technicians coming from various ministries, all early Internet users. The "Admiroutes manifesto" they published online set out their mission as follows:

> The world of public administration seems to be poles apart from that of the INTERNET.
> Administrative traditions are hierarchical and compartmentalized, with little openness to the private sector and citizens, and even less to the international arena.

> Networked information technologies, symbolized today by the Internet, are a permanent invitation to grassroots initiatives, crossing departmental boundaries, involving correspondents in the business world and individuals, both nationally and internationally.
> Administration is the world of instructions from above, of self-censorship in the face of creative possibilities. Senior civil servants, for their part, tend to think they have nothing to learn from anyone.
> The Internet is the world of bottom-up initiatives, of "do it yourself", of intelligent hacking. To take advantage of it, you need to be convinced that you know very little and that others can teach you a lot.
> The Internet's detractors portray it as a permanent zapping ground, discouraging all projects and creations. No doubt they haven't understood the added value that networking can bring to a project, however well-defined it may be from the outset. They only know how to react from a besieged fortress.
> The risks of superimposing the worlds of administration and the Internet on one another have been highlighted, particularly as regards the introduction of disorder, or even anarchy, into public policy.
> Wouldn't it be more useful to show the advantages of greater use of networks by the administration, on the understanding that departments and civil servants know how to respect and ensure respect for the indispensable rules of competence, confidentiality and reserve? (...)
> *Retrieved from Admiroutes.asso.fr, 1997, accessible from the Wayback Machine*, [our translation].

The Admiroutes manifesto is an emblematic example of the way the Internet and the State were conceived as opposite, even within the administration itself. It was built on the distinction between two "worlds" with fundamentally antagonistic features: hierarchical, compartmentalized, closed and top-down for the State bureaucracy; open, creative, disordered and bottom-up for the Internet. The text thus shows the spreading into the very heart of the French State of a critique of bureaucracy already formulated by Internet pioneers a decade before: it endorsed the concepts and principles of the cyberculture, detailed in the previous chapter, the praise of tinkering and individual initiative against a bureaucracy that suffocated them. Mimicking the 1970's computer clubs, Admiroutes members used to meet at *cybercafé*, or on dedicated mailing lists and exchanged computer tips and web discoveries.

For them, the bureaucratic defiance toward the Internet had more to do with a self-preservation instinct based on bureaucratic routines than with technical considerations or even public interest. Their website listed and denounced all these "reasons" for opposing the Internet heard within the administration. This section of the website, referred as the "beta-blocker dictionary", was modeled on Flaubert's *Dictionnary of Accepted Ideas* and took up its satirical tone to lampoon the clichés characteristic to the bureaucratic elite.

> *Going to the museum*: an activity that seems to have been made impossible for the beta-blocker, by the development of virtual museography on the Internet. Every year, the beta blocker visits the world's 15,758 museums, not to mention exhibitions. Example: "With the Internet, we no longer go to museums".
>
> *Anglo-Saxon*: this adjective, applied by the beta-blocker to the Internet, gives those of our citizens who feel overwhelmed by the phenomenon, an excellent reason to continue to understand nothing about it, and keep their heads in the sand. Example: "The French can't be interested in the Internet because it's an Anglo-Saxon network".
>
> *Bright Future* (there's still a): a formula that allows the beta-blocker to reassure himself about the durability of the old activities to which he remains emotionally attached (even though they have generally reserved nothing but annoyances for him, if we were to believe his imprecations). Example: "Despite the Internet, there's still a bright future for paper and the Minitel".
>
> *It's of no interest*: an argument used to avoid going to the trouble of putting information online. The beta-blocker uses it with all the more authority because he refuses to investigate what is or isn't of interest to the rest of the world. Example: "don't bother putting our reports on the web. It's of no interest to anyone."
> *Retrieved from Admiroutes.asso.fr, 1997, accessible from the Wayback Machine*, [our translation].

The alphabetical list was in fact quite long and gave a broad overview of the rationale and scope of the reluctance toward the Internet. While the definitions took stock of the justifications heard, they aimed above all to delegitimize their underlying logics, which ranged from the systematic rejection of technological novelty to national preference for the Minitel. For Admiroutes members, conservative attitudes and misjudgments were a consequence of the low level of dissemination of IT knowledge and practices within the bureaucracy. As a result, they disqualified the opposition to the Internet as ignorant reaction to innovative technology.

Although less visible than the Théry report, the Admiroutes website was a critical response to it, an evidence that French administration was probably less impervious to the Internet than some retrospective accounts of the period suggest.

In a heterogeneous and conflictual bureaucratic field, some French civil servants adopted the rhetoric of online communities as early as the mid-1990s. Their aim was less to establish the illegitimacy of state intervention on the Internet than to call for a reform of administrative practices and processes, particularly in the field of innovation and technology policies. The spread of the Internet was indeed part of a larger trend that, along with the liberalization of the telecommunication industry, favored an in-depth reform of the State's role in matters of innovation and communication.

3 Reforming Innovation Policies

The debates surrounding the Internet in France were part of bureaucratic conflicts and reflected a specific distribution of power structuring the administrative field. Up until the mid-1990s, government support for the Minitel and reticence toward the Internet indicated the key role played by civil engineers as the main decision-makers and implementers of innovation policies for the IT industry. The appointment of Gérard Théry as head of the Interministerial Committee dedicated to Information Superhighways in 1995 bore witness to their reputational power at the government. Telecommunication engineers also controlled local information networks, as the managers and top executives of the State's public monopoly, *France Télécom*. Along with the Minitel, a centralized vision of industrial policy was maintained, that guaranteed the key position of civil engineers and their management of innovation.

However, the rise of digital technologies and the liberalization of telecommunications fostered a global reconfiguration of intra- and extra-bureaucratic relationships in France. The opening up of IT markets strengthened international competition and the discussion of new ways of organizing the economy. The battle of networks laid foundations for a global reform of innovation and industrial policies, one that found widespread support from the European elite and challenged existing routines and positions in the French bureaucracy. In IT, these changes were marked by two concurrent evolutions: the emergence of a new model for the formation of civil engineers, and the advent of regulation, in place of investment or market intervention, as a new means of governing technology markets.

3.1 The "Little Deaths" of the Telecommunication Grand Corps

In 2010, Gabrielle Gauthey, former technical advisor at the ministry of Telecommunications (1995–1997), explained that the past decades had been marked by a series of crises, a series of "little deaths", calling into question the position of telecommunication engineers within the State.

This position had been won over a long period of time, following successive developments that had transformed an archaic, "technician" administration, marginalized within the Ministry of Postal Services, into an independent public organization and a symbol of administrative modernity (Vedel, 1984). Since the creation of the Telecommunications Department (DGT) in 1941, infrastructure and services had indeed been administered by civil engineers. The DGT was the sole operator of information and communication networks, the main investor in the sector, and was responsible for various public policies in this field, such as industrial development and research. During the 1970's and 1980's, the programs launched by the DGT had contributed to the rise of this administrative department, demonstrating its ability to define and implement a bold technological strategy. During the 1980s, the DGT acquired a high degree of autonomy, and gradually operated like an "entrepreneurial" administration, supported by multiple subsidiaries. The culmination of this process happened in 1990, when the Quilès law transformed the DGT into an independent public organization, named *France Télécom.* In 1995, *France Telecom* and its subsidiaries still employed more than 70% of all the telecommunication engineers.

Indicative of this momentum, the telecommunication sector was particularly attractive for graduate from the *École Polytechnique*. In this domain, civil engineers could enjoy autonomy, key positions of power over innovation, over the management of public resources and the decision-making process. In the 1990s, the telecommunication administration came across as a symbol of technocratic, highly specific and modernized public intervention (Jobert & Muller, 1987). However, unlike other technical *grand corps*, whose engineers occupy strategic positions in a wide range of administrative and economic departments, members of the Telecom administrations rarely moved outside of their specific domain. While the specialization contributed to the internal cohesion of the *corps*, it was also seen as a weakness in the bureaucratic world, all the more so as the domain was undergoing major changes. Indeed, the high level of specialization limited the *corps*'s "reach" and influence beyond the borders of the telecommunication industry. The vast majority of Telecoms engineers indeed spent their whole careers in the same administration.

Yet this highly specialized, state-integrated profession was challenged by technological upheavals and economic changes in Europe. The convergence of the telecommunication, audiovisual and computer industries, induced by the digital revolution , was blurring boundaries between sectors. At the same time, negotiations at the EU level, paving the way to a single continental market, had fostered the privatization of national industries and the opening up of telecommunication markets to competition. In 1996, the *Association des Ingénieurs des Télécommunications* (Telecommunications Engineers Association) published a memo to encourage its members to find positions outside of *France Télécom.* The forthcoming privatization of the public company raised questions about the status of its future employees, and telecommunication engineers feared becoming "employees like any other" within the future private company. The opening up of the sector to competition was welcomed with limited support among the *corps*. With liberalization, economic transformations would be entrusted to market forces, calling into question the strategic role that civil engineers had acquired in the organization of the industry and in the management of innovation. In addition, the expansion of the Internet, a network whose development had bypassed the public company and the technical expertise of the profession, was greeted with concern.

In many respects, the reaction of telecommunications engineers to the Internet was one of self-preservation: owing everything to the administration they belonged to, and outside of which they had little power, they were willing to defend it against any external reform that would threaten their position. Advocating for the "Minitel system" must also be understood as a defense strategy to preserve their expertise and status against a backdrop of economic and technological upheavals.

On the other hand, the reform of telecommunication was driven by other civil servants, often younger and mainly from other administrative bodies. They claimed alternative expertise and values to design telecommunications policies in the information society. In 1995, for the first time since its creation, an individual that did not come from the

Telecommunication *grand corps* was appointed as the CEO of *France Télécom*: Michel Bon, a graduate from the National School of Administration, had studied in the US and previously worked in the private sector before becoming *France Télécom* new leader. Like him, newcomers in the industry challenged the civil engineers' monopoly, as well as their vision of "modernity". They questioned the emblematic methods of steering the industry from above and promoted contrarily the development of market regulation instead of direct investment, top-down innovation and stabilization tools. They brandished the Internet as a new symbol of modern government, against the conservative reactions of Telecom engineers.

3.2 From Innovation Management to Market Regulation

The changing spirit of industrial policy can be captured by the difference between the Théry report in 1994 and the Miléo report on "Networks in the Information Society", published two years later by the State Planning Commission in France. Whereas the former called for proactive government action to develop the "information superhighways", the latter advocated a reduction of the State's influence on IT markets, relying on private initiative and fair competition.

The disparity between the two reports mirrored the differences between two organizational cultures—the Telecommunication administration versus the Planning Commission—and between the two men who presided over their elaboration. Thiery Miléo was born in Meknes in 1961, almost thirty years after Gérard Théry. After graduating from the *École Polytechnique* (class of 1984), he studied at the University of California, Santa Barbara, one of the cradles of the Internet. His career path went through the Ministry of Defense, then at the Ministry of Foreign Affairs, before briefly joining the Ministry of Post and Telecommunications as deputy director for industrial and international affairs. Between 1993 and 1994, he was a special advisor to the right-wing Ministry of Communication in charge of the "information superhighways". He was then appointed Head of Strategy at Bouygues Télécom, a subsidiary of the large transnational Bouygues group, who competed with France Télécom on the newly opened market of telecommunication services. Thierry Miléo and the young rapporteurs that wrote the report with him embodied a new generation of IT experts, with international and private-sector experience, favoring a European rather than a national strategy. The recommendations of the Miléo report indeed echoed the European strategy advocated at the same time by Martin Bangemann, Vice President of the European Commission and Commissioner for Industry. In 1994, Bangemann led a working group on "Europe and the global information society", which advocated the role of private initiative in the development of the information superhighways: "*it does NOT mean more public money, financial assistance, subsidies, dirigisme, or protectionism*"[8] (the capital letters appear as they are in the report). A little less assertive, Miléo advocated for a transformation of industrial policy, a transformation described as an "imperative" to avoid France lagging behind.

> The French government, whose room for maneuver is becoming tighter, particularly as a result of changes in the European Union, will soon have to choose between two strategies for developing the information superhighway: favoring an industrial approach (giving priority to setting up a "universal" infrastructure based on fiber optics), or preferring a competitive and incentivized development of innovative services, without determining a priori the types of media these services will use. [Mileo Report, 1996, p. 113]

It is clear in the report that the first solution refers to Gérard Théry's proposals, while the second is favored by the Planning Commission. The "innovative", "flexible" and "diversified" policy advocated by Mileo was much more compatible with the liberal European framework and came with a new approach regarding the Internet. Like the Théry mission two years before, Mileo tried to answer the following question: "Will the Internet become the next information superhighway?" In contrast to the clear-cut, negative answer given by Théry, his conclusion was much more favorable to the Internet. In just two years, the Internet had grown significantly worldwide, driven by the emergence of the Web and the first browsers. So, the expert of the Mileo commission set out to dispel the main concerns raised by Théry in 1994—security, business model, national sovereignty, etc. They pointed to recent experiments carried out in the United States to secure commercial transactions and develop new pricing models to show the ability of the Internet to address this kind issues.

[8] Bangemann, M., "Report on Europe and the global information society" European Commission, Brussels, May 1994, p.5.
https://op.europa.eu/en/publication-detail/-/publication/44dad16a-937d-4cb3-be07-0022197d9459/language-en

Although still in the minority, this pro-Internet stance found political support among a new generation of "reformist" right-wing politicians. In the Juppé government (1995–1997), such a position was embodied by François Fillon, the 41-year-old Deputy Minister for Telecommunications. His main task was to prepare the opening up of telecommunications markets, as provided for in European directives. The Telecommunications Regulatory Act was thus introduced and passed in 1996, bringing a new framework to address the global reorganization of the sector. The law wass emblematic of the slow shift of France toward a Regulatory State bound to replace the dirigiste State of the past (Majone, 1994). A new regulatory authority was created, the *Autorité de Régulation des Télécommunications* (ART), independent from the Ministry, to ensure fair competition and quality of services on telecommunication markets. Building on these evolution, François Fillon took up the "information superhighway" program launched by the Balladur government in the wake of the Théry report and tried to divert its aim: while the word "Internet" was absent from previous government communications, the deputy minister declared that "France had to take part in the development of the Internet". Yet in 1996, his words were not followed by action. His then technical advisor for new technologies recalled in interview that promoting the Internet was still largely discredited in the State, especially as the period saw the first cases of online piracy and pornography (see Chapter 4).

Although limited, these advances still showed that positions toward the Internet were gradually changing within the French bureaucracy, brought about by new modes of neoliberal governance promoted by the European Commission. But it was not until the opening of a new political conjecture, with the 1997 legislative elections, and thanks to the consolidation of groups of Internet promoters, that the general reform of government came to fruition and that the Internet made an official entry into the French administration.

* * *

In contrast to the expansion of the Internet network in neighboring countries in the 1990's, France was a latecomer to the Internet. This situation was not only the result of the Minitel success in the country but also reflected the features of French bureaucracy at the time. The Minitel was supported in particular by telecommunications engineers, who thereby defended their dominant position in the production of innovation at the government. A closer look at the development of industrial policies in IT also reveals that France's opposition to the Internet was less monolithic than it might seem at first glance. In the first half of the 1990s, the Internet entered the State, albeit marginally, and began to reconfigure relations between State elites, as liberalization programs and the convergence of technological sectors took shape. New combinations emerged between industries and public authorities, and new alliances were formed in the bureaucratic field, paving the way for the rapid development of the Internet in the second half of the 1990s. If the government had embraced the Internet earlier, would the role of IT expertise within the State have been strengthened? Would the illegitimacy of public intervention have been mitigated? Would the French Internet have taken on a different face? Looking at neighboring countries, and the period that followed, there is every reason to doubt it. In most European country, the Internet dissemination raised questions and fostered a global reconfiguration of state organizations, along with the European push for privatization.

The example of France and the Minitel enables mostly to emphasize the political properties of a socio-technical conjuncture in which several futures remained possible. Some commentators were wrong, most hesitated, and only a few really anticipated the advent of the Internet. Rather than handing out good and bad points after the battle, a situated and interactionist analysis of policymaking highlights the role of uncertainty, as well as that of expertise in shaping interpretive frameworks and instituted instruments to guide public intervention. While this episode is sometimes cited as an example of the inability of technocrats to predict and produce innovation, the chapter brings a more nuanced conclusion: in an uncertain context, the bureaucratic elite, much like economic or intellectual players, does not make "absurd" decisions, but tends to rely on tried-and-tested recipes and to defend its specific knowledge and means of action in an upturned environment. At the same time, alternative skills, such as knowledge in European law, computer science and foreign experience, can be mobilized by newcomers to subvert or even "dumb down" those in place. Finally, innovation is not incompatible with the framework of bureaucracy, but has better chance to take place at its margins. What happens then to these administrative experimentations and how is the Internet gradually incorporated into policymaking? Answering this question is the subject of the following chapters.

References

Bourdieu, P. (2018). *On the State: Lectures at the Collége de France, 1989–1992*. John Wiley & Sons.

Callon, M., Lascoumes, P., & Barthe, Y. (2011). *Acting in an uncertain world: An essay on technical democracy*. MIT Press.

Cohen, E. (1992). *Le colbertisme high-tech: économie des Telecom et du grand projet*. Hachette Education.

Ermakoff, I. (2008). *Ruling oneself out: A theory of collective abdications*. Duke University Press.

Gayon, V. (2016). Écrire, prescrire, proscrire: Notes pour une sociogénétique de l'écrit bureaucratique. *Actes de la recherche en sciences sociales, 3*, 84–103.

Goffman, E. (1974). *Frame analysis: An essay on the organization of experience*. Cambridge, MA: Harvard University Press.

Jobert, B., & Muller, P. (1987). *L'État en action: politiques publiques et corporatismes* (p. 242). Presses universitaires de France.

Keefe, P. R. (2006). *Chatter: Uncovering the echelon surveillance network and the secret world of global eavesdropping*. Random House Incorporated.

Lytel, D. (1989). The impact of Minitel on French politics. *Contemporary French Civilization, 13*, 22.

Mailland, J. (2015). 101 online: American Minitel Network and lessons from its failure. *IEEE Annals of the History of Computing, 38*(1), 6–22.

Majone, G. (1994). The rise of the regulatory state in Europe. *West European Politics, 14*(3), 77–101.

Morel, C. (2004). *Les décisions absurdes : Sociologie des erreurs radicales et persistantes* [Absurd decisions: sociology of radical and persistent errors] , 379 p. Gallimard.

Röhr, M. (2021). Der *lange Weg zum Internet: Computer als Kommunikationsmedien zwischen Gegenkultur und Industriepolitik in den 1970er/1980er Jahren*. transcript Verlag.

Schafer, V., & Thierry, B. G. (2012). *Le Minitel. L'enfance numérique de la France*. Nuvis.

Vedel, T. (1984). Les ingénieurs des télécommunications in Les ingénieurs. *Culture Technique,* (12), 63–75.

William, C., & Towsik, J. (1994). The French Videotex System Minitel: A successful implementation of national information technology infrastructure. *MIS Quaterly, 18*(1), 1–20.

CHAPTER 4

Geeks, Webmasters and State Technologists: Evangelizing the Internet

Remember that, at the time, when I talked about the Internet, people still thought I was referring to an American cleaning company.
André Santini, former MP and Mayor of Issy-Les-Moulineaux, member of the informal Internet working group at the French national Assembly, interviewed on July 27, 2016.

In the mid-1990s, the Internet was still largely unknown, even disparaged, particularly in the economic, political and administrative fields of France. In order to accelerate its development, net enthusiasts struggled to raise awareness on recent technological development, to convince people of the Internet's potential, as well as fight misconceptions and prejudices about the new network. This project brought together a surprisingly varied group of senior civil servants, political professionals, digital activists and business leaders. They converged in a common effort to promote a change in public policies toward the Internet in France. Often portrayed heroically as a "quarrel between the ancients and the moderns", their effort gradually contributed in the elaboration of the first Internet policies, as well as in the spread of new information and communication technologies throughout the administration.

The mobilization of the first Internet users against government interference (Chapter 2), on the one hand, and the resistance of French administrative elite to technological change (Chapter 3), on the other,

A. Bellon, *A Socio-History of Internet Policies*, International Series on Public Policy, https://doi.org/10.1007/978-3-031-69099-0_4

made the State and the Internet appear as two irreconcilable worlds. By emphasizing the differences between these social groups—senior civil servants versus computer scientists and hacktivists—we tend to artificially homogenize social spaces that are themselves fraught with tensions, as we have just seen in the previous chapter. What is more, the boundaries between these groups were in reality less impermeable than they appear at a first glance. In fact, at the intersection of the two worlds, a group of people was working to ensure mutual understanding and common strategies for Internet development. From the mid-1990s onward, they formed a coalition of common interest, they organized more or less formal meetings and promoted the exchange of expertise to support the development of Internet policies in France. Together, they formed an interstitial space interwoven in different social fields, a space to "evangelize" society about the Internet. In spite of their differences, these Internet advocates tended to legitimize each other and to collaborate around a common cause: the digital revolution, for everyone, and everywhere. Who were these "net evangelists", as they often called themselves, and above all, how and why did they manage to work together and promote Internet development in a country that was largely reluctant to the US network?

This chapter examines the formation of a group of "net evangelists" who sought to convert the public administration to the potential of the Internet. We endorse here the expression of "evangelists" as a way to underline the fundamental role of beliefs in these struggles "of the Internet against the rest of the world". Their activism was indeed part of an "institutional enterprise" (DiMaggio, 1988; Hardy & Maguire, 2008) that was as much material and political as it was symbolic, in that it aimed to establish public *trust* in the Internet. Hence, the battle was waged in and with the State, as producer and guarantor of the categories of perception of the social world (Bourdieu, 2014). The "evangelist" metaphor also allows for comparisons with other public policy innovations based on the collaboration of public and private players, and on the importation into the State of rationale and expertise at first external to the administration, such as shown in the case of new public management (Bezes, 2012; Dunleavy & Hood, 1996) and pro-market deregulation (Dixon, 1998). But even more than liberal reform, the Internet promotion relied on specific convictions, practices and cultural references. Because these references were almost as rare as computer expertise among the elite at the time, it enabled an astonishing fluidity of ideas and trajectories between distinct fields of power—economic, political and bureaucratic.

Public policy analysis has already highlighted the role of "epistemic communities" (Haas, 1992), "policy networks" (Rhodes & Marsh 1992) or "advocacy coalitions" (Sabatier, 1998; Sabatier & Jenkins-Smith, 1988) in transforming the modalities of state intervention. Often, however, these studies focus primarily on the impact of these networks on public policy outcomes, leaving aside the question of their formation. This chapter offers instead to understand how these policy networks are created, structured, and eventually dismantled. For the coalition of activists, IT researchers, senior civil servants, politicians and economic entrepreneurs in 1990's France was far from self-evident: Internet promoters indeed belonged to distant and more or less autonomous social fields. Their educational and professional backgrounds, their resources and the ideological traditions to which they subscribed more often distinguished them than bound them together. The aim of the chapter is thus to identify the social dynamics and common interests that brought Internet evangelists together and to understand the ways in which the different worlds they belonged to were intertwined. To explain the formation of this coalition, this chapter resort to two complementary methods: prosopography (Stone, 1971; Lunding et al., 2020) and social network analysis (Fischer, 2011).[1]

First, the trajectories and social characteristics of the net evangelists show how the promotion of the Internet became a common calling in a context when computer practices and technological culture were rare (1). Secondly, a social network analysis of the organizations where exchanges took place and of the relationships between players provide tools for measuring the relative solidity of this policy network and for describing its structure (2). Taken together, these two sections illustrate the ways in which the "State" and the "Internet" interpenetrated at the end of the 1990s. They also show the features of a policy network, its cultural characteristics and the social and political projects that come with its development at the intersection of various fields of power.

[1] For a combination of the two approaches see for example Keller (2018).

1 The Internet as a Calling

In the mid-1990s, the defense of the Internet prompted collaborations that seemed, to say the least, improbable. An interviewee, member of Prime Minister Lionel Jospin's cabinet, still recounts with amazement and amusement the first "Internet Festival" in 1998 "*when we invited the whole French Internet world. I remember there was even Valentin Lacambre [a hacker] smoking his joint on the steps of Matignon*[2]" [Interview 37, July 2017]. Beyond the amusing image of this young activist celebrating the Internet in his own way amid senior civil servants and members of the government, these relatively unprecedented curves of social space invite us to question their principle of operation and aggregation. During the interviews, a common "passion" for the Internet was presented as the main binding force. Contrary to usual representations and the sociology of cultural practices, it suggests shared interests and hobbies between seasoned senior civil servants, successful entrepreneurs and young IT technicians (Box 1). But how can we objectify this "interest for" the Internet, which is part and parcel of such different practices and professions? And how can we guard against a reconstruction in retrospect of this "passion" and its structuring effects on the trajectories of interviewees? After all, their stories are just as much about "presentation strategies" (Collovald, 1988)—which need to be thwarted—as they are about shared social experiences and beliefs—which need to be identified.

Far from confining ourselves to this observation, we need to examine what a "calling" for the Internet means in context and assess its effects on individual social trajectories. The sociology of professions has developed a critical approach to vocational discourses and provides avenues of analysis (Dubois, 2015; Gustafson, 1982). Existing research considers professional calling as the product of three elements: a reflective thinking of agents regarding their own determination, the definition of practices in reference to universal values and the conception of their job as a space for self-realization. We can take up and slightly amend this framework to study the activism of Internet promoters in the late 1990s. Indeed, the defense of the Internet was not associated with a single profession—that of computer scientist, for example, or technical expert—but rather fueled a specific relationship to one's work. This relation was at the same time endured, as a stigma, and endorsed as an opportunity to transform

[2] The Hôtel de Matignon is the official residence of the Prime Minister of France.

professional routines. In order to understand the commitment to defend the Internet, we look first at how this "calling" was embedded in early experiences of networked communities, then, at the values and norms it encompassed, and finally at the professional and social stigmas that came with it at the end of the 1990s.

Box 1 Identifying Net Evangelists at the End of the 1990s

This chapter is based on a prosopographic analysis of 100 individuals that were active in the development of the French Internet, insofar as they have, at a given time, influential properties to shape technological choices and public intervention. We have selected them by cross-referencing experts from 17 public reports and five newspapers of the time. More than activists, they were brokers who, through their position at the intersection of various social spaces and their collaboration with public authorities, contributed to the dissemination of ideas and expertise on the Internet within the State. The context is important, as the database does not name the "winners" of the digital revolution , but rather, without anticipating the "end of the story", gives an account of an ephemeral configuration of individuals involved in Internet promotion. They display a wide range of positions and resources, as well as early commitments that were unevenly invested and remunerated. We collected sociodemographic data for each individual and conducted interviews with 52 of the 100 individuals.

92% are men with an average age of 42 years old in 1998. They are also highly qualified, with 75% holding a Master's degree and 14% a PhD. Interestingly enough, 22% did spend part of their career in the US. Most of them (71%) come from well-off background, and only 10% of them have working-class parents.

1.1 "Fallen into Computing". From an Early Hobby to the Discovery of a New World

The precociousness and the intensity of computer hobbies have an important place in the personal stories of Internet promoters. Many of those interviewed consider themselves to have "fallen into" computing when they were younger. This metaphor even finds a quasi-literal transcription in the words of Jean-Michel Billaut, an economist at Banque Paribas, who ran a technology workshop attracting many Internet enthusiasts in the 1990s:

> In parallel with my economics thesis, I actually took a certificate in applied computer science, at the Place Philippe Lebon computer lab. In fact, I nearly killed myself there. We worked on an IBM 13-60, a machine that almost filled the entire room. One night, it was very hot, I wasn't careful, I caught my foot in a big cable, and I fell into the computer! [Interview 50, December 2016]

Like him, many of them recount a long-standing passion, sometimes tracing back to childhood. They recall vivid memories of their first computer—"an Apple II E I must have had in the early 1980s" [Interview 37]—or their first coded program—"a hypercard video game, when I was 13" [Interview 30, June 2016]. The precociousness of these practices justifies a posteriori a calling they consider rooted in their youth, and suggests a long-established expertise in electronics.

This enthusiastic relationship to computing technology then met the discovery of the Internet, a breakthrough experience to which genuine emotions were attached. The first connection to cyberspace was for them a "surprise", a "wonderment", that the respondents described in details. During the interview, they were asked about their first memories of the Internet and how they had discovered the network. Their answers provided an insight at the digital practices of that time. More generally, the question proved a successful strategy for bypassing a controlled discourse and for encouraging the interviewee to step out of their role, be it administrative, political or activist. The stories of these first steps online openned up the imaginary worlds associated with cyberspace: despite, and perhaps even because of, inevitable rewritings, they revealed a real enthusiasm for the Internet that still persisted at the time of the survey, almost fifteen years after their first encounter with newsgroups and websites.

Among several colorful accounts, Bernard Benhamou's story is particularly representative [Interview 24, May 2016]. A graduate in medicine and computer science, Benhamou became, after a few career wanderings, a freelance journalist specialized in new technologies. At a time when "the Internet community was extremely small in France", he quickly established himself as an "expert" on computer networks. He coordinated a special issue on multimedia technologies for a famous French magazine (*Télérama*) in 1996 and designed an exhibition on cyberspace at the National Science Museum (*La Villette*) in 1997. He also taught about information technologies at Sciences Po in Paris and at the National School for Administration (ENA) from 1998 onward. It was while looking for information on the new "American" network in the early 1990s that he bumped into the Internet. He then became an active member of Usenet newsgroups, some of which foreshadowed the future websites. In the following excerpt, he recalls, for example, attending the beginnings of the Internet movie database (Imdb.com), a comprehensive listing of films and their various contributors, revealing the encyclopedic vocation of early Internet communities:

> Usenet was a real phenomenon! There were newsgroups in all domains. I, for example, was passionate about cinema, I was a cinephile and a film critic at the time, and I discovered entire databases on cinema, for free. Did you know that imdb.com, which you may visit on the web, was born out of a Usenet newsgroup that was bought up by Amazon much later? I think it was a group of film students from Scotland who created the newsgroup. They would post cards about films, and as time went on, they allowed people to add all kinds of information. So, with the transition from the Internet to the web, it changed everything, in the space of a few years it became a worldwide database on cinema, long before there were specialized websites in French. [Interview 24]

His story conjures up the image of the "global conversation", developing across borders and enabling anyone to chat with people scattered around the globe, exchanging views on every subject matter. "Connected to the world", Benhamou considered the Internet as a new public sphere as vast as the range of its interest, which were not limited to new technologies:

> Back then, the first chatrooms I took part in were marked by a specific spirit, even though there were so many people you didn't know. Let me give you an example. I had the opportunity to talk to the producers of a famous US TV Show and their special effects directors. They didn't know me from Adam, and yet they were chatting with an obscure Frenchman, with no difficulty whatsoever. There was a gentlemanly spirit with the netiquette, which disappeared afterwards.

In this enthusiastic description, the possibility of new conversations—between an "obscure Frenchman" and Hollywood producers—overshadows the existing barriers to entry, whether economic or social. At a time when it was still possible to consign all Internet resources to a single repository, Bernard Benhamou saw the network as a "group of enlightened amateurs", a "gentleman's club" governed by a common etiquette, an ideal world structured by principles of sharing, respect and mutual understanding.

In a similar tone, Hervé Le Crosnier, who created the "biblio-fr" mailing list,[3] recounts his "encounter with the Internet" in 1993, through an access provided by his university: "What really appealed to me was the idea that, through the Internet, people could help each other. The medium itself was helping people navigating the medium. I was absolutely fascinated by this aspect at the time" [Interview 66, May 2020]. Once again, the social values of the network are put forward to explain both the intensity and the unexpectedness of the interest aroused by the Internet.

The stories of the French Internet pioneers are thus marked by the same romantic idea of a love-at-first that consecrated a lasting infatuation with digital technologies. These presentations reinforce the spontaneous, individual dimension of a "passion" that, in fact, owed little to chance. Socio-demographic data on the net evangelists shows indeed that the large majority of them were men, relatively young, highly educated, living in the Parisian region. These sociological features reflect and even amplify the characteristics of the first Internet users,[4] as well as they reveal the social conditions of an early connection to the cyberspace.

First and foremost, discovering the Internet at the time required access to computer hardware, the price of which was still very high (above the minimum wage). In addition, connection to electronic networks was expensive and often included a minute-based cost of communication. The comparison used by Laurent Sorbier, government advisor on new technologies, gives an idea of the economic barriers to entry: "I was 28 and a connection to Compuserve cost 200 francs a month. That was a lot for a student at the time, a bit like deciding to buy a 3D printer just for yourself" [Interview 22, May 2016].

Without surprise, the Internet promoters came predominantly from privileged backgrounds. Those whose computer experience predated the

[3] Created in 1993 for librarians and documentalists, this mailing list provided information on the Internet and a list of interesting web addresses, and quickly attracted members beyond the profession. With 15,500 subscribers in 2007, it was one of the most consulted mailing lists in France.

[4] Sociodemographic data on the 1990's Internet users were found in the professional literature that often referred to two main studies, one produced by Nielsen/CommenceNet in the US and in Canada, and one produced by MEdiangle for French online Services in 1997.

1980s often owed it to a parent, a close engineer relative, or, for the older ones, early professional experience in computer research. Moreover, the overwhelming majority of men is probably explained by the fact that electronics as a hobby, tinkering or even "hacking" was—and still is—more valued among young boys (Durndell et al., 1995; Collet, 2006; Wajcman, 2007; Abbiss, 2011). Among the interviewed women, their discovery of networked computing came later and often occurred in contact with male experts encountered in the course of their profession.

Beyond these shared practices and experiences, the promotion of the Internet was also based on the same vision of the transformative power of technologies, which converted a passion into a calling, extending into the professional and activist worlds.

1.2 "Something to Change the World". Norms, Beliefs and References about the Digital Revolution

The promotion of the Internet was often justified by a shared conviction that networked computing "was going to change the world". This conviction lied at the heart of the Internet activism of respondents. It was based on a body of cultural and intellectual productions that often preceded the arrival of the Internet, and which net enthusiasts would enrich in return. Far from a unified ideology, these productions formed a doctrinal puzzle that borrowed from computing science utopias and cyberspace pioneers, science fiction, as well as media and communication sociologists. Together, these hybrid references made up the basis of a strong belief in the revolutionary power of the Internet.

Science-fiction literature and cinema were the primary cultural vehicles for depicting the power of technology. Films and novels that explored social transformations linked to new technologies formed a set of references that still pervades current debates on artificial intelligence (Isaac Asimov), surveillance (George Orwell) or the virtualization of exchanges (Philipp K. Dick). Benoît Thieulin, who was in charge of Internet communication at the French Government Information Service in 2000, recounts, for example, that he was deeply affected by the movie *Wargames*, which depicts a young hacker about to unleash a nuclear war from his bedroom, by remotely entering and controlling a US army supercomputer: "*I've never re-watched it, maybe it's outdated now, maybe it's become rubbish, but the consequence of that movie is that I asked my parents to buy me a computer for Christmas. And if I tell you that, it is not just an anecdote, it's because I think that's what got me into computers, and then into the Internet*" [Interview 39, July 2016]. The film was released in 1983, the same year as the adoption of the Internet protocol. It was part of an abundant cultural production that fed the imagination of computer enthusiasts, from *2001: A Space Odyssey* to *The Matrix*.

Yet the common references of Internet promoters were not limited to works of fiction. Sociologist Patrice Flichy (2007) has attempted to define a corpus of texts that fueled the "Internet imaginaire": journalists—such as Howard Rheingold, who coined the expression "virtual communities"[5]—rub shoulders with authors of anticipation novels—William Gibson and Bruce Sterling—as well as futurologists and communication theorists, like Marshall McLuhan and Alvin Toffler. For these authors, the Internet was at the root of a global transformation of our civilizations, generating new social, artistic and political forms. The importance of these North American references also reveals a certain fascination for this region that was shared by French Internet pioneers. Almost a quarter of them studied or worked in the US and discovered the Internet network in the making, during their stay abroad. In the 1990s, Vice President Al Gore's speech on the "information superhighway" and the commitment of US cyberspace activists served as models for French activism. But while this influence was strong, the emergence of a freer, more transparent and united "information society" was more broadly based on a globalized imaginary that pervaded the intellectual, political and economic elites of industrialized countries.

In France, social upheavals brought about by information technologies were also a subject of growing attention in scholarly production. Since the 1970s, "information networks", "communication" and the "virtual" had been studied at the intersection of the academic, administrative and media fields. In academia, cybernetic thinking (Wiener, 1948) and the information theory (Shannon, 1948) inspired transdisciplinary research into artificial intelligence, self-organization and virtual communication. They were organized around a new discipline, "information and communication sciences", which was gradually institutionalized in France (Abbott, 2001). New research groups and academic journals emerged in the 1980s, including *Réseaux*, *Transversales Science Culture*, *Hermès* and *Terminal*. Although more critical toward technology than

[5] *The Virtual Community, homesteading on the electronic frontier*, Massachussetts, Addison-Wasley.

their Anglo-Saxon colleagues, their contributors were nonetheless attentive and enthusiastic commentators on the transformations made possible by information networks. Among them, Joël de Rosnay, a futurist writer, published in 1995 *The Symbiotic Man*, a visionary book on the social, political and cultural transformations brought about by the growing interconnection of individuals. That same year, he created with physician Jacques Robin a European Observatory of information superhighways, a group called *Vecam*, in order to "highlight and discuss the real issues and citizen's needs in the information society". *Vecam* became one of the first and foremost organizations in France to promote new policies adapted to the Internet age.

In the political and administrative fields, this conception of technology as a vehicle for progress raised many hopes for change. As early as 1977, the Nora-Minc public report on the "computerization of society" was a publishing success in France (Walliser, 1989). Among the interviewees, a vast majority acknowledged the influence of this report, which raised awareness on the issues and possibilities entailed by information technologies. For Maurice Ronai, reading the report even triggered a change of trajectory [Interview 35, June 2016]. An audiovisual study graduate, he was working at the time as director of a TV news program, and was active in a Trotskyist left-wing movement "where there was a great deal of interest in the scientific and technological revolution". The discovery of the report came as a "real shock" to him. In his own words, "everything changed" and he began working as a journalist specializing in information and communication technologies. He became editor-in-chief of niche publications such as *Vidéotex* and *Infotecture* before founding *Le Courrier International* with Jacques Rosselin, a weekly newspaper that translated and published excerpts of articles from over 900 international prints. He also broke with Trotskyism and started gravitating in political circles close to the French Socialist Party, where he took part in a number of experiments in digital activism, such as the "Computer-Assisted Left-wing" organization. Yet, "his commitment was above all to public administration" and he gradually gained recognition as an expert in the field of public data dissemination. In 1982, he joined a committee on scientific and technical information that worked on the digitization of administrative documents. The integration of IT and new means of communication had indeed triggered ongoing reflection within the State: the Nora-Minc report was only the first of a long series of parliamentary and administrative reports dedicated to information technology, whose authors often became among the most ardent promoters of the Internet in the political field.

The promoters of the Internet identified with this hybrid intellectual heritage of fiction, academic and political production. In the 1990's, the "digital revolution" they heralded was not so much a social reality than the expression of a conviction: information and communication technology would bring about a global transformation of society. They contributed in their own way to nurturing this conviction, publishing works that present the Internet as the endpoint of social change through technology. These works—papers in technology law, textbooks, essays on the virtual world and expert reports—were all part of the "evangelization battle" they intended to wage. They presented the potential of the Internet and its ability to transform social relations, making them more democratic, more horizontal and less dependent on status and hierarchical positions. Some even embarked on concrete experiments in social change through technology. For example, Christian Paul—MP member for the French Socialist Party—"tinkered" with a Minitel server to facilitate exchanges between local and regional authorities, when he was doing his internship for the National School of Administration. Tech Lawyers, such as Lionel Thoumyre, then a PhD student, created websites to enable free access to legal documents and databases (juriscom.net). In addition, journalists such as Laurent Mauriac at *Libération* or Michel Colonna d'Istria at *Le Monde* struggled to put their daily newspapers online. From access to information to cross-sectorization and activist coordination, the Internet "calling" shaped professional practices and work relations of the net evangelists. However, their efforts were still little appreciated and sometimes even mocked by those—the great majority of society—who did not yet succumb to the Internet.

1.3 Techno Stigma and Dealing with It

The initiatives of net evangelists were not always positively received. More often than not, they elicited indifferent or even hostile reactions. Reluctance toward the Internet was not confined to the public bureaucracy: in many social fields in France, the new network remained unfamiliar, its installation costly, its dangers real, its commercial potential hazardous. In addition, Internet promoters also displayed an interest in computers and information technology that was still uncommon at the time, notably in the fields of power. Passion for the Internet departed from approved standards of behaviors and social norms in the bureaucratic, legal or economic fields, where it tended to become a "stigma", in Goffman's sense (1963).

In today's digital age, it may be difficult for the reader to recall—or imagine—a time when, as one respondent recounts, "a self-respecting office manager didn't have a computer: it was a thing for the office assistant" [Interview 52, former digital advisor in a ministerial office (1999–2002), December, 2016]. While today sending e-mails, using the web to search for information, or publishing online are required skills in any job position, they were disqualified at the time. Valérie Sédallian, a lawyer who took part in one of the first associations to defend French Internet users, talks at length in interviews about the mockery and discredit she suffered because of her interest in technology:

> At the time, I was looking for a job, which means, as a young lawyer, that I was looking for a collaboration. I remember, once, I said to a lawyer who had called me back after I'd sent her my CV: "ah well at the moment, I am developing a legal information website". Do you know what her reaction was? She hung up on me. Those were the early days of the Internet. When I talked about it, she thought I was crazy. And believe me, I'm far from being a cuckoo. [Interview 51, December 2016].

Valérie Sédallian learnt to use the web and to publish content online outside of her legal training, thanks to her partner, an IT entrepreneur. Yet, at the time, the Internet was seen by her professors and colleagues as "a fading trend", and practical computer skills were deemed incompatible with "what one expects of a good lawyer".

Computer use and promoting the Internet were particularly stigmatized in the French bureaucratic field. Specific interest in information technologies ran against the "generalist" thinking valued in the training and recruitment of French senior civil servants (Biland & Kolopp, 2013; Eymeri-Douzans, 2001). Knowledge about information technologies was perceived as a hybrid, and therefore muddled, skill—not intellectual enough (understanding how computer networks really work) and too practical (ability to use computers and surf the web). By the end of the 1990s, the expert and the technician merged into the little-valued figure of the "technologist". Net enthusiasts in the State sometimes took advantage of this equivocal position to install by themselves an Internet connection or to create a website, while giving their opinion on the regulation of information networks. But more often than not, this label contributed to degrading the perception of their activities into manual labor. One interviewee, technical advisor in the Prime Minister's office, recalls that it was not uncommon for a colleague to come to him for advice on the purchase of hardware, or for help with repairing a broken computer. "We didn't ask Claude [advisor in charge of Agriculture] to plant flowers and look after the garden", he protests [Interview 37].

Eventually, the stigma brought closer individuals who were sociologically and ideologically distant, but suffered from the same disqualification in their own professional field. Hence, promotion of the Internet underpinned a "reconciliation through technology", defined by one respondent as "the solidarity of those who believed in something new against those who didn't" [Interview 52, former digital advisor in a ministerial office (1999–2002), December, 2016]. It referred to an alleged agreement between innovators facing a multi-faceted conservatism, "conservatism being trans-political in the same way that innovation was trans-political" [Ibid.].

Indeed, the Internet fostered a replacement of traditional oppositions with new principles of division. At a time when the vast majority of politicians were not interested in technological issues, the "calling" for the Internet led to ephemeral coalitions that overlooked partisan affiliations and ideological positions. For example, in 1996, a cross-party working group on the Internet was set up at the French National Assembly. Other activist organizations promoting the Internet were deliberately "apolitical", like *Admiroutes* which gathered civil servants with opposing political affinities (see previous chapter). Likewise, interviewees recall unprecedented reductions in social distances: a young lawyer was astonished to have been able to talk easily with a member of the French *Conseil d'État*, a young hacker remembered with amazement discussions in the office of a leading MP, and a member of the administrative elite found more in common with computer scientists than with some of his colleagues. This understatement of social and political differences gave ground to the idea that "the shared passion transcended all divisions".

In fact, interest in the Internet had as much to do with a "shared passion" as with homologies of position in various fields (Bourdieu, 1984). Net evangelists were often "the least elite among the elite", or newcomers into the economic, political or bureaucratic fields of power. They had experienced a sudden shift in their career path, had not always attended "the best schools" or had only recently (and illegitimately) acquired economic capital. This was particularly true of young entrepreneurs involved into the development of Internet services: most of them had been Minitel players who made a fortune with adult erotic message services, such as Xavier Niel[6] or Rafi Haladjian, who created one of the first Internet service providers (FranceNet). Likewise, Henri de Maublanc, a civil engineer, went from "3615 ALINE"—an erotic chat service—to respectable e-commerce, founding the first online flower sales websites, Aquarelle.com. Among these early Internet entrepreneurs, one could also find activist and hacker profiles, such as Valentin Lacambre, an independent computer engineer who created one of the first French web hosting services, altern.org. In the telecommunication industry, this early transition from the Minitel to the Internet was nonetheless viewed with suspicion, the prevailing belief being that it was impossible to develop reliable commercial services on the web. Besides, these Internet pioneers were sometimes directly implicated in the "Net affairs" of 1996 (Box 2), which contributed to the network's poor reputation in France.

Box 2 A Series of "Scandals" Against the Internet

In 1996, no less than three "scandals" shook the still nascent French Internet. Firstly, in January 1996, the book published by François Mitterrand's personal doctor, Dr. Gubler, revealing the early diagnosis of the former President's cancer, was released on the Internet. However, *Le Grand Secret*, published just a few days after François Mitterrand's death, had in fact been withdrawn from sale on the orders of the family. An Internet user had scanned the book, which was being reproduced and distributed on numerous French and foreign websites. The distribution of Dr. Gubler's book was one of the first cases of copyright infringement on the Internet in France. However, neither the author nor the publisher lodged a complaint. Two months later, the French Jew Students Association filed an injunction against nine Internet service providers, claiming that Holocaust denial content was available on the web. The complaint was finally rejected by the Paris Court. Finally, in May, two ISPs were

[6] See profiles in the international Press: "A billionnaire who breaks the Mold", Kevin O'Brien, *The New York Times*, May 5, 2013; *Garside, Juliette* "Xavier Niel: rebel storms bastions of Gallic elite". *The Guardian, 23 February 2012.*

accused of making pornographic content available on a Usenet discussion forum. Their managers, Rafi Haladjian and Sébastien Socchard, aged 35 and 27 respectively, were charged with "distribution of pornographic images". The investigation lasted three years and eventually led to the case being dismissed. While the Internet was still in its infancy in France, early Internet users took up the cause to defend the network. Through petitions and tribunes, they criticized the technical ignorance of the plaintiffs and denounced dangerous obstacles to the development of the Internet in France caused by these judicial attacks.

These cases highlighted, as early as 1996, the main issues in Internet content regulation—copyright, hate content, child pornography—and showed how difficult it was to adapt the existing legal framework to the digital context. At the same time, the lack of convictions and legal decisions fed the myth of a "legal vacuum" on the Internet, contributing to a certain mistrust in the new network.

In the mid-1990s, the defense of the Internet led to uncanny encounters based on early experience and practices of networked computing, but above all on a shared belief in the revolutionary power of the Internet. The uncanny, which the interviewees marvel at in retrospect, should not, however, obscure the converging interests that motivated these coalitions. The "calling" for the Internet emerged in a specific context marked by the low diffusion of technological skills among the French elite, the reconfiguration of market positions in the information industry, and the uncertain future of network development. While "net evangelists"—both expert users and promoters of the Internet—were stigmatized for their passionate, vocational relationship with technologies, they also saw the Internet as an opportunity to abolish the "privileges" of the technocratic elite and fight for their own recognition in the fields of power by presenting themselves as modernizing figures. Net evangelists fought the "stigma" through their identification as "innovators" and tried to emphasize, alongside their technical skills, their "atypical" backgrounds or their "anti-conformism". As such, the vocation for the Internet was not just a purely disinterested cause: it was also an opportunity to challenge power relations, in the service of social and/or professional advancement. Hence, the battle of ideas was also a battle for positions, as Internet promoters attempted to assert themselves in competitive fields and influence the future of public policies. They found common interest not only in the new network but also in asserting the pioneering role they played in its development.

2 An Interstitial Space for Internet Activism

"How's good old Yolin?" [Interview 50], "And what's become of dear Bruno?" [Interview 52]. As we would ask for an old friend, the net evangelists constantly referred to their "buddies" in interviews. Beyond the similarity of their trajectories, the strength of the feeling of belonging to this group of "evangelists", still alive more than twenty years later, is striking, particularly in view of the poorly structured Internet scene at the end of the 1990s. Public institutions were practically non-existent, associations recent and often short-lived and initiatives scattered. Advocating for the Internet did not happen in a single place, in a single organization. It relied on a plurality of more or less ephemeral collectives and the organization of formal and informal meetings. These intermediary institutions favored the circulation of knowledge and the consolidation of the Internet cause: a social network emerged at the crossroads of the business, administrative, technical and political fields organized around a global project of social transformation through networked technologies.

Made up by varied organizations, supported by a community that was as limited as it was heterogeneous, this social space declined with the widespread diffusion of the Internet and the transformation of digital issues. Many of the institutions that constituted this space were short-lived: some splintered, others reformed or specialized. Most did not take the time to safeguard their archives. Yet it would be erroneous to study only the institutions that have withstood the test of time and impose present issues on a teeming and unconsolidated space of commitment and encounters. "Internet parties", meetings in cybercafés, online discussions, colloquia and exhibitions, all provided opportunities for new technology enthusiasts to get together. To grasp the structure and features of this nebula, today's researchers have no other option than to collect traces of these places in digital and media archives or to call on the personal memories and recollections of interviewees, who are quick to evoke the often-unconventional atmosphere of these venues. While the latter method provides an opportunity to gather representations and "impressions", the former has often made it possible to compensate for the respondents' failing memory, and even to amend retrospective reconstructions and oversights as to who was present and what was discussed in these organizations.

Taking part in the Internet "evangelization" enrolled the net promoters in a network of organizations. The latter offered social affiliation, reinforced identification with shared values and beliefs, but above all weaved links between distinct social groups. In this section, we provide a map of these organizations, showing an unprecedented picture of the Internet cause in France as it entered the twenty-first century.

2.1 Garages, Festival and Workshop Studios. Meeting French Net Enthusiasts in the 1990s

In a context of weak technological acculturation and defiance toward the Internet, bringing together supporters of the new network was an imperative for the cause. Some venues thus became central meeting places for net promoters: from the "Internet festival" to the Summer Conference on Communication in Hourtin, these events played a major role as spaces and occasions for new sociability, bringing to life the idea of a reconciliation through technology. Among several emblematic events of the period, the Internet Meetings in Autrans enjoy a prominent place in the memory of interviewees. They were organized by the French chapter of the Internet Society, an organization created in 1996 whose main goal was "to promote the use of the Internet in France by highlighting experience gained, providing a first level of information, and encouraging contacts between French and international ISOC members"[7]. The first French Internet Meetings took place from January 9 to 11, 1997, with this question as sole program: "Why and how should French society be networked? The aim is to win over Net skeptics...". Among participants, one could find government officials, politicians, technical experts and association representatives, as well as some of the leading figures of the global Internet, such as Vinton Cerf, one of the "fathers of the network" (see Chapter 2). This eclectic mix became one of main characteristics of Autrans, confirming its vocation as a networking venue for French Internet pioneers. Christian Paul, "who must have been there four or five times" [Interview 14, Socialist MP (1997–2017), March 2016],

[7] Retrieved from www.isoc.asso.fr (via Wayback Machine of the Internet Archive).

recalls a convivial atmosphere, where the discovery of the latest technological innovations mingled with the elaboration of a common agenda for the development of Internet policies: "It was here that I first heard about Wifi, for example. It was a meeting place for enthusiasts—we weren't yet talking about geeks back then. We used to get together every year, in the snowy and cozy atmosphere of the small village of Autrans" (Fig. 1).

In these venues, sociability patterns partly reproduced the characteristics and values of Internet virtual communities and helped to spread them beyond their milieu of origin. Another emblematic *rendez-vous* was *l'Atelier*, a new technology open workshop based at the Paris headquarters of Banque Paribas. It was founded and run by Jean-Michel Billaut, an analyst within the bank, who describes *l'Atelier* as follows:

Fig. 1 Autrans Internet Meetings Poster found in the personal archives of Bruno Oudet, founder of the French Internet Society

> It was just a studio, a room rather, in a filthy basement where I started inviting people who were doing interesting things. (…) Some came more for the free whisky than the ideas, but whatever happenned, it was a pretty weird and extraordinary place. To caricature it, it was perceived as a bunch of anarchists squatting the basements of big bank Paris Paribas.

For more than twenty years, *l'Atelier* was conceived as a "garage" where a team of "youngsters"—in fact graduates of top-ranked schools with extensive computer experience—developed electronic applications to "revolutionize" the banking sector [Interview 50]. The story told by Billaut summons up the myths of the Internet Revolution. The "youngsters" refer to the "hackers" and their "garage" to the popular myths of Silicon Valley success stories, allegedly started in the garages of students like Bill Hewlett and David Packard (HP), Steve Wozniak (Apple) or Larry Page and Sergueï Brin (Google). Gradually, and against the advice of his superiors, Billaut opened *l'Atelier* to outside members. In the mid-1990s, the studio gathered the main promoters of the Internet in France, counting politicians as well as activists or academics.

Conviviality, presented as a feature of the "Internet spirit", was thus used to explain as much as to justify the lowering of barriers to entry at these ritual gatherings of net promoters. Internet promoters also created organizations which, while working collectively for the development of new technologies in France, differed both in their objectives and in their political and militant culture. Taken together, they structured the network of Internet activism.

2.2 A Profusion of Groups and Affiliations

In the mid-1990s, the need to unite Internet promoters, and to protect the first users, led to the creation of numerous organizations that gradually took on the task of representing and defending the interests of the French Internet. The development of digital uses favored the coordination and the profusion of structures, some of which had a purely virtual existence. This was the case, for example, of the *Association of Internet Users*, founded in 1995 by an "electronic constituent assembly" that brought together a small group of pioneering online users. The reflexive use of information technologies and the transformation of militant practices had a crucial importance within many organizations, such as the Socialist Party's digital section, *TemPS_réels*. Set up in 1998, it played a key role in the "evangelization" of political staff and gathered a large number of net enthusiasts, recruiting well beyond the party's boundaries. Finally, the democratization of technological knowledge was at the heart of associations of computer scientists and free software advocates—such as the *AFUL* and the *APRIL*—which promoted, with the Internet, the values of openness and free flow of information.

Other organizations followed in the footsteps of long-standing groups of IT and Minitel players, which had been reconfigured with the emergence of the Internet. This was the case, for example, of *AFNet*, the former French Association of Unix and Open Systems Users (AFU), that became the Association of Net Users in 2001. Similarly, *AFTEL*, a lobby for telematic service providers, became *ACSEL* in 2000, to mark its conversion from the Minitel to the Internet. It was also at this time that the first organizations for start-ups, such as *Silicon Sentier*, emerged to defend the innovative small businesses of the information economy.

Through their formal and thematic diversity, these structures formed a social space in the making, at the end of the 1990s. To account for and study this teeming environment, we selected a wide range of institutions, including entrepreneurial groups, militant associations, administrative commissions and partisan sections. This diversity testified to the enthusiasm and profusion of the early days of the Internet, but also to the heterogeneity of Internet activism in France, emerging at the crossroads of various social fields. With a fledgling Internet and weakly-structured institutions, net promoters tended to join several organizations at the same time. This interplay of multiple affiliations ensured the networking of different institutions and the coordination of their actions. Affiliations indeed linked various structures via their common members.

The resulting network allows us to visualize the social space of Internet activism as a graph with two types of nodes: individuals on the one hand, and organizations on the other (Fig. 2). Central nodes appear on the graph, around which Net evangelists organized themselves in clusters, such as the *FING*, *Isoc-France* or *TemPS-Réel*. For the period under study, these organizations were indeed strategic venues for those working on Internet development in France. Unlike other organizations (such as professional associations or administrative institutions), they were open institutions whose main purpose was to coordinate efforts and spread knowledge about the Internet.

Co-membership in the same association can also be understood as a link between two individuals. Admittedly, co-membership was just one dimension of multi-dimensional relations—professional, academic, personal—that gathered Internet promoters. But contrary to others, it is easier to substantiate and verify in retrospect, thanks to the archives of the organizations. It also enables to emphasize the structuring role of organizations, as vehicles for the circulation of political, intellectual and social resources. Hence, we can derive from the first graph a second one with only Internet activists (Fig. 3).

This network reveals the central players of Internet activism at the end of the 1990s. First and foremost, we find intensely involved individuals, active members of up to seven Internet advocacy organizations. For example, Jean-Michel Billaut was a founding member of the *Club de l'Arche*—a think tank on the information economy—and of the Association for the Internet festival, as well as one of the early members of *Vecam* and of the *AFNET*. He also took part in *ACSEL*, *FING* and *club.senat.fr*, think tanks bringing together net entrepreneurs and politicians. Other prominent figures include Bruno Oudet, founder of *Isoc-France*, Cécile Alvergnat, a former Minitel entrepreneur, and Jean-François Abramatic, researcher at INRIA and first president of the World Wide Web Consortium.

The graph also enables us to identify pivotal intermediaries that connected different social spaces around Internet activism. Among them, Daniel Kaplan played an important role as an intermediate between public and private Net evangelists. A former student at Sciences Po Paris, he was then a classmate of the future Socialist deputy Christian Paul, with whom he set up a left-wing union section. Interested in new technologies, he "cobbled together" a Minitel service for the orientation of students. Building on this first experience, he created in 1986 a telematics service company (*JKML*) and joined the *AFTEL*, the professional association of Minitel players. In 1993, he became an independent consultant in new technologies. During a trip to the US, he discovered the Internet and immediately began advocating the relocation of Minitel services to the new network. In 1995, he wrote a pioneering report for the AFTEL entitled "Internet, challenges for France". He also took part in the creation of the Internet Society-France, becoming its first General Secretary in 1996. He was above all convinced of the potential of the Internet for public

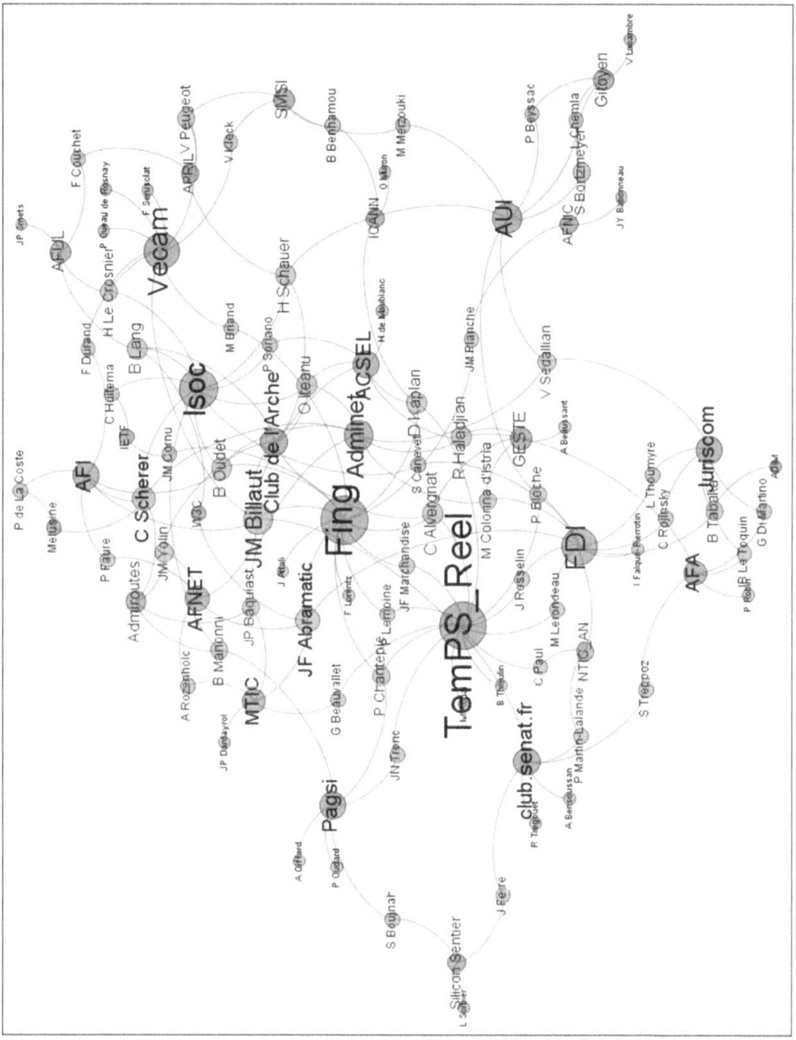

Fig. 2 Bi-partite network of Internet activists and their affiliations (*Legend* the size of the nodes is proportional to the number of connections with other nodes. Blue nodes are individuals and green nodes organizations)

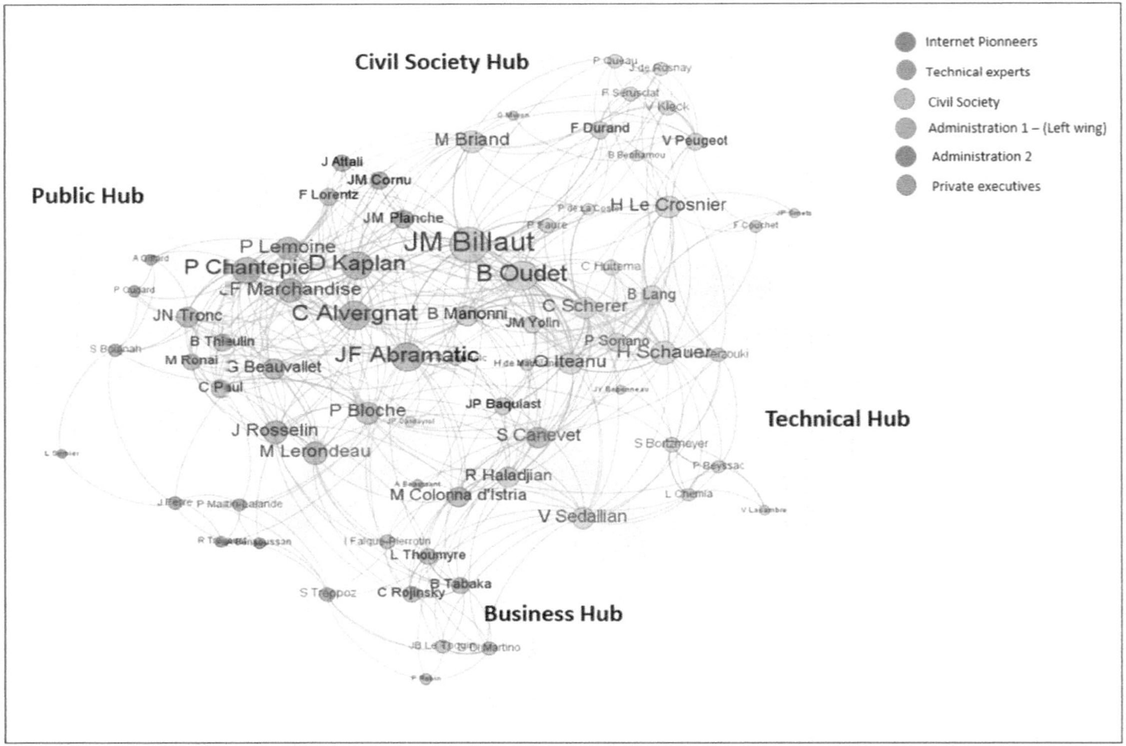

Fig. 3 The network of net evangelist at the end of the 1990s (*Legend* the size of the nodes is proportional to the number of connections with other nodes (degree-centrality). Color of the nodes refers to their class of modularity, according to the Louvain algorithm)

services and gradually consulted for administrations and public companies. In 1999, he founded the "Internet new generation initiative" (the *FING*), in order to bring together private, non-profit and public-sector players, and facilitate their exchanges around Internet issues. He also produced many studies on Internet uses and users and regularly wrote in national newspapers about these issues. Daniel Kaplan's multiple commitments and interventions in social fields as diverse as politics, the media and digital entrepreneurship made him a key player in the circulation of ideas within the space of Internet activism. This ability to build "bridges" between social groups is not a mere function of the number of his affiliations. For example, Christian Scherer, senior civil servant at the Ministry of Industry and founder of *Adminet* (see previous chapter), took part in as many collectives as Daniel Kaplan, but most of them are situated in the administrative field: he remained little connected to other social groups. Conversely, Valérie Sedallian, a young lawyer and pioneer of technology law, was in contact with various groups as an active member of *AUI*, a contributor to *Juriscom* and a legal consultant for *Adminet*. Without being a central figure in the network, she connected distinct and distant communities—jurists, lawyers, IT specialists and civil servants[8].

The graph displays a network structured into different hubs. It is divided into six distinct communities,[9] revealing as many modes and logics of promoting the Internet in France.

At the heart of the network, we distinguish the community of the French "pioneers", early adopters and experts of the Internet. They include a large number of computer scientists, such as Christian Huitema, chairman of the Internet Advisory Board, and Bruno Oudet, who founded a social network for French expatriate researchers in the US, as early as 1991. This first group of experts yet stands apart from another technical community, made up of computer engineers with less formal education and further removed from the corridors of power. We find here free software advocates, hackers and tech activists such as Stéphane Bortzmeyer, precursor of electronic exchange encryption, and Laurent Chemla, a historic figure of French hacking and the co-founder of one of the first independent ISP with Valentin Lacambre. Together, these two

[8] In the language of network analysis, it means that the betweenness centrality of the node "Valérie Sedallian" is higher than her degree-centrality.

[9] Community detection was achieved with a louvain algorithm on the grap (De Meo et al., 2011).

groups form the technical hub of Internet activism characterized by an intense and reflexive use of new technologies, the defense of the Internet's open architecture and of the free flow of information.

If they often fight together as representatives of Internet users and defenders of online freedoms, it is precisely this technical dimension that distinguishes this hub from another group of activists at the top right of the graph. This opposition is echoed in the discourse of the interviewees that also suggest a gendered relationship to technologies: for example, Valérie Peugeot, members of *Vecam* remembers that "the computer engineers had a lot of contempt for us "Vecam girls", because we were not technical enough..." [Interview 25, May 2016]. This third group gathers academics and intellectuals, close to political and administrative players, such as Joël de Rosnay or Philippe Quéau. Their mobilization was based on the production of essays and public reports about the socio-technological changes underway. While this group was mostly active in France, their members were also connected to transnational movements. Following the World Summit on the Information Society (WSIS), they participated in the discussions on the global governance of the Internet. They positioned themselves as representatives of a "civil society" that had to conquer its place alongside multinational corporations and national states in international forums. They promoted the advent of a non-profit Internet and raised awareness on the risk that economic and industrial interests would capture the digital revolution to the detriment of the common good. *Vecam* was particularly active in the community network movement that was developing in Europe, building on the pioneering experiences of citizen networks in cities such as Bologna, Cardiff, Brighton, Amsterdam and Barcelona.[10]

In this, they were opposed to the private hub, whose members defended the advent of the information economy with the Internet. This other group included Internet service providers such as Patrick Robin, creator of Imaginet, as well as online media pioneers such as Michel Colonna D'Istria (*LeMonde.fr*) and Jacques Rosselin, who created the first French webTV, *Canalweb*. We also find here young lawyers (6 out of the 13 members of the group) that reflected on digital law and created legal watch websites. Taking advantage of the lack of institutionalized expertise on these subjects, they also consulted for professional associations.

[10] See brochure of the European Association for Community Networks on the archived Vecam website: https://vecam.org/2002-2014/article209.html.

For example, Benoît Tabaka, a key member of this group, got a master's degree in law from a second-rank University but launched an "electronic review of French legal news" at the age of 21 and became president of the small *Association des Internautes Médiateurs* (ADIM). He then joined the IT department of the *Conseil Constitutionnel* (French Supreme Court) to develop the institution's website. In 2000, he was elected member of the steering committee of the *Forum des droits sur internet,* a newly created public institution for Internet regulation. He left in 2006 to join the private sector, notably as head of legal affairs for major digital groups (Price Minister then Rakuten). After 8 months as Secretary General of the *Conseil National du Numérique* (National Digital Council), an independent committee created by the French government in 2011, he was hired by Google France where he joined the "public policy and institutional relations" team in 2012. His professional career is emblematic of the upward social trajectories experienced by some Internet pioneers in the 2000s.

Finally, on the left-hand side of the graph, a large community forms the public hub of Internet activism whose members were involved in government, political parties or administrations. The proportion of graduates from prestigious schools (8/24) and/or from Sciences Po Paris (13/24) is higher in this group than in others. Individuals in this group were particularly attentive to public issues surrounding the development of the Internet and the digital transformation of political and administrative organizations. They found themselves at the heart of the digital policymaking process in the 1990s. A sub-community that stands out in the center of the graph was characterized by its left-wing political orientation, with MPs from the Socialist Party such as Christian Paul or Patrick Bloche, and public affairs consultants close to socialist political networks such as Daniel Kaplan or Jacques-François Marchandise.

The detection of communities thus reveals dividing lines that structured and sometimes fractured Internet activism during the 1990s and 2000s. The identified communities were indeed separated by both social and ideological features. These distinctions were potential principles of division, sometimes euphemized, sometimes reaffirmed, by the Net evangelists. They constituted powerful centrifugal dynamics between collectives defending the Internet, whose convergence was primarily conjunctural, as one interviewee reminds us: "Splits have occurred among internet actors. For sure, there was a moment when the idea was that all political divides were erased. But at some point, people who are very left-wing, defending a participatory Internet, find it quite difficult to align with the neoliberal figure of Jean-Marie Messier [CEO of the mass media holding company *Vivendi*]." [Interview 52, digital advisor to the government (1999–2002), December 2016]

Identifying these diverse communities allows us to put into perspective the narratives collected in interviews about the reduction of social distances thanks to a "common passion" for the Internet. Behind the enthusiast recollections of a single-hearted defense of the Internet, this method reveals dissensions that would continue to assert themselves in subsequent periods. The exchanges and interactions that took place at the end of the 1990s were indeed the result of a particular conjuncture: the early stages of the French Internet, marked by the limited diffusion of computer practices and of technological knowledge in the fields of power. While we must take seriously the uncanny convergences that took place in this context, they should not be confused with a homogeneity of discourses nor projects regarding public policies. Internet activism remained an aggregation of various goals and political concerns—administrative modernization, democratization of participation, free circulation of information—that would fuel the first Internet policies.

* * *

The promotion of the Internet at the end of the 1990s is based on interactions that call into question the supposed permeability of the boundary between the State and the Internet. Civil servants and political players on the one hand, Internet activists and entrepreneurs on the other, found themselves working together, despite their differences, on the same project to develop the French Internet. Crossovers and interconnections between these groups were encouraged by the reluctance toward the US network in the fields of power. The emergence of an Internet "calling" was underpinned by shared practices and beliefs as well as by common difficulties. The net evangelists suffered from a "technologist stigma" and struggled to conquer bastions of resistance to "modernization", in both the public and private sectors.

At the end of the 1990s, they created hybrid places at the intersection of various social fields, places that fostered the exchange of ideas and the formalization of public demands and political programs for the digital transformation of society. Historically defined, this network of organizations characterizes a specific moment in the development of digital policies in France, marked by great porosity between sectors and the understatement of political and social differences around a common activism in favor of the Internet. This cross-sectorial approach would mark the first Internet public policies which drew from this nebulous movement the seeds of a new public intervention for the development of the French Internet, and which are studied in the next chapter.

References

Abbiss, J. (2011). Boys and machines: Gendered computer identities, regulation and resistance. *Gender and Education, 23*(5), 601–617.

Abbott, A. (2001). *Chaos of disciplines*. University of Chicago Press.

Bezes, P. (2012). État, experts et savoirs néo-managériaux: Les producteurs et diffuseurs du New Public Management en France depuis les années 1970. *Actes de la recherche en sciences Sociales, 193*(3), 16–37.

Biland, É., & Kolopp, S. (2013). La fabrique de la pensée d'État: Luttes d'institutions et arrangements cognitifs à l'ENA (1945–1982). *Gouvernement & action publique, 2*, 221–248.

Bourdieu, P. (1984). Espace social et genèse des" classes". *Actes de la recherche en sciences sociales, 52*(1), 3–14.

Bourdieu, P. (2014). *On the state: Lectures at the Collège de France, 1989–1992*. John Wiley & Sons.

Collet, I. (2006). *L'informatique at-elle un sexe?: hackers, mythes et réalités*. Harmattan.

Collovald, A. (1988). Identité (s) stratégique (s). *Actes de la recherche en sciences sociales, 73*(1), 29–40.

De Meo, P., Ferrara, E., Fiumara, G., & Provetti, A. (2011). Generalized louvain method for community detection in large networks. In: *2011 11th international conference on intelligent systems design and applications* (pp. 88–93). IEEE.

DiMaggio, P. J. (1988). Interest and agency in institutional theory. *Institutional patterns and organizations*, 3–21.

Dixon, K. (1998). *Les évangélistes du marché: les intellectuels britanniques et le néo-libéralisme* (p. 117). Raisons d'agir.

Dubois, V. (2015). *Culture as a vocation: Sociology of career choices in cultural management*. Routledge.

Dunleavy, P., & Hood, C. (1994). From old public administration to new public management. *Public Money & Management, 14*(3), 9–16.

Durndell, A., Glissov, P., & Siann, G. (1995). Gender and computing: Persisting differences. *Educational Research, 37*(3), 219–227.

Eymeri-Douzans, J. M. (2001). *La fabrique des énarques*. Economica.

Fischer, M. (2011). Social network analysis and qualitative comparative analysis: Their mutual benefit for the explanation of policy network structures. *Methodological Innovations Online, 6*(2), 27–51.

Flichy, P. (2007). *The internet imaginaire*. MIT press.

Goffman, E. (1963). *Stigma: Notes on the Management of Spoiled Identity*. Prentice Hall.

Gustafson, J. M. (1982). Professions as" Callings". *Social Service Review, 56*(4), 501–515.

Haas, P. M. (1992). Introduction: Epistemic communities and international policy coordination. *International Organization, 46*(1), 1–35.

Hardy, C., & Maguire, S. (2008). Institutional entrepreneurship. *The Sage Handbook of Organizational Institutionalism, 1*, 198–217.

Keller, F. B. (2018). Analyses of elite networks. In H. Best & J. Higley (Eds.), *The Palgrave handbook of political elites* (pp. 135–152). Palgrave Macmillan UK.

Lunding, J. A., Ellersgaard, C. H., & Larsen, A. G. (2020). The craft of elite prosopography. *Researching elites and power: Theory, methods, analyses* (pp. 57–70).

Rhodes, R. A., & Marsh, D. (1992). New directions in the study of policy networks. *European Journal of Political Research, 21*(1–2), 181–205.

Sabatier, P. A. (1998). The advocacy coalition framework: Revisions and relevance for Europe. *Journal of European Public Policy, 5*(1), 98–130.

Sabatier, P. A., & Jenkins-Smith, H. (1988). An advocacy coalition model of policy change and the role of policy orientated learning therein. *Policy Sciences, 2*, 129–168.

Shannon, C. E. (1948). A mathematical theory of communication. *The Bell System Technical Journal, 27*(3), 379–423.

Stone, L. (1971). Prosopography. *Daedalus*, 46–79.

Wajcman, J. (2007). From women and technology to gendered technoscience. *Information, Community and Society, 10*(3), 287–298.

Walliser, A. (1989). Le rapport" Nora-Minc". Histoire d'un best-seller. *Vingtieme siecle. Revue d'histoire*, pp. 35–47.

Wiener, N. (1948). *Cybernetics, or control and communication in the animal and the machine*. The MIT Press.

CHAPTER 5

A Revolutionary Moment? Experimenting E-Government in France

> And it is because the State cannot remain in its superb isolation in the face of a technological transformation that concerns all countries and society as a whole, that the government has decided to make the State, not only be a major player, but also an example, in the development of information and communication technologies.
> *L'État et les technologies de l'information et de la communication*, Public report to the Prime Minister, December 2000, p.17.

On August 25, 1997, Lionel Jospin, who had just been appointed Prime Minister in France, announced at the Summer University on Communication in Hourtin, France, that information technology was now an "essential concern" of his government. Above all, he presented the Internet as a fundamental innovation compared to the "technologically limited" Minitel, and as an opportunity for a positive transformation of the State. While reluctance toward the new network was still pervasive in France, the Hourtin speech was hailed by Internet promoters as a "miraculous accident" [Interview 24], "a call to arms – similar to De Gaulle's on June 18, 1940" [Interview 50]. Years after the Hourtin Speech, they have never ceased to refer to this event as a major breakthrough in the history of French Internet policies, marking a significant shift in official discourse and heralding new policies for the development of information and communication technologies in France.

A. Bellon, *A Socio-History of Internet Policies*, International Series on Public Policy, https://doi.org/10.1007/978-3-031-69099-0_5

Indeed, a few months later, the French government adopted a large-encompassing "Government Action Plan for the Information Society" (PAGSI) targeting six policy domains: education, culture, state reform, e-commerce, innovation and networks regulation. The PAGSI had a strong impact on Internet development in France. Between September 1996 and July 1999, the number of Internet users increased tenfold, and while less than 1% of households were connected in 1997, this number had risen to more than 20% by 2002, the end of Jospin's mandate.[1] While France was lagging behind in terms of Internet use, it gradually made up for his delay compared to other European countries in the first decade of the twenty-first century. This change was particularly marked in the public sector, with institutions receiving new hardware, setting up websites and creating e-mail addresses for their employees. Surfing on the transformative potential of the Internet, experimentations were also conducted within the State: computer scientists leading administrative missions, technological teaching considered for the training of upper civil servant, extra-administrative forms of regulation tested, etc. Witnesses and players in these changes, Internet promoters we interviewed enthusiastically recall the period as a "revolutionary moment" in the development of Internet policies.

The date of the Hourtin speech and the publication of the PAGSI are convenient landmarks in the chronology of French Internet public policies. Yet, the role of socio-history is to question these sometimes over-enthusiast recollections and to unveil the conditions through which paradigmatic policy change (Hall, 1993) is made possible as well as to assess its true impact on the actors and instruments of public intervention. The very concept of "turning point" is the subject of growing mistrust in recent studies in political science and historical institutionalism. They point to the need to question the temporality of institutional evolution (Palier & Surel, 2010; Thelen, 2000), to document "structural effects", to shed light on the conflicts and uncertainties that preside over change and to nuance the power of political alternation (Aldrin et al., 2016). Any political change could rather be understood as the product of a combination of ruptures (what changes abruptly), conjunctural evolution (what changes progressively), irreversibility (choices that constrain the future) and inertia (what does not change). In the case of Internet in France,

[1] At the same time, Internet usage in Germany goes from 4% in 1996 to 23% in 1999, and from 7 to 21% in the UK (Source: International Telecommunication Union).

how can we explain such a shift within a State field that was still largely reluctant to adopt the US network? How can the ethos of the Internet and its open features be accommodated within the bureaucracy when, as a public report pointed out in 2000, "*built around highly hierarchical structures, designed to enforce a rule of law enacted at central level, the State is not spontaneously at ease in the world of networks, where the circulation of information is transversal and more informal*"[2]? How can the government intervene in this online territory, whose main actors reject public regulation?

According to the same report, quoted in the chapter heading, to become a key player in the information society, the State had to become an exemplary locus for the use of computer network technologies—a "Virtual State" (Fountain, 2001) as well as an Internet user—and thereby regain a legitimacy of intervention that had been partly abandoned to technical experts and scientists. Before assessing the role played by national governments in the digital revolution , we need to look at the very possibility of a "bureaucratic revolution" within the State, its mechanisms and limitations, its advances and setbacks.

In this chapter, we challenge the idea of a national State as an immovable dike erected against the Internet wave. We will show that the Sate as a field must rather be understood as a permeable terrain where technology and ideas infuse to transform modes of organization and intervention, here and there coming up against still-closed doors. As Pierre Bourdieu has shown in his classic study of the State (2014), a "bureaucratic revolution" is first and foremost a subversive enterprise led by newcomers who challenge existing hierarchies and boundaries within the bureaucracy; in this respect, it can be accompanied by organizational changes or new forms of governance. The "revolutionary heroes" of our period were top civil servants or young ministerial advisors with notable social dispositions, seeking recognition and power in the bureaucratic and political fields. Far from a spontaneous transformation, the policy change in favor of the Internet came along a claim of legitimacy by net promoters, to the detriment of old hierarchy in innovation and technological policies. At the turn of the twenty-first century, they conquered decision-making

[2] Our translation, from Bruno Lasserre (dir.), *L'État et les technologies de l'information et de la communication*, Rapport du Commissariat général du Plan, handed to French Prime Minister in December 2000, p. 17.

positions and engaged the State in new actions to develop, organize and police the Internet.

Yet the success of their enterprise did not owe solely to their "heroism" (Bezes, 2000; Gaïti, 2002). It lay as much on collective strategies for triggering policy change as to a specific context conducive to the renewal of innovation policies; in a fluid conjuncture where ideas circulated between activists, scientists and civil servants (see previous chapter), coalitions between administrative reformers and digital pioneers enabled a series of institutional changes. The first Internet public policies thus bore the dual hallmarks of an imperative for reform, advocated by national and international institutions, and a creative use of networked technology in the administrative field. E-government programs, software development and co-regulatory bodies that burgeoned at the turn of the century, were characteristic of the import of Internet's tools and ideas into government, in the service of State reform. While the first Internet public policies testified to the enthusiasm that reigned over this period, they also revealed its limits. The differences between the worlds of the Internet and of the State did not cease to exist with the dissemination of information and communication technologies in the administration: with the expansion of networks, the State also faces new challenges that called into question the possibility of a government modeled after the Internet.

Looking back at early Internet policy experimentations in France, this chapter traces the conditions favorable to the transformation of public intervention and the emergence of new policies based on the technological modernization of the State. It also provides an understanding for the ephemeral nature of some experiments, explaining why the institutional traces of these early programs are short-lived in political memory, and why policy development in the realm of the Internet took a much longer time to be implemented.

1 Political Alternation and Administrative Modernization

In the aftermath of the Hourtin speech, several newspapers and magazines ran headlines on Lionel Jospin's Internet Program. On the cover of the newsmagazine *Le Point* (Fig. 1), the Prime Minister appeared pixelated as a new figure of modernism, symbolizing a policy shift at the head of state. The Hourtin speech was not, however, the result of a single-person enterprise. Lionel Jospin had not previously shown any real enthusiasm for network technologies, a subject that was also relatively absent from the 1997 legislative campaign in France.

Rather, the elaboration of innovative policies in favor of the Internet was the result of multiple mobilizations, both within and outside the State, in a context that was favorable politically—the 1997 alternation—administratively—with a movement for State reform—and economically—the resumption of economic growth in the second half of the 1990s, thanks in particular to technological innovations. The turning point symbolized by the Hourtin speech and the adoption of the PAGSI lay at the intersection of these different evolutions, or "streams", which contributed to the opening of a "window of opportunity" (Kingdon, 1984) seized by institutional entrepreneurs. From ministerial cabinets to expert missions, they gradually joined key loci of policymaking and promoted the development of Internet within the State. If there was a rupture or a "revolution", it was only made possible by the convergence

Fig. 1 "Goodbye Minitel, Hello Internet", Front Page of *Le Point* n°1302, August 30, 1997

of these movements of transformation in the political and administrative fields notably, that the following section explores.

1.1 A New Power Elite

Following the dissolution of the National Assembly by right-wing President Jacques Chirac, the Socialist Party won the 1997 legislative elections in France. The government formed by Lionel Jospin reflected the heterogeneity of the "plural left", and the ongoing reform of the *Parti Socialiste*. Alongside the close relations to former President Mitterrand, ministers and their *cabinets* also gathered a new generation of socialists, inspired by the New Labor or the pragmatic new Social Democracy in Germany. Among these reformers, the new government included Dominique Strauss-Kahn, at the head of a large and renewed Ministry of Economy, Industry and Finance. Despite their mentor's absence from the government, a number of young "rocardiens", that had long been advocating for more decentralization and less State control over the economy, also made their way into ministerial offices.[3]

The renewal of government's staff also marked, albeit marginally, a renewal of typical career paths of government advisers, moving away from the figure of the politicized technocrat (Mangset, 2015). In Dominique Strauss-Kahn's cabinet, for example, a number of advisers had previously worked in the private sector and abroad, and enjoyed a training in economic as well as a law and politics. This was the case, for example, for Frédéric Lavenir, a policy advisor who graduated from a business school, and Stéphane Boujnah, the technological policy advisor of Strauss-Kahn who was previously a corporate lawyer specializing in mergers and acquisitions in an international firm. These newcomers brought with them new rationale and interests at the government: they were particularly interested in the democratization of state institutions, administrative reform and European policies. They also bore a fascination for the social liberalism embodied—in a highly heterogeneous way—by contemporary left-wing figures such as Bill Clinton, Tony Blair and Gerard Schröder. All of these terms were gradually combined with the promotion of the Internet as a global network for Europe, and a focus on information technologies as

[3] Michel Rocard was prominent figure of the Socialist Party in France. He is known for his positions, sometimes controversial, in favor of the self-governance model, or a reshuffling of the right/left opposition in France.

a factor in economic growth, employment and democracy. These ideas were particularly defended by Jean-Noël Tronc, the new technical advisor in charge of the information society at the Prime Minister's office.

Born in 1967, J.-N. Tronc discovered computer science at the age of 9, on the computer of his father, a nuclear physicist. Despite this heritage, Jean Noël Tronc repeatedly points out in interview the distance that separated him from the "scientific" engineers like his father: "I hadn't had an above-average grade in math since 4th grade" [Interview 37, July 2016]. Involved in politics from an early age, he became president of the *Jeunes Rocardiens* at eighteen. In parallel with his studies at Sciences Po, he worked as an assistant to Gérard Fuchs, socialist member of the French National Assembly and then member of the European Parliament. A graduate from a business school, Tronc started his professional career as a business consultant with the US firm *Andersen Consulting*. Like other recruits, his contract began with two months of programming training at the University of Chicago. "In my view, the US lead in IT starts from there: the elite knows how to program and to type on a computer, which made them both more productive and, above all, more 'tech-savvy' than its French counterpart" he says in interview. The experience had a lasting impact on his vision of technology and of the digital revolution . For two years, he worked on the evolution of the telecommunication sector, notably for *Motorola* and *France Télécom*. In 1995, he was recruited by the French National Planning Committee (*Commissariat général du Plan*), as a project manager for information society networks. There, he became a strong support of the Internet: as rapporteur for the Miléo Committee (see Chapter 3), and as leader of an expert group for the coordination of government websites, at the origin of the ".gouv.fr" domain extension. In January 1997, he was invited as a speaker at the first Autrans Internet meetings. He also pursued his militant career at the *Parti Socialiste* and in 1996 contributed to the drafting of a program on information society. One year later, he joined Prime Minister Lionel Jospin's cabinet.

Jean-Noël Tronc was the main figure behind the Hourtin speech and the PAGSI. More generally, he played a central role in the emergence of Internet policies at the end of the 1990s. His trajectory was paradigmatic of the net evangelists (see previous chapter), as well as of a new generation of socialists who joined the Jospin government in 1997. With his expertise in IT, his youthful political commitment and his experience abroad in the private sector, his career path epitomized the specificities of Internet policy entrepreneurs at the turn of the twenty-first century.

Just before his appointment, Jean-Noël Tronc detailed in a programmatic note his agenda for the future Internet policies.[4] He defined the digital revolution as "a challenge for the future, but also a political motto for modernization, from which the government could derive great benefit. Indeed, among a section of the population, particularly young people, there is a strong expectation of a proactive and ambitious commitment on the part of the State to these issues, the examples of President Clinton and the new British government having shown that they can be a prime object of political mobilization" (our translation). The whole note anticipated the main lines of the Internet Government Program, cleverly defended as an opportunity to modernize the image of the French left and appeal to a younger audience. Its impact confirmed how much bureaucratic note-writing constitutes a key form of expertise that yields authority within the French government (Mangset & Asdal, 2019).

At a time when the Internet and information technology in general was still little-known, J.-N. Tronc also organized careful "presentation" of the Internet to other cabinet members, presentations that showcased his expertise, as well as his vision, on the subject:

> In the room next to the Prime Minister's personal office, on the second floor, we hurriedly installed a special telephone line and a modem 56 to connect the computer to the Internet. I presented a dozen websites that I had selected to introduce the Internet to Jospin, *in concreto*. I could find you the exact date: it was the day of the World Youth Day, when Pope John Paul II was on the Champ de Mars in Paris. I remember it vividly, as it was very hot and the windows were open, so we could hear the clamor of the crowd outside. On the subject of culture and innovation, I showed him a little experiment of the first French "web TV". At the time, the video was the size of a postage stamp, and it was actually broadcasting the WYD. So it was funny: through the window, you could hear the sound of images we were discovering online, and with a slight delay, images of the Pope. I also showed him e-commerce websites, and websites with illegal content. For example, I pointed to a website, I wonder if it was Aaargh.com or another, in any case it was a website where you could find Holocaust denial content (...) [The idea was to show] him the issues of security and content

[4] I would like to thank Jean Noël Tronc for all the personal archives he allowed me to consult for research purposes.

> regulation. And then, I visited for him one or two administrative websites, at the time practically devoid of interest, those of the first ministries present on the Internet, with a few speeches by ministers and press releases. Then I moved on to the much more interesting Admi.net. The website was hosted on the *École des Mines* server, against the will of the Secretary General of the Government, because it broadcasted the *Journal Officiel* [Official Bulletin].

Being the sole knowledgeable about Internet in the cabinet, Jean-Noël Tronc demonstrated his expertise regarding the new network and his ability to frame related public issues, which were to form the lineaments of the government action program for the Internet. The scene was emblematic of the "bureaucratic revolution" underway: it was indeed a key moment of role reversal, when the youngest member of Prime Minister's cabinet—only 30 years old at the time—revealed to senior civil servants the challenges of the information society. Following the words of Pierre Bourdieu (2014, p. 43), Tronc displayed here a "surprising resource", that enabled him to "impress" the political and administrative elite. The demonstration described above was part of a series of performances "played out" by Internet pioneers, sometimes aimed less at raising public awareness than at overturning hierarchies and legitimizing the urgent need for a new kind of public intervention.

Besides, Jean-Noël Tronc could count on many supporters within the government. Minister of Economy Dominique Strauss-Kahn, for one, was in favor of converting to the Internet, but also promoted the information economy in the fight against unemployment. An "emblematic geek of the government", as many interviewees recall him, Strauss-Kahn liked to bring out his "PSION" (pocket microcomputer) at inter-ministerial meetings, and welcomed in Bercy, against the advice of part of the government, major tech CEO such as Steve Jobs (Apple), Bill Gates (Microsoft), John Chambers (Cisco) and Michael Lynton (AOL). Strauss-Kahn's cabinet at large was also pushing for incentive measures to support young innovative companies, notably through a global tax reform more favorable to venture capital—the infamous "DSK life insurance contracts". In his pioneering study of French innovation policy at the turn of the twenty-first century, political scientist Gunnar Trumbull (2004) even considers that "without Strauss Kahn, it is likely that much of the French program to promote start-ups during this period would not have been launched" (p.13).

At the Ministry of Culture and Communication, new political advisers also saw the Internet as a means to revitalize and modernize the flagging "democratization of culture": Minister Catherine Trautmann spoke out loud and clear in favor of the development of the French Internet, both at Hourtin and at the major Internet forums where she represented the French government, notably at the ISOC international conference in 1998. Her cabinet gathered several Internet pioneers, including Alain Giffard, former IT director at the *Bibliothèque nationale de France* (French National Public Library), who became the Minister's special advisor on the information society.

Spread across several ministries and administrations, the promoters of new Internet policies met at informal "PAGSI" meetings organized by Jean-Noël Tronc. The latter also included a few right-wing agents who had long been involved in Internet activism—such as Patrice Martin-Lalande, a MP and founder of the Internet working group at the French National Assembly. PAGSI meetings also provided a springboard for newly-elected deputies such as Christian Paul and Patrick Bloche, who relayed government initiatives in favor of the Internet in the Assembly and within the *Parti Socialiste*. Indeed, the Internet was seen by these younger MPs as an opportunity to modernize the left-wing movement. The party's digital section, *temPS-réels,* proposed to "experiment with new forms of political action and organization made possible by information technologies".[5] At a time when the Internet was still an "unidentified political object", the aim was to defend a "fair and just" information society and to steer Internet policies to the left. In 2002, Jean Noël Tronc, Christian Paul, Maurice Ronai and Dominique Strauss-Kahn wrote a programmatic report for the leftist think tank *Fondation Jean Jaurès*, where they described the digital revolution as an opportunity to adapt the socialist tradition to "a changing world", and proposed "several avenues for bringing to life the values of freedom, equality, solidarity, democracy and sovereignty, while renewing modes of public intervention".[6] On this last point, socialist modernizers converged with another growing movement for state reform in the administrative field.

[5] Retrieved from www.temps-reels.net/_qui_index.php, available through the Internet Archive.

[6] *Vers la cité numérique*, Notes de la Fondation Jean Jaurès, mars 2000, 29, p. 10.

1.2 Deepening State Reform with the Internet

In the administrative field, the 1990s saw a profound deepening of the State's "self-concern" for legitimacy and efficiency (Bezes, 2009). The decade marked the advent of a new "configuration of reform", symbolized by the shift in public discourse from "administrative modernization" to the large-encompassing notion of "State reform". Carried out by political professionals, experts and senior civil servants, "State reform" differed from previous programs in its comprehensive, proactive nature, and its effects on the design and production of public policy. State reformers set themselves the goal of "reformatting administrative capacities and modes of control, by resizing the State, modifying its competences and calling into question some of its bureaucratic rules" (our translation, ibid., p. 342). In the early 1990s, several reform committees were created in France, notably the Committee on "State Efficiency" in 1989 and, above all, the administrative mission entrusted to Jean Picq in 1994 on "The State in France". It led to the establishment of a State Reform Commission in 1995, tasked with implementing the recommendations from these expert public reports.

The political alternation of 1997 did nothing to slow this trend—quite the contrary. In 1998, the State Reform Commission grew into an inter-ministerial department, directly reporting to the Prime Minister. And eventually, in 2001, an organic law on public finance, the LOLF (*Loi organique relative aux lois de finance*), was adopted under the impetus of Economy Minister Laurent Fabius, leading to a profound redefinition of budget management rules and budget control in France.

The 1990s programs of State reform are characterized by the import of private management and efficiency assessment tools into public services, as well as by an increased control of bureaucracies. It prompted a functional reorganization of the state administration, to the benefit of the most central institutions of the executive government—the Ministry of the Economy or the Prime Minister's Office—becoming strategic loci of power from which State policies were steered. Although this movement began before the arrival of the Internet, State reformers found new opportunities and instruments in the technological advances underway to accelerate the implementation of this agenda. By the mid-1990s, the development of information and communication technologies, and above all the Internet, was advocated by national and international administrative reform bodies alike. As part of the European Union's "e-Europe 2002" and "e-Europe 2005" plans, the Internet was to be used to interconnect national administrations and improve public services. At the OECD, the Public Management committee (PUMA) included information technologies in its recommendations for improving the "performance" of national administrations. In 2003, a new PUMA report made the use of information and communication technologies, and the Internet in particular, an "imperative" for "better administration".[7] Far from resisting this trend, French reports published between 1998 and 2003 quoted these foreign and international examples to push for the digitization of the State.

Dunleavy et al. (2006) have argued that this trend marks the end of NPM reforms and the beginning of a new "digital-era governance" for public administration. We defend a slightly different argument here. In many countries and France in particular, information technologies were rather combined with than opposed to new public management tools. It was even *through* this hybridization that the Internet had gradually been accepted and absorbed within the administration. Indeed, the dematerialization of procedures was first and foremost presented in public reports as a source of budgetary and time savings. At a 2000 seminar on e-government, the Socialist Minister for Civil service and State reform, Michel Sapin, declared: "the emergence and extremely rapid spread of ICTs are greatly increasing citizens' expectations of the State. Like businesses, whose offerings are increasingly flexible, scalable, targeted and personalized, the State must take these developments into account". Generally speaking, reports and speeches on state reform aimed to demonstrate how the Internet could be used to introduce a "results culture", "evaluation and performance" tools and countless "productivity gains" into the heart of the administration, an imperative that echoes the mottos of New Public Management.

The use of information technologies to rationalize and modernize the bureaucracy was nothing new: from the introduction of the typewriter (Gardey, 2008) to the computerization of the administration (Agar, 2003), research has shown how the deployment of information technologies goes along the development of state action. In fact, until 1997, the Internet was considered as one technology among others in information-processing within the State, even arousing the reluctance of some IT

[7] OCDE (2003), *The e-Government Imperative*, OECD e-Government Studies, Éditions OCDE, Paris, https://doi.org/10.1787/9789264101197-en.

departments. In the late 1990s, however, a shift took place: the "computerization of the administration" was replaced by the larger encompassing project of an "electronic administration", conceived as a systematic use of technology to modify the organization of the State and its relations with citizens and businesses. With the transformation of government in Western countries, the Internet provided as much a technical support as a model for reform. The flexibility, adaptability and generativity of the network were used as references to "imagine forms of State that [were] not the sole bulwark of conservatism".[8]

Reformers of the 1990's criticized sectoral boundaries, top-down communication and administrative fragmentation as sources of inefficiency within the State. On the contrary, the connection of administrative departments was supposed to ensure accountability and better coordination between departments. At the time, the image of the network was already a common reference in managerial reforms (Boltanski & Chiapello, 2005), to which the Internet culture provided new ideas of openness, transparency and inclusivity. In French public reports, the whole architecture of the Internet and the Web was conceived as enabling new organizational and informational processes in a networked administration:

> We give this concept, which should mobilize citizens and civil servants, a name that translates this ambition into an appropriate term: the "Hyper-Republic". The hyper-republic would be decentralized, thanks to its network organization. In fact, only the spirit of hypertext makes it possible to give coherence to the information conveyed on the administrative Internet, to pool it, while respecting the autonomy of decentralized communities. [Hyper Republic: building a networked administration around the citizen, Public report, 2003, Paris: La documentation française, p. 6].

The pre-cited public reports promoted a new vision of the State based on the Internet, which dialogued with citizens and relied on the collective intelligence of the network, prefiguring what would later be referred as the "platform State" or "Government as a Platform". These new administrative mottos contributed to the ongoing advent of a "New public

[8] Jean-Paul Baquiast, *Proposition sur les rapports de l'Internet à la modernisation du fonctionnement de l'État* (Proposals on the contribution of the Internet to the modernization of government), Rapport to the Ministry of State Reform, 1998.

management" and added to a vast reform dictionary. Information and communication technologies became a major instrument of administrative reform at the turn of the century, fostering new alliances between reformers and Internet promoters.

1.3 Net Evangelists and Reformers, a New Alliance in the Administrative Field

The integration of new technologies into reform programs gave visibility to the experiments launched by Internet pioneers in the early 1990s. As a late recognition of their pioneering role, they were consulted by the Prime Minister's services to give their insight on the technological transformation of the State (Table 1): Jean-Paul Baquiast, founder of *Admiroutes*, was commissioned to write a report on the "contributions of the Internet to the modernization of government operations", and Bruno Oudet, founder of Isoc-France, who had to leave the French Ministry of Foreign Affairs after the introduction of an Internet service at the Embassy in the United States, was in charge of the report on "Internet and administrations abroad". In their contributions, the net evangelists defended the strategic role of information technologies and "computer network" expertise in the implementation of State reform. Gradually, net evangelists were integrated at the center of the bureaucratic field, from which they had hitherto been marginalized (see Chapter 3). At first stigmatized or, at best, ignored, these individuals were rehabilitated and even congratulated starting from 2000. For example, Bruno Mannoni and Jean-Pierre Dalbéra were awarded the *Légion d'Honneur* in 2001 for having contributed "to the reputation and international influence of the French Ministry of Culture in the Internet sector".[9]

Internet pioneers, modernizers of the *Parti Socialiste* and state reformers may have come from different political and social backgrounds, the context allowed, to paraphrase Max Weber (2010), the development of "elective affinities" between the net ethics and the spirit of reform. On the one hand, the belief in the transformative power of technology and, on the other, the conviction that State had to adapt to economic and social changes underway, converged toward new reform programs. These affinities called into question the idea that the Internet

[9] Extract of the speech delivered by the Ministry of Culture Catherine Tasca on presentation of the medal in 2001, Personnal Archives of JP. Dalbera.

Table 1 A proliferation of public reports on state reform and ICT

French title	*English title*	*Date*	*Authors*
Proposition sur les apports d'Internet à la modernisation du fonctionnement de l'Etat	Proposals on the contribution of the Internet to the modernization of government	1998	Jean-Paul Baquiast (M), senior civil servant, Ministry of Economy
Usage pratique des NTIC dans l'administration	Practical use of NICT in administration	1999	Daniel Kaplan (M), JacquesFrançois Marchandise (M), Charly Dupuis (M), private consultants
L'Etat et les technologies de l'information : Vers une administration à accès pluriel	The State and information technologies: Towards a multi-access administration	2000	Bruno Lasserre (M), senior civil servant, coordinator; Olivier Japiot (M), civil servant, Philippe Chantepie (M), private contractor, Jean-Philippe Mochon (M), civil servant, Laurent Sorbier (M), private consultant, authors
Internet et les administrations à l'étranger : une source d'idées	Internet and public administrations abroad : a source of ideas	2000	Bruno Oudet, IT professor, founder of Isoc France
Pour une administration électronique citoyenne : contributions au débat	An e-Government for citizens: contributions to the debate	2001	Thierry Carcénac (M), Socialist MP, coordinator, Bruno Mannoni (M), Head of IT department, Ministry of Culture, main author
L'Hyper-République : bâtir l'administration en réseau autour du Citoyen	Hyper-Republic: building a networked administration around the citizen	2003	Pierre de La Coste (M), journalist and IT activist

community was uniformly committed to dissolve the bureaucratic state. In France, strong alliances developed between Internet pioneers and state reformers to debunk the concerns of part of the elite against the Internet, while fostering new forms of state action in the information society. Indeed, the programs promoted by the e-administration reports were less about reducing the State's influence than preserving its role through a radical transformation. Most reports even defended the importance of public services, in order to answer the challenges generated by rapid network development and to ensure the permanence of the Internet's emancipatory and democratic culture in front of market predation.

One of the most symbolic examples of these new alliances was the Commission on "State and information technologies" launched by the Socialist government in 2000 and led by Bruno Lasserre, a top civil servant previously involved in the reform of the telecommunication sector. With six thematic workshops, and numerous international comparisons, the commission gathered a hundred of experts in order to define the future organization and forms of government for the State in the information society. The Commission included both net evangelists and members of the administrative elite, coming from central state institutions (such as the General Planning Committee, the Ministry of Economy, the Ministry of State Reform), as well as politicians and trade union representatives. The Commission was organized as a vast forum where different experiences and areas of expertise met and confronted each other. It favored the translation of "digital revolution " discourses into the technocratic vocabulary of bureaucratic renovation: horizontality and interoperability of administrative departments mirrored the structure of the network, openness and interactivity of public services echoed the imperative of online participation, decentralization and de-sectorization the critique of bureaucratic hierarchies and silos. State reform gave a new meaning to the connection of the administration, and more prosaically, also helped to remove some obstacles to the penetration of the Internet, by devoting financial and symbolic resources to hardware equipment and IT development. In fact, the final report proposed a number of "cross-functional projects" designed to firmly anchor public administrations into the information society.

The four rapporteurs of the Commission epitomized the alliance between net evangelization and state renovation. Laurent Sorbier and Philippe Chantepie were non-civil servant "experts" and network pioneers, while Olivier Japiot and Jean-Philippe Mochon were promising graduates from the National School of Administration. Aged between 30 and 37, these four young "innovators" shared a common vision of information technologies, combined with a desire to "make things change". Their common beliefs and aspirations transcended their professional and political affiliations, as Chantepie explains in interview:

> Laurent, Japiot, Jean-Philippe and I met during the Lasserre Commission. We formed a band, not just because of internet promotion, we were also friends, regardless of party or political affiliation. I didn't even know they were right-wing at the time. Japiot, it was perhaps a little more obvious, but then I met him again when he worked for the right-wing government and we were both working on digital culture policies, and he was the one who helped me. In fact, we were pioneers of digital technology and we were buddies, well, we got on really well. [Interview 43, September 2016].

At the end of the 1990s, digital pioneers and state modernizers tended to merge around a shared vision of reform. Like the four rapporteurs of the Commission on "State and Information and communication technologies", political differences were then minimized in favor of a new conception of State enhanced by the Internet and new technologies. This consensus enabled lasting alliances that even went beyond e-government projects and contributed to rethinking the modalities of State intervention, notably regarding Internet regulation, as we will see in the following section.

2 From Electronic Administration to Co-regulation: The New Internet Policies

More than just a change in rhetoric, the break in public treatment of the Internet was symbolized by a range of new government interventions. From connecting schools to the creation of "public access to Internet houses", the liberalization of electronic encryption or the support for the IT sector, public policies concerning the Internet and encouraging its development multiplied at the end of the 1990s, not to mention the many initiatives taken by local authorities. In many cases, Internet policies provided an opportunity to experiment with new forms of public action called for by state reformers and Internet pioneers. More generally, they were part of an ongoing movement to transform the State: the deepening of administrative reform and the advent of a regulatory State in Europe (Majone, 1994; Moran, 2002; Thatcher, 2002), described as an increased use of legal authority by governments to the detriment of redistribution or stabilization tools. Internet policies of the 1990s were emblematic of these major changes, as much as they contributed to them. In this section, we will particularly focus on two domains revealing the contribution of Internet policies to the reinvention of State: electronic administration programs and Internet regulation. In both cases, innovation was based on organizational procedures, technological tools and even discourses inspired by the Internet culture. In both cases, the policies implemented called into question traditional modes of intervention and offered concrete translation to the ambitions of State reformers. In both cases, they also revealed an enduring resistance to the "digital revolution", showing that, despite the advent of state reform was never completely unequivocal.

2.1 E-Government Policies and State Reform

It is difficult to summarize the profusion of initiatives launched in the context of "e-government" programs, ranging from the creation of an e-mail address for each civil servant to the establishment of a web platform giving access to all public services in France: service-public.fr, opened in 2000. These initiatives can be grouped under three main headings, which were guiding administrative policies at the turn of the century: the dematerialization of procedures, the reorganization of workflows and the opening up of public data. Taken separately, these three dimensions were not unprecedented in administrative polices but they were newly articulated around the "e-government" label, that borrowed from discourses, principles and organizational forms of the Internet.

The first dimension of "e-government" programs consisted in continuing and improving the development of electronic services, from the Minitel to the Internet. To this respect, advances in information technology and the development of the Internet breathed new life to the digitization of public services. Within five years, all public administrations were equipped with a website. This transition from Minitel to web services was also intended to modernize the relationship with users by making digital public services "more direct and interactive". Government websites now offered discussion forums—on the changeover to euro or the 35-hour workweek reform—real-time information and mailing list subscriptions. In government programs and reports, these projects were presented with a "revolutionary" rhetoric, as witnessed by the ambitious "Copernic" project to create a platform for online tax payment, launched by the Ministry of the Economy and Finance in 2001. The reform of the tax administration took on the main objectives set for the dematerialization of procedures: simplification, accessibility and decompartmentalization of services. An "exemplary project" for the e-government, it gathered a team of almost 600 people and a budget of one hundred million euros per year for ten years. In terms of ambition and resources, the "Copernic" program was yet a project in a class of its own, at a time when many administrations made do with online forms that were hastily digitized and not even interactive. Likewise, the Ministry of the Economy and Finance's website boasted more than 100,000 pages, a forum, directories and applications, while many administrations only duplicated their Minitel services on the web. It pointed to strong inequalities in terms of digitization that also mirrored the unequal distribution of IT skills and resources within the administration.

The introduction of e-mail, the construction of ministerial intranets and the development of cross-sectorial applications were part of a second dimension of e-government program targeting organization and workflows. "Networked cooperative working" was introduced as one of the most radical innovation enabled by the Internet, intended to establishing "more interactive and egalitarian relations between departments". It took its inspiration from the collaborative tradition of computer science labs and the cyberspace, to which administrative reports even referred directly. For example, Bruno Manonni, main rapporteur of the report on Electronic administration in 2001, pointed to the free software movement as a model for the administration, while the Baquiast report referred to the example of the online cooperation of Internet activists: "It is obviously necessary to start with flexible formulas in complex structures where a rigorous method of cooperative work cannot be imposed. This is how the heads of various associations steered the organization of the first Internet Festival. Everything was done via the Internet, but improvised" (1998, p. 62). Both reports insisted on the role of technological devices that could foster cooperation between administrations, such as discussion platforms, joint working software and online meetings. Here again, however, the mixed achievements revealed the instability of institutional forms behind e-government programs: from the simple introduction of e-mail to the rare experiments with videoconferencing meetings or collaborative publishing, the involvement of administrations depended on individual willingness as much as material equipment.

A final aspect of e-government program was the emergence of open data policies. In France, the right of access to administrative documents was enshrined in the law since 1978, with the creation of a special

Commission to ensure access to public documentation, the *Commission d'accès aux documents administratifs*. Yet digital technology and its culture of free flow of information further pushed principles of open access and transparency in the elaboration of reform policies. As an emblematic decision of the ongoing policy change, the free online distribution of the Official Bulletin, symbol of conflicts between Internet pioneers and the French bureaucracy in the previous period (see Chapter 3), was finally authorized in 1998. The distribution of legal texts, speeches, reports, even budgets and administrative decisions contributed to the propagation of new culture of transparency and participation largely inspired by Internet communities. The creation in 1998 of three new websites, *légifrance.fr, ladocfrançaise.gouv.fr* and *admifrance.gouv.fr*, which respectively gave access to legal documentation, public reports and a directory of public services, symbolized this new turning point. The Lasserre Commission in 200 even envisaged the legislative introduction of an "obligation of information availability" for administrative authorities. Provisions for the compulsory and free dissemination of "essential public data" were included in a large-encompassing bill on the "Information Society", prepared from 2000 onward and finally abandoned in 2001, due to a lack of cross-ministerial support and an overcrowded agenda of reforms in the months preceding the presidential campaign of 2002.

E-government programs led to numerous reorganizations within ministry departments. They were also an opportunity to create new, innovative inter-ministerial structures. In 1998, the MTIC (*Mission interministérielle de soutien technique pour le développement des technologies de l'information et de la communication*—Interministerial technical support mission for the development of information and communication technologies) was set up to promote interconnections between the government and its various departments. Once again, setting up MTIC was not a straightforward matter: difficult negotiations happened between the Prime Minister's office, the Ministry of Civil Service and the Ministry of the Economy, all of which were vying to gain control over State reform. It took a reduction of the ambition of the MTIC and the demonstration of its strategic importance for the management of e-government programs argument, to finally set up the mission department:

> I tried to explain [to Dominique Strauss-Kahn] that the MTIC was intended to be very light, a small administration, tasked with implementing

> standardization, with guaranteeing the interoperability of systems developed by administrations, and above all creating an intranet that didn't even exist at the time. I appealed to his interest in IT, but also to his sensitivity to security issues. Dominique Strauss-Kahn was more or less convinced, although he accepted to say a few words of support to Lionel Jospin, who eventually agreed to the creation of the MTIC. [Interview 37, male, digital advisor to the Prime Minister (1997–2002), July 2016].

Jean-Pierre Dardayrol, a civil engineer who had taken an early stand in favor of the Internet in the 1990s, was appointed head of the MTIC. He recruited a team of Internet mongers and "young geeks", including Godefroy Beauvallet, a recent graduate from *Ecole Polytechnique* and *Telecom Paris*, and who had discovered the Internet during a research internship at the University of California, San Diego, in 1993. In interviews, Godefroy Beauvallet described the MTIC as a "hotbed of network engineers", Internet users and open-source advocates. They joined the close circle of PAGSI "innovators", created by Jean-Noël Tronc, whose members were trying to "get things moving" and create new forms of administrative cooperation [Interview 30, male, MTIC member, digital advisor to the Minister of Civil Service and State Reform (2000–2002)]. MTIC engineers were developing technological devices to foster collaboration and information sharing between administrations. Although poorly received by sectorial IT department, the MTIC managed to build the first cross-ministerial intranet, the "AdER" (*Administration en réseau*). They also organized training sessions and seminars to spread the Internet culture into the administration.

A multi-faceted government program broken down into multiple measures and goals, e-government enabled the development of experiments and new routines in the administrative field. E-government program was also key to understand the appropriation of the Internet within the administration, by encouraging the State's presence online, imposing the adoption of open standards and encouraging IT uses by administrators and citizens alike. Yet behind their stated ambitions, e-government entrepreneurs also recalled the numerous obstacles they faced, from poorly trained agents to non-cooperation. In a field where IT equipment and skills were still unevenly distributed, the digital reality of the time was catching up with the revolutionary rhetoric. The technology in itself did not fully disrupt administrative routines: it was only slowly adopted, integrated into existing practices and even subverted, producing incremental changes in the bureaucracy. Bruno Mannoni, head of the IT department at the Ministry of Culture gave us a striking example of these mixed impacts of the Internet: "Of course, I wanted to know what people were going to do with it. Well, they definitely used it for stuff. Either to visit porn sites, or to visit research sites, or administrative sites. Like everyone else in fact. They made the tool their own, and not exactly what we expected of it" [Interview 54, January 2017]. The uptake of digital technologies was not always commensurate with the great transformative project championed by the reform elites, whether in the field of e-government or the protection of online rights.

2.2 The Invention of "Internet Co-regulation"

Faced with the rapid development of the Internet, defining a regulatory framework for web-related businesses and activities became the second major policy concern for the government. The creation of a legal framework for the Internet bore witness to both the difficulties inherent to public action in the cyberspace and the gradual privatization of regulation that marked the period (Büthe, 2011; Vogel, 2008). A central dimension of the neo-liberal transformation of the State, the globalization and privatization of rule-making during the 1990s and early decades of the twenty-first century were marked by the alleged economic benefits of common standards for global markets as well as the realization that governments often lacked the expertise and resources to deal with increasingly complex and urgent regulatory tasks. This apprehension was even stronger for the Internet: the international nature of the network, the speed of its technical evolution, the attachment of virtual communities to the principle of "self-regulation", all contributed to the illegitimacy of traditional public intervention. These ideas were in fact shared by Internet pioneers and State reformers alike, who took up the rhetoric of digital activists regarding the limited regulability of the Internet. Adding to that the legal impasses of the first Internet affairs (see previous chapter), government regulators thus preferred to discuss regulation with private actors and entrust them with the implementation of common rules.

In 1996, French government charged Antoine Beaussant, President of the Syndicate of online services providers, with the task of drafting an "Internet Charter" in consultation with other web players: together they defined a set of rules whose observance was to be guaranteed by a private body representing the main web players, the "Internet Council".[10] A few months later, the authors of PAGSI enshrined this principle of self-regulation as the best way of ensuring rights and freedoms on the Internet: " *Experimentation by players will be encouraged. The existence of a strong ethic of behavior, sometimes referred to as "netiquette", which is widespread among users, is a dimension of the Internet that should be emphasized and encouraged*".[11] In parallel with these national reflections, experiments for the self-regulation of content were also being carried out by European web players, such as the "Code of Practices and Uses" set up by the Association of Internet Service Providers (AFA), or the "Code of Conduct" drawn up on by seven consumer associations in Europe.

Yet the impacts of self-regulation proved insufficient. Charters and codes of conduct were just as much criticized by some digital activists, who denounced a dangerous "privatization" of the Internet, as by international organizations themselves, with the OECD speaking out in 1997 to warn against the "risks of self-regulation: excessive influence of private interests, barriers to market entry, lack of transparency and weak accountability of players".[12] Taking advantage of the impetus given by the Hourtin speech, French policy entrepreneurs tried to push for a return of public intervention in the cyberspace, in order to ensure online rights and freedoms against the reign of private interests.

While the US adopted a "safe-harbor" principle against any liability for harmful content published online, a mixed approached emerged in Europe (MacKinnon, 2012; MacKinnon et al., 2014). In France, this hybrid framework developed around the idea of "co-regulation", as a compromise between experiments in self-regulation and the extension of media and audiovisual regulation to the Internet. The concept of "co-regulation" first made its appearance in a 1998 report by the *Conseil*

[10] *La Charte de l'internet. Règles et usages des acteurs de l'internet en France*, Public Report to the Prime Minister, Paris: La Documentation française, 1997. https://www.vie-publique.fr/rapport/26075-charte-de-linternet-regles-et-usages-des-acteurs-de-linternet-en-fra.

[11] *Programme d'action gouvernemental pour la société de l'information*, Personal archives of Jean-Noël Tronc, 1997, p. 54.

[12] *The OECD Report on Regulatory Reform: Synthesis*, Paris, OECD, 1997, p. 28.

d'État on "Internet and digital networks".[13] For the two authors—Isabelle Falque-Pierrotin and Jean-François Théry—it was urgent to restore State power over the Internet, the State being the only legitimate institution to arbitrate between various players. The expression was then taken up in 1999 by Socialist MP Christian Paul, who was commissioned by the French Prime Minister to write a report on Internet rights and freedoms. Slightly diverging from the *Conseil d'État*, he defended co-regulation as a "method" rather than an additional source of legal authority. According to his report, co-regulation should be entrusted with a new type of organization, conceived as "a meeting place between public regulation and self-regulation, between the expectations of economic players and network users"[14] (p. 19). This institution would be called the "Internet Rights Forum".

Yet, the conditions under which the Forum was created bore witness to the instability of the first Internet policies, and by the same token, to an enduring feeling of illegitimacy when it came to exercising government authority over cyberspace. Isabelle Falque-Pierrotin, who was commissioned by the Prime Minister to set up the new organization, even speaks of an "unacknowledged birth", as the legal contours of the institution were bitterly negotiated, and the resources required for its operation snatched away. In her account of the Forum's creation, she reveals the hesitations surrounding the setting up of a such an institution, whose status and mission were considered too experimental in the administrative field:

> Many things had to come together to make [the Forum] a reality. For example, a lease had to be signed. We're getting down to the nitty-gritty of things, but it was fundamental, because the lease provided a place for employees to work. To sign a lease, you have to be able to commit yourself, and I couldn't personally commit myself on behalf of the State. So, I needed authorization from the Budget in this case, that I was going to have subventions. But these people... Everyone was waiting a greenlight from everyone else. I ended up calling the Director of the Budget, saying "I'm calling you, you certainly don't know what the Internet Forum is, but you should know that...and here's the story. If I don't sign this lease,

[13] https://www.conseil-etat.fr/publications-colloques/etudes/internet-et-les-reseaux-numeriques.

[14] https://www.vie-publique.fr/files/rapport/pdf/004001056.pdf.

> I'm not going to be able to take over these premises, I'm not going to be able to recruit people, so this whole extremely fragile house of cards is going to fall apart, so I need a written agreement from you that I'm going to get the subsidy". (...) And so I said to her: "As I'm signing tomorrow, I need to have this document by 9am tomorrow morning, otherwise you'll have to take responsibility for it in front of the Prime Minister." It was a bluff, because of course, she could always refuse. And what happened, I found out afterwards, was that same evening there was a meeting, a rather exceptional meeting that took place between the director of the Budget, and the head of the Prime minister cabinet, and they finally agreed on this issue. When you think about it, my God, how hazardous it all was. And so, the next morning, I got a fax which arrived at 8.45am stating "the budget for the Internet Rights Forum will be one million one hundred I don't know how much, on such and such budget line", and that was it.

Isabelle Falque-Pierrotin's account is typical of the heroic rhetoric used by Internet pioneers and institutional entrepreneurs: they described long struggles fraught with pitfalls and accomplishment against all odds, to emphasize the difficulties of creating new policies in a bureaucratic field still wary of the Internet. Although one need to handle this rhetoric carefully, it shows nevertheless in concrete terms just how fragile the first public institutions of the Internet were: the result of ongoing negotiations, small conquests and "bluffing", at the end of an uncertain process in which each missed step could mean the abandonment of the project.

The Forum indeed enjoyed a unique status in the administrative field: a private non-profit association, it recruited young pioneers in technology and Internet law, such as Lionel Thoumyre of juriscom.net and Benoît Tabaka (see previous chapter). The marginal position of the Forum enabled its agents to eschew bureaucratic routines and operational constraints, encouraging institutional innovations. The former members we interviewed never ceased to point out the "visionary" nature of this new form of regulation: " *even the website was a very exciting project insofar as it involved institutional news, but also and above all, it included participative working groups and consultation sections in the forum's standard operation. It may not seem like much today, but this was 2001, and it's very, very avant-garde. We started very, very interesting things. For example, thinking about how design matter for participation, how previous contributions lend credibility to a contributor's profile, how you technically organize the debate, and so on*" [Interview 23, male, Forum staff (2001–2006), May 2016].

The staff also created an online mediation service (MediateurDuNet.fr) to settle disputes between users or between service providers—access providers, hosts, publishers—and their clients. They organized consultations between the various stakeholders on the protection of intellectual property and privacy. In the mid-2000s, following international recommendations for "multistakeholder" web governance, the Forum managed to bring together the main digital interest groups, both activists and Internet users associations—APRIL (a Free software association), Isoc-France—and web companies. The Forum was indeed the first contact point between public players and tech giants—such as Google, Ebay, Paypal, Facebook, etc. In this way, the organization became a source of expertise, as yet poorly identified, on regulatory issues, producing consultation-based recommendations. Its scope of interest was very broad, crossing several ministerial domains, addressing technical (naming and referencing) as well as legal (privacy and intellectual property) issues. The establishment of the Forum fixed regulatory expertise at the borders of the State and developed the first public–private dialogue with US web companies. But this accumulated knowledge and social capital only partly made up for the Forum's institutional weakness in terms of administrative power. Although supervised by a member of the very legitimate *Conseil d'État* and gathering State representatives among its members, the Forum struggled to gain recognition for its expertise and faced increasing difficulties, leading to its demise in 2010.

3 From Modern Paragon to "Minister of Bad News": A Chapter Closed

In March 2000, after a constant growth of valuations in IT start-ups and online shopping companies, the dot-com bubble burst: many companies had to shut down after burning through their venture capital. In the US, the future giants were not in full growth yet and many companies that had invested in IT were in a fragile state. In Europe, the massive investments made by telecoms operators following liberalization and the opening up to competition were revised downward. After several years of speculation and enthusiasm about the digital revolution and the information economy, the weakness of online business models and the financial burden of technological investments were pointed out by economists and analysts. These economic difficulties had a strong impact on Internet policies, all the more so as new technological inequalities were pointed out in political arenas. What is more, in the administration, the promises of e-government reform started to nurture disappointments: the heavy costs of IT equipment and the weakness of digital expertise in the State slowed down the completion of projects. Many programs were postponed or merely abandoned, ambitions mitigated. In the domain of law, co-regulation started to appear as a partial and unsatisfactory answer to the development of illicit online practices, exacerbating tensions between activists, administrative agents and representatives of private enterprise.

After a period of enthusiasm and dynamic experimentation, the government's handling of the Internet turned into a "ministry of bad news", as put by a responsible of digital policy after 2002 [Interview 22, male, digital advisor to the Prime Minister, May 2016]. Of course, the French government did not question the choice of the Internet anymore, nor the need for technological modernization of public systems, but the chapter opened by PAGSI closed from the mid-2000s onward, leading to a reconsideration of the experiments carried out by Internet pioneers within the State.

3.1 E-Government Runs Out of Steam?

While the introduction of Internet technologies in the administration was initially seen as an opportunity for budget savings, e-government projects proved in fact to be very costly, as suggested by the amounts allocated to the development of online tax payment, presented above. In 2000, the Lasserre report estimated that budget appropriations for State IT had increased by 10% between 1997 and 1998, and by 5% in 2000. In all, more than 270 million euros were allocated to the technological modernization of public services between 1998 and 2000 alone. The bursting of the "Internet bubble" in the early 2000s also revealed that the productivity gains generated by information technology had been greatly overestimated. At a time when the introduction of budgetary control of public policies was gaining ground—with a new framework for spending bills adopted in August 2001—e-government projects were reassessed, and even criticized, in the light of new performance indicators. For example, a 2009 parliamentary report by the Finance Commission severely criticized the Copernic project for online tax payment, saying that the evaluation of benefits had been "approximate" and performance "poorly measured", resulting in heavy cost for the public.[15]

The development of managerial and budgetary imperatives in government reform also contributed to a relegation of IT expertise to the background. As an agent of the Ministry of the Civil Service and State Reform recalls: "the spread of the Internet in the administration was understood first and foremost as a tool to save the French people money and time" [Interview 30, male, MTIC member, digital advisor to the Minister of Civil Service and State Reform (2000–2002)]. He thus deplored the fact that technical challenges of e-government were gradually subordinated to budgetary considerations, as soon as the expected savings were not demonstrated. In 2005, the Agency for the Development of E-government (ADAE), which had succeeded the MTIC, was dissolved into a new Department for State Modernization (DGME), attached to the Ministry of Economy. This change testified to the gradual subordination of technological policies to economic logic, as the State reform was now controlled by Budget and Finance departments. While in 1998, political arbitration had been favorable to computer scientists and network experts who enjoyed relative autonomy at the MTIC, from 2005 onward, the Ministry of Economy absorbed e-government institutions, indicating a new balance of power in favor of economic rationalization in the bureaucratic field.

The budgetary burden of IT projects was not the only factor contributing to the slowing down of e-government programs. Resistance to "cooperative networking" initiative and information sharing was legion in sectorial departments, either from previous engineers who balked at changing their routines as well as directors, who saw the ever-increasing interconnection of departments as a loss of autonomy. For example, the "SOLON" project for co-writing legal documents, launched by the MTIC, came in for heavy criticism [Interview 66, *Conseil d'État* member, January 2019]. Intended to reduce the time needed to prepare texts, to promote the circulation of information between administrations, and improve the legislative process, this "groupware" was denounced as an excessively costly and intrusive "digital cathedral". The project was finally abandoned in 2002 (but resumed after 2010).

[15] Parliament Report, Finance Comittee, Bernard Angels (Socialist MP), *Programme Copernic: la révolution informatique de l'administration fiscale n'est pas achevée*, october 2009. https://www.senat.fr/rap/r09-070/r09-070.html.

In many respects, the ambitions claimed by e-government also seemed out of step with the actual spread of digital technologies in society. In 1999, only 3.9% of French households were connected, and less than 30% of administrative workstations had Internet access. The unions also pointed to the lack of training for employees, who, while welcoming the arrival of new technologies, deplored the lack of consultation and technical assistance in getting to grips with these new tools. It's true that, from the 2000s onward, computer use grew (in 2000, 13% of the French population had access to the Internet at home, rising to 41% in 2006), but the theme of the "digital divide" was also gradually gaining ground in public debate. It was increasingly being mobilized by political professionals: faced with the fear of seeing the development of "two-speed" access to public services, the administration could not be content with being present on the Internet. This issue of digital inequality was not absent from reports on technological modernization, but from the mid-2000s onward, its political takeover led to the abandonment of an all-encompassing vision of "e-government" in favor of the notion of "multi-access" services, articulating counter, telephone and website.

3.2 Co-regulation Reaches a Dead-End

The same types of difficulties affected the co-regulation project. In spite of, and sometimes because of, the experiments carried out by the Internet Rights Forum, the legitimacy of the institution began to erode in the mid-2000s. Faced with the challenge of controlling online practices and content, with the increase saliency of copyright infringement issues, the Forum was criticized from all sides.

Criticism came first and foremost from Internet activists, who started to see co-regulation as the "holy alliance of government and economic lobbies".[16] While they had welcomed the creation of an institution that embraced the principles of limited government intervention and multi-stakeholder governance, they deplored the growing weight of private companies in the discussion of Internet regulation issues. Some more libertarian association of engineers also criticized the "excessive" bureaucratic control exercised by the Forum's secretary. In 2007, a major free software association, the APRIL, opposed the reappointment of Isabelle

[16] Press Release of IRIS association (Imaginons un Réseau internet solidaire) on coregulation. http://www.iris.sgdg.org/documents/rapport-coreg/rapport-coreg.html.

Falque-Pierrotin as President of the Forum, as well as the revision of the association's bylaw to place it more formally under the authority of the government.

Isabelle Falque-Pierrotin, head of the Forum between 2001 and 2010, was indeed seeking to "strengthen the institutional legitimacy" [Interview 36, July 2016] of the Forum through its formal integration into the bureaucratic field. The Forum was indeed increasingly contested by administrative departments, who saw the organization as an embarrassing thorn in their flesh. At the beginning, the Forum's acceptance by political and administrative elites was based on the novelty of digital issues and the astonishment they aroused in most public institutions. But as ministries accumulated resources and developed their own digital doctrine, the Forum's marginal position and its sometimes "radical" recommendations became less and less accepted by the bureaucracy. Not a formal regulatory body, the Forum could no more than try to influence the policymaking process, often competing with other institutions, closer to the executive governement: "The idea that the general interest could be represented by something other than a ministry department was something that gave rise to a great deal of debate, and the Forum constantly had to prove its added value", says Isabelle Falque-Pierrotin [ibid.].

Tensions between the Forum and ministerial departments intensified from the mid-2000's onward, especially when co-regulation agents ventured into new policy domains. In 2005 for example, the Forum issued an opinion strongly opposed to the "electronic identity card" project, launched by the Ministry of the Interior, warning the government about the risk entailed for citizen's privacy. Not only did the opinion irritated the ministerial agents but it also infringed on the domain of the French data protection authority, the CNIL (*Commission Nationale Informatique et Libertés*). Conflicts were also vivid with the Ministry of Culture on copyright issues. In 2003, the Forum produced a summary report to explore the possibility of a flat-tax to finance the non-commercial exchange of creative works online. This proposal was sharply criticized by the cultural administration, which was introducing at the same time a new law on the protection of intellectual property on the Internet. The fact that the Forum declared itself competent on a subject which, in the ministry's agents view, fell within their exclusive prerogatives was particularly unwelcome. The association was forced to abandon the discussion with web players on this matter, as Isabelle Falque-Pierrotin recalls: "The Ministry of Culture and the public authorities told us: 'It's out of the question for you to continue to deal with this subject, it belongs to us, the Ministry of Culture, we'll deal with it'. And so, we were forced to close the file".

This call to order revealed once again the institutional weakness of the Forum, at a time when competition between administrations for the production of Internet policies was increasing. The lack of "reputation" (Carpenter & Krause, 2012) of the Forum, from the point of view of Internet activists as well as from ministerial administrations became more pronounced in the late 2000s, and finally led to the dismantlement of the organization. In 2010, the public subsidies that had sustained the association were not renewed. At the last General Meeting, members voted for the "early dissolution of the association", putting an end to the Internet co-regulation experiment.

The former agents of the Internet Rights Forum only euphemistically referred to the "political" dimension of the decision: in 2010, the right-wing government closed an experiment that had begun during a Socialist government ten years earlier. But the Forum's dissolution was due above all to the lack of support both within and outside government, to defend this new form of extra-administrative regulation for the Internet. This dissolution also revealed the evolution of vision regarding the role of the State in terms of Internet governance. It is particularly perceptible in retrospective interviews we conducted in 2016 and 2017: when the Forum was mentioned, respondents distanced themselves from the co-regulation model they had yet supported twenty years before. Jean-Noël Tronc, for example, declared: "I absolutely don't believe in this idea of co-construction of norms and all that. At some point it has to stop, and the State has to assume responsibility and provide a vision for Internet regulation" [Interview 37, July 2016]. More nuanced, Daniel Kaplan, private consultant, founder of the think tank FING and a former member of the Forum, reckoned that "All of us [Internet pioneers] got a bit lost with this idea. The co-production of regulations was in fact an idea very much driven by companies, and it almost gave rise to institutions... and then it kind of fell by the wayside" [Interview 19, May 2016].

The interviews allow us to measure the shift in discourses and representations about Internet regulation over the past 20 years. The institutionalization of co-regulation and experiments in multistakeholder governance was indeed the product of a particular context marked by the relative novelty of the Internet as a socio-political phenomenon and the legal uncertainty created by the first Web affairs when the future Internet giants were still in development. This context of enthusiasm, combined with international pressure for digital market development, favored the adoption of soft-regulation for digital markets, presented as a loyalty to the principles of Internet pioneers. The end of the Forum in France signaled the questioning of this soft-regulation approach and the beginning of a new period, characterized by a stronger control exercised by sectoral administrations on the Internet, with the fight against piracy becoming an emblematic example of this attempt to increase government intervention. Yet, as we will also see in the next chapter, it also shows the difficult tendency of administrative agent to turn back the wave of private and technological governmentality.

* * *

At the end of the 1990s, two political agendas converged to favor the emergence of the first Internet policies in France. The joint mobilization of Internet pioneers and reform-minded civil servants—who sometimes blurred into the figure of the technophile technocrat—led to a policy shift that ensured Internet technology dissemination within the French administration. Indeed, the implementation of "e-government" projects and the development of Internet co-regulation practices introduced durably new tools, organizational and regulatory practices largely inspired by Internet communities and companies. Eventually, the period was characterized by a hybridization of Internet culture and administrative practices, involving a acknowledgment of the limits of the State in the information society, and the incorporation of digital tools into reform processes.

Yet the heroic rhetoric describing this period as a "revolutionary moment" needs to be nuanced. In many respects, we have shown that these changes were limited. First, new Internet policies recycled projects "already in the pipeline", while offering them visibility and even unprecedented resources, under the banner of a new "Virtual State". Second, Internet pioneers and state reformers were still faced with many obstacles slowing down or even impeding the implementation of state digitization.

More than an historic break, the 1990s were above all a formative period for the French State: the projects launched at that time laid the foundations for future digital policies and were often taken up, almost identically, by subsequent governments. The Hourtin speech, the draft law on the Information Society and the short-lived RE/SO plan of the following government—for a Digital Republic in the Information Society

(2002–2007)—have become references for future digital policy officers. Above all, the gradual neo-liberalization of the State, that came with reform programs and new modes of regulation at the turn of the century, was still under construction.

In contrast to a "Copernican revolution", as heralded by the online tax payment program, the enthusiasm generated by the spread of the Internet within the State is more akin to a "Galilean revolution", that is to say a global transformation that is far from institutionalized within the State, still struggling to gain recognition and support. In fact, it will be many years before we see the general spread of IT practices in French society, and the completion of state modernization projects outlined as early as the late 1990s. The digital transformation of public services and administrative work announced by Internet entrepreneurs arrived maybe "too soon", coming up against the slow evolution of IT practices in government and society alike. In the first decade of the twenty-first century, there was still a great deal of friction between Internet principles and bureaucratic reform, around the questioning of administrative boundaries and the role of activists and private enterprises in regulation. Weakly institutionalized, the first structures dedicated to Internet policy disappeared, along with a vocabulary inevitably associated with the era, that of the "information society". But the seeds of change had been sown in administrative soil and were about to produce radical transformations of the State, with advanced bureaucratization of Internet-related issues and technologies in the next period.

References

Agar, J. (2003). *The government machine: A revolutionary history of the computer*. The MIT Press.

Aldrin, P., Bargel, L., Bué, N., & Pina, C. (Eds.) (2016). *Politiques de l'alternance. Sociologie des changements (de) politiques*. Éditions du Croquant.

Baquiast, J.-P. (1998). *Proposition sur les rapports de l'Internet à la modernisation du fonctionnement de l'État (Proposals on the contribution of the Internet to the modernization of government)*. Rapport to the Ministry of State Reform. Paris: La documenttion française.

Bezes, P. (2000). Les Hauts fonctionnaires croient-ils à leur mythe? L'apport des approches cognitives à l'analyse des engagements dans les politiques de réforme de l'État Quelques exemples français (1988–1997). *Revue française de science politique*, 307–332.

Bezes, P. (2009). *Réinventer l'État: les réformes de l'administration française (1962–2008)*. Presses Universitaires de France.

Boltanski, L. & Chiapello, E. (2005). *The new spirit of capitalism*. Verso Books.

Bourdieu, P. (2014), *On the State. Lectures at the Collège de France, 1989–1992*. Polity.

Büthe, T. (2011). *The new global rulers: The privatization of regulation in the world economy*. Princeton University Press.

Carpenter, D. P., & Krause, G. A. (2012). Reputation and public administration. *Public Administration Review, 72*(1), 26–32.

Dunleavy, P., Margetts, H., Bastow, S., & Tinkler, J. (2006). *Digital era governance: IT corporations, the state, and e-government*. Oxford University Press.

Fountain, J. E. (2001). *Building the virtual state: Information technology and institutional change*. Brookings Institution Press.

Gaïti, B. (2002) . Les modernisateurs dans l'administration d'après-guerre l'écriture d'une histoire héroïque. *Revue française d'administration publique, 102*(2), 295–306.

Gaïti, B. (2014). L'érosion discrète de l'État-providence dans la France des années 1960: retour sur les temporalités d'un «tournant néo-libéral». *Actes de la recherche en sciences sociales, 1*, 58–71.

Gardey, D. (2008). *Écrire, calculer, classer. Comment une révolution de papier a transformé les sociétés contemporaines (1800–1940)*. La Découverte.

Hall, P. A. (1993). Policy paradigms, social learning, and the state: The case of economic policymaking in Britain. *Comparative politics*, 275–296.

Kingdon, J. W. (1984). *Agendas, alternatives, and public policies*. Brown and Company.

MacKinnon, R. (2012). *Consent of the networked: The Worldwide struggle for internet freedom*. Basic Books.

MacKinnon, R., Hickok, E., Bar, A., & Lim, H. (2014). *Fostering freedom online: The Roles, challenges and obstacles of internet intermediaries*. United Nations Educationa.

Majone, G. (1994). The rise of the regulatory state in Europe. *West European Politics, 17*(3), 77–101.

Mangset, M. (2015). What does it mean to be part of the elite?: Comparing Norwegian, French and British Top Bureaucrats' understandings of the elite concept when applied to themselves. *Comparative Sociology, 14*(2), 274–299.

Mangset, M., & Asdal, K. (2019). Bureaucratic power in note-writing: Authoritative expertise within the state. *The British Journal of Sociology, 70*(2), 569–588.

Moran, M. (2002). Understanding the regulatory state. *British Journal of Political Science, 32*(2), 391–413.

Palier, B., & Surel, Y. (2010). *Quand les politiques changent: temporalités et niveaux de l'action publique*. L'Harmattan.

Thatcher, M. (2002). Analysing regulatory reform in Europe. *Journal of European Public Policy, 9*(6), 859–872.

Thelen, K. (2000). Timing and temporality in the analysis of institutional evolution and change. *Studies in American Political Development, 14*(1), 101–108.

Trumbull, G. (2004). *Silicon and the state: French innovation policy in the Internet age*. Brookings Institution Press.

Vogel, D. (2008). Private global business regulation. *Annual Review of Political Science, 11*, 261–282.

Weber, M. (2010, Revised Edition). *The Protestant ethic and the spirit of capitalism*. Oxford University Press.

CHAPTER 6

The Pirate Years: Copyright Policies in the 2000–2010 Decade

> The Internet is a new frontier, a territory to be conquered. But the Internet must not be a high-tech Wild West, a lawless zone where outlaws can plunder creations without limit, or even worse, trade on the backs of artists. On the one hand, brand-new networks, ultra-perfect equipment, and on the other, medieval behavior, where, under the pretext that it is digital, anyone could freely practice shoplifting.
> President Sarkozy Speech, for the signature of an agreement between creative industries and Internet service providers to protect cultural works online, Élysée Palace, November 23, 2007

While the first Internet policies were marked by enthusiasm and an attempt at subverting traditional boundaries and hierarchies within the State, this period rapidly drew to a close as new public issues regarding Internet regulation became more salient. They provided an opportunity for the government to reassert its power over a digital territory presented as a "new frontier to conquer", a social space where public authority should be reaffirmed. In contrast to the innovations around co-regulation, the 2000–2010 decade displayed concurrent attempts to develop more traditional forms of state intervention in order to control online practices. Nothing was more emblematic of this intervention than the fight against "piracy", a central concern of Western governments throughout the 2000s.

A. Bellon, *A Socio-History of Internet Policies*, International Series on Public Policy, https://doi.org/10.1007/978-3-031-69099-0_6

Online "piracy" covers a wide range of practices, from peer-to-peer exchanges to illegal streaming and direct downloading. Of course, the adaptation of copyright to technological change is a long-standing issue that was not discovered with the Internet. Printing press, television and radio have raised long before similar issues about the protection of creative works in front of the constant reduction of reproduction and distribution costs (Lessig, 2004). But with the development of the Internet and the web, the possibilities for copying and sharing creative works became massive. Illegal downloading first affected book and music industries, with peer-to-peer file sharing applications such as Napster, released in 1999 (Menn, 2003), or the Pirate Bay in 2003 (Li, 2009). The fight against piracy was then waged in courts, with a number of emblematic trials that more than often demonstrated the slowness and inadequacy of legal proceedings: the closure of Napster in 2001, followed by the conviction of the four Norwegian operators of the Pirate Bay in 2009, did nothing to halt the growth of copyright infringements online. For example, just after it was condemned to be shut down, the Pirate Bay was still accessible via multiple mirror websites hosted on foreign servers. What is more, with increasing connection speed, piracy started to affect the film industry, while illegal streaming websites such as Megaupload appeared in 2005.

Throughout the 2000s, Western governments struggled to strengthen the protection of intellectual property online (Box 1). In France, no less than two laws were passed in three years to curb the growth of illegal downloading and to protect copyrighted works on the Internet: the Copyright and Related Rights in the Information Society law (*Loi Dadvsi*) in 2006 and the "Creation and Internet" law, known as the *Loi Hadopi*, in 2009.[1] At the time, the fight against piracy was the most visible tip of a new regulatory arsenal organized within the State in the field of content regulation. Much less visible, the fight against terrorist propaganda or child pornography raised issues that were often similar to copyright: should the State cooperate with Internet service providers? how can we identify the authors of infringements? What should be the responsibility of Internet intermediaries? But piracy was more directly

[1] "Hadopi", refers to the name of the agency created by the law to regulate copyright infringement online, the Haute Autorité pour la diffusion des oeuvres et la protection des droits sur Internet.

related to one central cause of Internet communities: the free flow of information and access to knowledge. As such, it became emblematic of new positions and oppositions played out around Internet regulation. It brought back the antagonism between the "State" and the "Internet" in Europe, at a time when there was no longer a resistance to the "US" network per se. In France, the antagonism centered around two visions of culture and cultural policies. On the one hand, Internet activists were defending "free culture", i.e. a concept of culture and creation that was based on the principle of freedom and democratic access (Lessig, 2004). On the other hand, institutionalized cultural policy in France was based on a wide range of instruments associated with specific goals (Dubois, 1999), notably the defense of the "cultural exception". Culture was seen as a state-regulated economic sector, underpinned by an institutional dialogue between public and private players. With file sharing and illegal downloading, this complex regulatory ecosystem featuring French cultural policies was thus called into question.

Box 1 Copyright Battles in the European Union

Fighting the development of online piracy was a common concern of European governments in the 2000s, especially with countries displaying among the highest rates of piracy in the world, such as Sweden or Poland. In 2001, the European Union's Directive on the Harmonization of Certain Aspects of Copyright and Related Rights in the Information Society (2001/29/EC) or the "Information Society Directive", initially intended to implement the WIPO treaties, strengthened the rights of copyright holders within the EU. It raised concerns among various civil society organizations, spanning from digital rights activists to library associations, and led to the creation of the Pirate Party in Sweden (2006) (Fredriksson, 2015). Debates intensified in 2009 when the equally contested Intellectual Property Rights Enforcement Directive (2004/48/EC), known as the IPRED Directive was implemented, requiring member States to provide more effective tools against piracy. Much like in France, these directives were followed by far-reaching changes in national IP legislations and aggressive enactments. With its strong cultural industry and public intervention tradition, France undoubtedly took the lead in terms of anti-piracy policy in Europe. Yet France's choice to entrust an independent administrative body with copyright enforcement was rarely followed. In most countries, the matter was rather taken to court, leading to sometimes spectacular legal actions such as The Pirate Bay trial in Sweden (2009–2010) or the YouTube trial in Germany (2009).[2] Later on, the fight against piracy in Germany increasingly leant on private intermediary firms specialized in tracking shared data and asking for the destruction of links. This choice proved much more successful in reducing illegal downloading.[3] In other countries, such as Spain, a more progressive approach was adopted, with the recognition of peer-to-peer file-sharing as a form of fair use. The salience and concomitance of copyright debates in Europe favored the circulation of arguments among digital activists and joint protestations: in 2012, various European organizations participated in a vast campaign against the Anti-counterfeiting Trade Agreement (ACTA), that aimed at fostering an international legal framework against copyright infringement. The campaign successfully ended with the rejection of the proposal by the European Parliament.

In this chapter, we will study anti-piracy laws as a strategic case to understand the tensions between sector-based public intervention and Internet policies. While Internet policies were conceived by Internet pioneers as a cross-cutting project for the reinvention of state action, this project ran up against the boundaries of well-established categories of public intervention. The strength of these categories (the established policy domains) lay in the fact that they were based not only on administrative institutions—the ministry departments—but also on norms, statutes and beliefs shared by the agents of the administrative field. While the digital revolution , like the climate crisis or the fight for gender equality, is a political dynamic that cuts across sectors and areas of specialization, it questions the common jurisdictions of ministerial departments and raises issues about the organization of State itself. Taking the cultural administration and the fight against piracy as an emblematic case study, this chapter analysis how "bureaucratic politics" (Allison & Halperin, 1972, Peters, 2018) intersects with Internet policymaking. This notion refers first and foremost to the weight of organizational cultures, which means that agents tend to adopt the interests and perceptions of the

[2] In 2009, a German court indeed stated that Google's subsidiary could be held liable for damages when hosting copyrighted videos without the copyright holder's permission, resulting in major labels' videos being blocked in Germany.

[3] https://en.unifrance.org/news/14762/the-fight-against-piracy-lessons-to-be-learned-from-germany.

administrations that employ them. It also takes into account the competition and sectoral resistance that hinder the convergence of practices and objectives assigned to cross-sectorial Internet policies. How, then, did the digital revolution encounter and transform cultural intervention? And to what extent did it stumble over the boundaries of ministerial department?

In just a few years, the cultural administration went from a pioneer department launching many Internet-based experimentations to a symbol of the French government's anti-Internet stance. These developments should be understood as a gradual dilution of Internet policy goals in sectoral policy domains. Bureaucratic politics was not so much about preventing the digital transformation of cultural action, than adapting it to administrative constraints: in the domain of cultural policy, administrative reorganization, creation of new agencies, and the development of ministerial expertise merely answered the challenges raised by the Internet in terms of financing creation, access to culture and heritage protection. Caught up in new bureaucratic routines and norms, digital issues were eventually shaped by the cultural administration. While these new issues truly contributed to the Ministry's digital transformation, they were in turn "sectorized", i.e. refracted into a policymaking process marked by intra-administrative struggles, established alliances and a specific way of elaborating state action.

Empirical data for this chapter were collected during a long fieldwork in and around the French cultural administration. It draws on observational data from ministerial cabinets,[4] as well as numerous interviews with special advisors, civil servants and political staff who were in charge of digital cultural policy between 2000 and 2017. At the same time fieldwork among hackers and Internet activists that fought against the strengthening of intellectual property offered a symmetric vision on digital cultural policies. Starting with the debates surrounding the Dadvsi and Hadopi laws, which crystallized a new opposition between the State and the Internet (1), the chapter explores the reconfiguration of digital activism in the face of copyright and anti-piracy laws (2). Finally, it shows the gradual adaptation of the cultural administration and its appropriation of digital issues, and how it became part of new bureaucratic routines (3).

[4] Between January 2014 and April 2014, the author spent four months as a participant observer in the ministerial cabinet of Minister of Culture Aurélie Filippetti.

1 From Dadvsi to Hadopi: Looking Back at a "Political Imbroglio"

In the 1990s, the advent of the information economy, combined with the development of new technologies, led to an international review of intellectual property rights. This agenda was driven in particular by transnational alliances between lawyers, politicians and representatives of the creative and information industries (Sell, 2003). It resulted to the adoption of the 1996 treaty on the protection of works in the digital environment, signed by the fifty-two member States of the World Intellectual Property Organization (WIPO). The treaty provided additional protection for copyrighted works and prohibited the circumvention of technological measures of protection. The treaty was then transposed into national laws in Northern America and Europe, sometimes further strengthening intellectual property rights. In the European Union, the 2001 European Directive incorporated the principles of the WIPO, while harmonizing copyright law between member States. Circumventing "digital locks" or "digital rights management" became illegal throughout the Union, as well as the use of software or online services that ran counter to these restrictions.

In 2003, the "Copyright and Related Rights in the Information Society" bill or *Loi Dadvsi*, which transposed the provisions of the European directive, was first introduced in French Parliament by Jean-Jacques Aillagon, then Minister of Culture in the Raffarin right-wing government. The law was finally adopted three years later, in June 2006, and by 2008, a new draft for the protection of online copyright, was already in preparation. In 2009, the discussion of the "Creation and Internet" law or *Loi Hadopi* in the French National Assembly gave rise to long and stormy debates, echoing protests in the street against the "graduated response" system. Upon the Hadopi debacle, Culture Minister Christine Albanel lost her position at the government, replaced by Frédéric Mitterrand. In both cases, the laws were censured by the Constitutional Council on one of their essential aspects: the introduction of a fine for copyright infringement for Dadvsi and the cutting-off of Internet access for Hadopi. It took another passage through Parliament in September 2009 for a new Hadopi 2 draft to finally inscribe the "graduated response" system in the law.

Throughout the whole 2000–2010 decade, cultural and political players were thus mobilized by the fight against piracy. In many respects, the content and length of the debates sparked by these two bills were referred as an unprecedented "political imbroglio". Firstly, because the subject was relatively new in both assemblies and only a handful of members of Parliament got involved in the debates, while often declaring themselves ill-equipped to deal with questions of technological regulation. Secondly, because the debates were unexpected, as the government tackled with copyright infringement, an issue that appeared, at first glance, politically consensual and supported by a majority of artists. As a reminder, the previous copyright law of 1985 had been passed unanimously in France. Finally, the discussion blurred traditional political boundaries and divided *throughout* the majority and the opposition.

The debates on copyright reveals the Internet's ability to shake up well-established dividing lines in the political and administrative fields. The emergence of digital issues in the legislature led to new and sometimes surprising coalitions in defense of sharing and online freedoms, but also encouraged political professionals to define new strategies to take back control on the Internet. The Dadvsi and Hadopi debates thus provide a strategic insight into the politicization of digital causes and Internet regulation, studied in this section.

1.1 An "Unidentified Political Object" in Parliament

In 2000, the Internet was a new subject for French MPs, a subject which, in the words of a former deputy, "was of no interest to anyone" [Interview 28, PC Deputy (2002–2007), June 2016]. At the end of the list of issues that one should address to gain political visibility, Internet was left to a few specialists, often newcomers in Parliament. In 1996, they decided to create a multi-partisan group on the "Information society". As a mere working group, they did not enjoy the resources and visibility of a standing committee. It was more a matter of informal sociability, discussions in the refreshment room, exchanges in the corridors and attendance at joint events. As such, these interactions did not show up in the official record of the National Assembly but were often mentioned in interviews:

> There was this group, I remember this story quite well, it was a cross-current group, practically autonomous. We met regularly, had meetings in the refreshment room, people from the right, from the left, and yet the whole group functioned well together. We exchanged arguments, information (...) We almost had the impression of belonging to the same political

> group (laughs), us against all the others, fiercely against, allegedly, what was interpreted as 'against copyright'. [Interview 28]

This working group was indeed one of the first political arenas to discuss intellectual property policies in the digital age, but also to dialogue with the free software movement and discuss the legality of peer-to-peer exchanges, which were assimilated to "private copying".[5] Lawrence Lessig was even invited by the members of the working group as the sole US speaker at the Parliamentary Meetings on the Information society in 1999. He warned the attending politicians and senior civil servants: "You cannot act as if a simple act of Parliament could make the software work differently. You need to learn the ins and outs of the code and how it works". Long before new copyright bills were introduced and debated in public sessions, the members of the working group had thus developed a critical view of the reinforcement of copyright, which they felt was ill-suited to the evolution of online cultural practices. On the contrary, they stood up for "cyberpirates", who were prosecuted in the early 2000s. For example, French socialist MP Christian Paul wrote in 2004 a vibrant tribune in defense of a young Internet user who, in his view, had become the scapegoat for a new "crusade" led by creative industries. It started as follows:

> August 18, the home of a young teacher, music enthusiast and Internet user was searched, and "Alexis" - a pseudonym - prosecuted for counterfeiting, because he owned 600 albums downloaded via the Internet. The "Alexis" case had begun yet this man is not an organized criminal reselling reproduction of pirated tracks on the Net. Like millions of French people, he was taking part in *pair à pair* networks (P2P in John Lennon's language) whose members share files of musical works. "Alexis" faces a maximum sentence of 3 years in prison and a fine of 300,000 euros....[6]

The working group also enabled MPs to become more knowledgeable regarding digital issues, to the point of being considered specialists within

[5] Private copying is an equivalent of fair use. In France a **private copying levy** is charged on purchases of recordable media in exchange for the authorization of sharing in the private sphere.

[6] « L'affaire Alexis», opinion by Christian Paul, published in *Le Monde,* October 2, 2004.

their own political parties. These include Patrick Bloche (PS), Christian Paul (PS), Frédéric Dutoit (PC), Martine Billard (EELV), Richard Cazenave (UMP) and Alain Suguenot (UMP), who played a key role in the Dadvsi and Hadopi debates. In the highly codified and hierarchical parliamentary arena, the discussion of anti-piracy laws offered an unprecedented spotlight on these less-known political figures, and an opportunity for them to showcase their still rare computer-related knowledge.

Digital copyright policies were indeed based on new IT concepts, often unknown to political professionals. In the Dadvsi law, for example, the protection of "DRMs" ("digital rights management"), a technological lock that could prevent access depending on the medium or the geographical area, raised a number of technical issues. As early as 2005, only a handful of MPs were able to debate on "interoperability", "IP addresses" identification or "flow measurement", to clarify the functioning of peer-to-peer systems and distinguish between "MP3" and "MP4" formats. All these terms increased the cost of entry into a debate that sometimes echoed expert discussions.

Among MPs, ignorance of Internet technology was often coupled with a feeling of powerlessness. Technical approximations were pinpointed by activists and opponents alike, and relayed by journalists in the context of well-attended, high-profile debates. Against this backdrop, a number of MPs advocated for extra-parliamentary delegation of these issues and supported the creation of independent expert agencies: "We are witnessing very rapid technological developments. The debates are extremely technical. We need to be clear about Parliament's ability to legislate and make decisions on these issues. We are coming up against our limits—as the examination of this bill has illustrated" (Laurent Wauquiez, UMP MP, Minutes of the Parliamentary Debate, March 16, 2006).

Especially during the Dadvsi Debate (2005–2006), the technical framing of copyright policies favored an under-politicization of parliamentary discussion. When partisan allegiances became blurred, the discussion was marked by the unexpected irruption of new proposals directly inspired by Internet communities.

1.2 A "Crazy Evening in Parliament": Breaking with and Subverting Political Institutions

The Dadvsi debate holds a special place in parliamentary memory, particularly among the few MPs who participated the most. The discussion was indeed marked by numerous imprecisions, confusions, backtracking and innovations, all of which represented a break with the usual parliamentary practices. While debates had to follow the rules of parliamentary deliberation, the novelty of the subject enabled these rules to be circumvented, opening up new political opportunities in a decision-making process often portrayed as closed and constrained.

When the Dadsvi law was introduced in Parliament in December 2005, the government saw its adoption as nothing more than a formality that should be dealt with before the holiday break. What is more, the text belatedly transposed the 2001 European directive on copyright, making its adoption even more urgent for France, for fear of being submitted to penalties from the European Union. Yet, on December 21, in a sparsely-populated assembly, an amendment from the majority, legalizing peer-to-peer file sharing, was adopted against the government's advice, to everyone's surprise, by a group of deputies from both the right and the left wing of the chamber. The measure voted, assimilated to a form of "global licensing" for the exchange of creative works, was in complete contradiction with the bill and called into question its future adoption. In the upper galleries, digital activists exulted and, on the parliamentary benches, MPs looked at each other in bewilderment:

> It was an extraordinary night. I remember it well because my daughter had come to see the debates. It was just before Christmas so she was there on holiday and I told her: "Come and see, it's fun". And on that evening, just before Christmas, I was one of the MPs that had to defend the amendment, it was just one amendment in the middle of a bundle of others. And when we came to the vote, I remember that moment very well, because we suddenly realized it had passed. There weren't many of us, maybe twenty or so in the Assembly. I don't remember who was chairing the meeting, but he didn't catch it immediately. The session secretary, who in principle is suposed to detect this kind of thing, he didn't tell him anything right away, and moved on to the next amendment, giving the floor to the minister, who also continued, as if nothing had happened. But everyone was thinking about the consequences of the amendment, and I think that at some point, it was the secretary general of the session who started to stand up and said: there's something wrong, this is bringing down the whole text. And in fact, it did bring down the whole bill. [Interview 18, Socialist MP (1988–2012), April 2016]

One must realize what this vote represents regarding traditional political references in France: conservative Christine Boutin had just defended a completely unprecedented political proposal alongside her traditional political opponent, progressive MP Patrick Bloche; the government's project was overturned by an amendment from its own party, and all the political groups were in fact divided on the issue of peer-to-peer legalization. The coalition of voters was completely cobbled-together, as if nothing was premeditated about it: right-wing opponents to the text had just sought to convince within their own ranks, right up to the last minute, while the Socialist deputies supported the proposal in the absence of any group consultation. This was not so much the case of organized dissention on behalf of right-wing deputies, but rather one of the too-rare success among many parliamentary attempts to contribute to change government proposals.

The vote also came as a surprise to the government—notably the minister of Culture and his political advisors. In interview, Olivier Japiot, the government commissioner for the law, used the same words as above to describe the disarray of government actors as they realized what had just happened. To avoid the dropping of the bill and further disavowal by members of the majority, they decided to "cobble together a new amendment, on a corner of the bench". This amendment, that reduced the penalties associated with illegal downloading,[7] is the first appearance of the concept of "graduated response" in the law, as a compromise between the legalization of file sharing and the criminalization of piracy. The new provision was yet introduced "in haste" to pander to the majority's opponents and demonstrate the government's concern not to penalize Internet users. The "graduated response", a concept bound to become central in the fight against piracy thus emerged almost by accident, during a session jostled by the unexpected. The Dadvsi debate saw a proliferation of such moments of confusion and cobbled-together solutions, to which the interviewees returned at length, giving the example of the last minute introduction of the idea of a public downloading platform or the adoption of several amendments to promote free software use. In this respect, this first parliamentary discussion of digital copyright policy was an exemplary case of the ability of digital issues to disrupt political discussion. Several

[7] At the time, "counterfeiting" was punishable by up to three years' imprisonment. The new amendment proposed by the governmentoki reduced sanction for counterfeiting to a fine between €38 and €50.

institutions were subverted: the hierarchy of issues, partisan opposition and the division of labor between administration, political representation and the government.

A series of overflows finally led the government to completely alter the timetable for discussions. The examination of the text was suspended and only returned to the Assembly in March 2006, after a three-month interruption. At this time, a dubious but legal procedure was used to re-vote the first article of the bill, canceling the vote of December 21. A long and heated discussion followed, that lasted until June, when a disciplined majority finally adopted the Dadvsi law. But it was a mere victory for the government because, with looming presidential elections, a revision of copyright policy was already prepared by both political camps.

1.3 Hadopi and the Paradoxical Politicization of Copyright Policy

Barely passed, the Dadvsi law was already showing limitations: the creative industries were indeed turning away from "technical locks", while the first version of the "graduated response" was censured by the French Constitutional Council. As early as 2007, the newly elected president Sarkozy promised to draft a new law against piracy. This presidential endorsement marked a strong politicization of copyright issues, with many speeches and declaration by members of the government against the "uncivilized Internet" and its "culture of gratuity". In 2008, an agreement was signed at the Elysée (French Presidential Palace) between French ISPs and representatives of the creative industries, to join their effort in the fight against copyright infringement. In the agreement, the principle of the "graduated response" received a new meaning, as a gradual process from notification to suspension of Internet connection, also known as the "three strikes and you're out" in English-speaking countries. The scheme was advocated as a "soft" and "pedagogical" approach to online copyright enforcement, more fitted to the expansion of peer-to-peer exchange and downloading in France. It was included in the new "Creation and Internet" bill, introduced in front of the Senate on June 18, 2008. It was then adopted by the upper house after only two days of relatively consensual debate, with only 14 votes against. Yet, the passage through the French National Assembly gave rise to a heated controversy, transforming the bill into a true political battle (Fig. 1).

In contrast to the Dadvsi debate, partisan opposition was more pronounced when it came to the *Loi Hadopi*. Rejected by the right-wing majority, the "creative contribution", an updated version of "global licensing", was defended by Socialist MPs as a unified group. In March 2009, they introduced an amendment to create "extended collective licenses in the form of a creative contribution" in the music industry. The amendment was put to a public vote: its politically clear-cut outcome shows the political work that separates December, 2005 from March, 2009. From confusion and blurring of political boundaries to partisan polarization, the Hadopi debate bore the mark of a new political appropriation of digital issues (Fig. 1).

The debates moved away from technical disputes to general political values inspired by Internet communities: opponents mentioned free access to the Internet, the right to communicate and opposition to citizen surveillance. By shifting the stakes of the debate, MPs were able to criticize the Hadopi law without opposing the principle of copyright

Fig. 1 Protest against the Hadopi Law in Paris, May, 2009

protection. This counter-argumentation was also underpinned by recent social transformations in digital use: with 71.6% of the French population regularly using the Internet in 2009—compared with 42.9% at the time of the Dadvsi debate—occasional or regular downloaders were no longer considered as lone wolfs, but were referred as emblematic figures of a new tech-savvy generation. Some opponents even reversed the stigma of the "pirates" in favor of a more positive image of curious and eclectic cultural consumers, who were developing new ways of accessing and using creation.

Above all, the "creative contribution" or "global licensing" suggested by the Socialist group provided a technical alternative to the "graduated response". As defined by Barthe (2003), technical alternative are socio-technical object that enables "in a situation that seems saturated with irreversibility, to find the room for manoeuvre necessary for compromise and political negotiation". Major artistic figures from the movie industry, such as Catherine Deneuve and Chantal Akerman, supported this solution and openly criticized the Hadopi bill in the press. The "creative contribution" re-established opponents' concern for the remuneration of creators. At this stage of the discussion, the details of this alternative policy were of little importance. A reading of the debates even reveals the vagueness that surrounds the definition of the solutions grouped behind this generic term of "global licensing": partial or total, compulsory or optional, reserved for music or extended to all works available online, financed by a tax on ISP or by a fee linked to website subscriptions, none of these precisions were really clear-cut. Yet even after the Hadopi debate, the global licensing craze carried over into the 2012 presidential elections: during the campaign, many candidates took up the principle of a global licensing, sometimes under different names,[8] showing how much influence this political solution, developed mainly among Internet communities as a counter-argument to the Hadopi, gained political attention at the time.

Despite President Sarkozy's direct involvement and the accentuation of partisan divisions in Parliament, the politicization of copyright policy was yet fragile, even paradoxical. Indeed, while the Hadopi debate revealed

[8] In his "Humanist Project", François Bayrou recommended a "flat-rate, unlimited global license-type system"; Marine Le Pen defended "a global license for private exchanges on the Internet"; François Hollande spoke of remunerating authors "according to the number of accesses to their works, thanks to funding based on both users and all players in the digital economy".

new political oppositions, divisions still existed within political parties. Several members of the majority unofficially criticized the "graduated response" system. And despite their apparent unanimity in the National Assembly, many Socialist figures feared losing the support of artists in the Hadopi battle. These difficulties no doubt explain the closing of the Hadopi chapter in 2012, after the election of Socialist President François Hollande. The Hadopi agency, a new regulatory authority for content, remained in place throughout the five-year term, and the adoption of the "creative contribution" was abandoned as early as the summer of 2012. It marked the erosion of alliances forged between digital activists and politicians during the Dadvsi and Hadopi debates, as well as the consolidation of bureaucratic control over these issues, two phenomena explored in the following sections.

2 Digital Activists and Contentious Politics

Legislative struggle to fight copyright infringement reconfigured the relationship between government, politics and Internet activism. After the early years of Internet policies during which many activists contributed to policymaking, digital activism took on a more central role in contentious politics (McAdam et al., 2001), that is to say a social movement that opposed digital government policies.

The criminalization of peer-to-peer exchanges and illegal downloading directly impacted idiosyncratic practices of the digital world. The defense of free software, and the free flow of information, central causes of Internet communities (see Chapter 1), led to a more general questioning of intellectual property rights. While new legislations were adopted in many Western countries to strengthen and extent intellectual property rights, counter-arguments and contentious practices also traveled globally between activists to fight these copyright policies. In France, protests against the Dadvsi and Hadopi laws favored a reorganization of digital activism around a new association created in 2008, *La Quadrature du net*. The latter centralized and symbolized the inclusion of Internet activism in French social movement.

2.1 *From Transnational to National Contention*

Since the WIPO treaty in 1996, the strengthening of intellectual property rights in the information economy had been strongly criticized by transnational Internet communities. Following in the footsteps of the pioneers, the first Internet users defended the free flow of information against the attempt of major content industries to lock down creative practices and peer-to-peer exchanges on the web. The contention was inspired by the free software movement and its emblematic associations, such as Richard Stallman's Free Software Foundation, and by cyberspace advocacy organizations like the Electronic Frontier Foundation (see Chapter 1). As early as 1994, one of its founding members, John Perry Barlow wrote a manifesto for a new "economy of ideas" in *Wired* magazine, with the following proposition: "Copyright is dead in the digital age".[9]

Alliances between Internet activists and legal scholars were forged to discuss the foundations of intellectual property and its future in the digital environment. In the US, the issue pitted representatives of Internet and Society studies against the Law and Economics vision of intellectual property, based on the economic rationality of agents: for the latter, patents played as essential incentives for individuals and organizations to take risks and invest in research and creation. Yet, this framework was undermined by the study of new models of innovation without patents, notably the free software community (Benkler, 2006), while the extension of the duration of intellectual property rights was criticized as an attack on the public domain and a hindrance to the very process of creation (Lessig, 2004). A leading figure in this legal critique, Professor Lawrence Lessig published a series of three books (2001, 2004, 2008) in the first decade of the twenty-first century, where he presented sharing and remix as constitutive of creation, and denounced the stranglehold of cultural lobbies on congressional decision-making process. These alliances between legal scholars and Internet activists were consolidated around the contestation of copyright policies in the US. In 2001, two pieces of legislation strengthening intellectual property protection and extending the duration of rights were passed by Congress: Digital Millennium Copyright Act and Copyright Term Extension Act were strongly criticized by digital communities and legal scholars alike. Professor Peter

[9] http://groups.csail.mit.edu/mac/classes/6.805/articles/int-prop/barlow-economy-of-ideas.html.

Jaszi of the University of Washington even founded the Digital Future Coalition to bring together lawyers and activists to exchange expertise and arguments in the contention. The protest against DMCA and CTA prompted Lawrence Lessig to strengthen his ties with computer scientists and hackers. In 2002, he prefaced Richard Stallman's book, and in 2004, he founded, with other digital activists, the Creative Commons association, to promote the legal sharing of creative works on the Internet. These alliances culminated in 2011 and 2012, with the contention of SOPA (Stop Online Piracy Act) and PIPA (Protect International Property Act). A broad coalition of media, intellectuals, activists and companies—among which Google—managed to have the two bills withdrawn (Benkler et al., 2015).

Dadvsi and Hadopi debate in France thus took place in an effervescent international context, when discussion and contention around the strengthening of intellectual property were happening in many Western countries. In the EU, the adoption of the Copyright Directive in 2001 gave way to the negotiation of a new, highly controversial text on software patents, finally rejected by European Parliament in 2005. Debates and legislative actions overlapped, encouraging the circulation of arguments and modes of contention in different countries. Transnational fora were also key to this circulation: international hacker meetings—such as the annual Chaos Computer Club Congresses in Europe[10]— and the World Summit on the Information Society, organized by the UN in 2003 and 2005. Some activists involved in these international arenas, such as *Vecam* members in France, played a central role in structuring the international movement against the reinforcement of copyright and in importing new ideas into the French discussion. The free flow of information, the right to communicate and the defense of the "commons"—principles that structured Internet activism transnationally—thus traveled between transnational and local arenas. That was especially the case for the notion of "commons", quite new to the French public sphere. Drawing on the pioneering work of economist Elinor Ostrom on the collective governance of the shared resources (1990), the commons refers to community-based practices of self-governance, opposed to government and market-driven governance. Largely unknown in France prior to her

[10] The Chaos Computer Club (CCC) is one of Europe's largest and oldest association of hackers, founded in 1981. Since 1983, it has hosted the annual Chaos Communication Congress, Europe's biggest hacker gathering.

Nobel Prize in Economics in 2009, her work was introduced by Internet activism organization *Vecam*,[11] whose members organized several colloquia and workshops about the future of Intellectual Property. In 2003, association member Hervé Le Crosnier set up a publishing house dedicated to digital culture and citizen governance—C&F Editions.[12] The publishing house played a great role in the dissemination of international works on free culture and the commons in France. In the context of Dadvsi and even more of Hadopi, the defense of sharing and creative commons formed a powerful counter-argumentative to address the stigma of "piracy" and cybercrime.

2.2 Reorganizing Digital Activism in France

In France, protests against copyright policies developed on an online platform managed by APRIL, an association of computer scientists promoting the use of free software. Launched in 2001 in opposition to the European directive on the harmonization of copyright, EUCD.info became the main coordination point for Internet users against the reinforcement of intellectual property. The website relayed information on parliamentary debates, developed counter-arguments, coordinated collective actions and hosted a discussion forum. In 2005, they also created a petition calling for the withdrawal of the Dadvsi bill that gathered 53,335 individual signatures and 930 collective signatures in two months. Behind this large participation, a handful of committed activists started to work more closely with MPs: Frédéric Couchet, president of APRIL, Christophe Espern, an employee of the Free Sofware Foundation in France, Jérémie Zimmerman, a young hacker and free software activist, and Gérald Dinet, free software activist. All were computer engineers with no previous political involvement.

The contest of copyright policies provided these digital activists with an opportunity to develop new political skills. Hence, Dadvsi and Hadopi debates led to a slow professionalization and politicization of Internet organizations in France. While hackers were sometimes characterized by their distant relationship with politics (Coleman, 2004), they entered with

[11] See full archives and timeline of the organization on its website: https://vecam.org/

[12] The publishing house translated in French the work of Fred Turner, David Bollier, Elinor Ostrom, Helen Nissenbaum.

these debates the political game and discovered its backstage. As holders of key technological expertise, they were able to advise MPs opposed to the law, "squatting their offices" between two sessions to fine-tune the most complex arguments and providing "technical vigilance" over the debates. They attended every debate, drawing up extensive reports for their online communities, registering the presence of lobbies or unofficial exchanges. These moments constituted a fast-paced and sometimes exhilarating political training for French hackers:

> I had an extraordinary moment with Christophe during Dadvsi! We were in a UMP [right-wing party] MP's office, explaining a technical trick to her. She understood very well. At one point she said, "OK, listen, I'm going to call Renaud". We looked at each other, a little, hum...amazed. Because she was indeed calling the minister, and she got him directly. And then we witnessed this scene where she was actually lecturing the minister about technical aspects of the law (laughs). And when she hesitated, we would put words in her mouth. We were hallucinating! [Interview 33, male, engineer, delegate of April, June 2016]

Accessing the backstage of political games offered a sense of proximity to the decision-making process for these activists. While the Internet was still an unidentified political object, they were able to play a central role in the political discussion and to make the claims of Internet communities heard and voiced in the national political arena. These very informal interactions with MPs, based on personal or ideological affinities, were further encouraged an uncertain political context and the blurring of traditional political reference points, as mentioned above.

Relations between hackers and politicians became more formal during the Hadopi debates, as the protest movement was now structured around a new organization, *La Quadrature du Net*. Dedicated entirely to the protection of rights and freedoms on the Internet, the new association had been created in 2008 by former APRIL members and hacktivists to consolidate the protest against the Internet policy program announced by President Sarkozy. Founding members included Jérémie Zimmerman, who became the association's first spokesperson, Christophe Espern and Laurent Chemla, a figure of the French hacker movement. They were joined by Philippe Aigrain, a computer scientist, who had directed several research programs at the European Commission, where he had distinguished himself as an ardent defender of free software policies. The latter was also part of the I3C network for a cooperative, creative and civic Internet in France. A graduate of the prestigious University of California at Berkeley, Philippe Aigrain played a major role in bridging the gap between French and international movements against the reinforcement of Intellectual Property rights. A strong advocate of the commons, he also published an essay for the defense of the "information commons", and a detailed plan for the implementation of a "creative contribution", a sort of global license fee for the remuneration of artists (Aigrain, 2012). His proposal was taken up by Socialist MPs during the Hadopi debate, showing the strong influence of the association on the political discussion. Besides, the *Quadrature du Net* fueled the repertoire of contention with new digital tools of coordination and intervention, such as websites monitoring the legislative process, online petitions, wikis for collaborative analysis and the writings of arguments (Breindl & Briatte, 2013).

The Hadopi debate favored the institutionalization of *La Quadrature du Net*, from a hacker collective to a legitimate organization, a sign of the gradual professionalization of digital activism in France. This process was underpinned by a diversification of both recruitment and modes of action. Between 2009 and 2013, new members coming outside of the hacker movement, such as young lawyers and political scientists, joined the team. With their experience of institutionalized lobbying, they brought in new ways of campaigning and advocating political leaders. The first non-computer scientist to be recruited was a doctoral student in political science, and initially responsible for "legal watch". He soon offered to take charge of communication and public relationships, in order to change the collective's image:

> Following them from a distance, I thought the group was a bit arcane. I couldn't figure out who was really behind the association. So, when I joined them, I gave them a little brief on how to present themselves on the website, how to organize communication, I looked at what Free Press or the EFF were doing in the United States, to create content on the website so that it would be more appealing, in terms of image, to try to define the institution, its main goal, etc. [Interview 15, male, activist and *La Quadrature* staff member, March 2016].

New recruitments thus prompted the metamorphosis of an "arcane" group of hackers into a more legitimate organization representing and defending Internet users. In 2013, *La Quadrature du net* became an official association under the French law of 1901, organized around a "Strategic Orientation Council" and a permanent team in charge of legislative monitoring, fundraising and campaign coordination. Besides, the new organization normalized its modes of intervention, moving away from the confidentiality or even border-legality of hacker practices. Of course, these transformations did not go without provoking tensions within the collective, notably coming from a first circle attached to the centrality of technology into activism. Yet these evolutions also strengthened *La Quadrature*'s reputation in the French and international social movements. The association notably forged lasting alliance with French civil rights associations such as the *Ligue des droits de l'Homme* and the *Syndicat de la Magistrature*, and with transnational organizations such as the Electronic Frontier Foundation and Amnesty International. Now well-identified by political institutions, *La Quadrature du net* nonetheless continued to pursue a contest policy, notably after Hadopi, as the new *Parti Socialiste* government turned away from activists' proposals that had fueled the parliamentary debate and the argumentation of its MPs.

3 Copyright Policies Seen from the State

At the end of the 1990s, "internet policies" referred to a series of scattered initiatives at the Ministry of Culture and Communication in France: it confused the impetus for technological equipment of the administration, the digitization of cultural heritage, the democratization of access, as well as the adaptation of copyright to the new technological environment. These different aspects were managed, sometimes jointly, by a few pioneering administrators, who criticized the lack of resources at their disposal to tackle these new issues. The Ministry was indeed initially ill-prepared for the upheavals caused by the Internet to the creative sector: the administration lacked trained staff with specific expertise to understand the impact of digital transformation and to define solutions for the creative industries.

The unpreparedness of the administration contrasted with the growing importance of Internet-related issues at the Ministry, and in particular the protection of intellectual property online. Following the WIPO treaty of 1996, the adaptation of copyright policy to the new digital environment was a major concern of the administration. The preparation and implementation of the Dadvsi and Hadopi laws kept the Ministry's departments busy for over ten years. In the end, it contributed to the integration of digital issues into cultural policy and established the French Ministry of Culture's predominance in this area, contrary to other countries.

This section studies the mechanisms through which Internet became part of sectoral administrative routines at the Culture Department: by selecting experts, stabilizing bureaucratic language to discuss internet-related issues, and linking new systems to existing ones, the ministry's agents *translated* the digital issues they were confronted with to ensure that they fitted the prerogatives and instruments of their departments. Here, we delve on the work of Pierre Lascoumes, that showed that "translation" has become a key process in policymaking: "*To become governable, to give rise to political choices, complex issues need to be reformulated as problems for public action. This presupposes, on the one hand, the production of a certain type of knowledge about them and, on the other, the accomplishment of a particular process of mobilization and legitimization of the envisioned public action*" (Lascoumes, 1996, p. 334). Applied to Internet policy, this process contributed to the gradual dilution of the Internet into bureaucratic routines and management.

3.1 Expertise Development

Following the adoption of the 2001 European Directive on copyright, the Ministry of Culture had to prepare the legislative transposition of intellectual property protection measures. The task was entrusted to the ministerial *cabinet*, and to the small Intellectual Property Office in the administration. Created in 1985 and staffed by a handful of legal experts only, the department was quickly overwhelmed by the breadth of debates sparked by the Dadvsi and Hadopi laws. The "surreal lack of resources" and the absence of consolidated expertise are systematically recalled by interviewees: "At the time—and I have to say it's less serious now, but at the time we were really struggling in this policy domain, hence the multiplication of external missions, if you like - it's because the Ministry didn't have the human resources enough" [Interview 17, male, digital advisor to the government, March 2016].

To address the difficulties encountered by the administration, the Ministry launched several expert missions to discuss new rules for the digital distribution of creative works and the public funding of creation. First, expertise was sought outside the ministry department, from legal scholars specialized in IP law. Among them, Professor Pierre Sirinelli from University Panthéon-Sorbonne, wrote no less than three reports between

1994 and 2012 to adapt the literary and artistic property code to the digital environment. He was also heard during the preparation of the Dadvsi law, and became a member of the short-lived public authority for the regulation of DRMs, the *Autorité de regulation des mesures techniques* (ARMT).

Representatives of the cultural sector and creative industries also contributed to put new measures on the ministry's agenda. Their direct involvement in cultural policymaking has long been demonstrated by French political sociology (Dubois, 2013; Surel, 1997). In the field of copyright policy, they framed online piracy as a public issue that threatened the whole ecosystem of creation in France. Copyrights management companies notably played a central role in defining problems and solutions, such as the powerful SACD (copyrights management for the movie industry), headed since 2004 by Patrick Rogard, and the SACEM (copyrights management for music industry), whose president in 2012 was Jean-Noël Tronc, Jospin's former advisor on information and communication technologies. During the Dadvsi and Hadopi debates, these companies orchestrated the mobilization of artists through the publication of tribunes and petitions in favor of anti-piracy legislations. Advocacy on this issue was also performed by leading figures of the creative industries: in 2007, Denis Olivennes, then Chairman of *FNAC*,[13] published a pamphlet against the "culture of freebies" that was allegedly developing on the Internet (Olivennes, 2007). He was then entrusted by President Sarkozy with a commission on copyright policy, laying the ground for the Hadopi law. Following in his footsteps, Patrick Zelnic (Chairman of Virgin France and founder of the Naïve Records label), Marc Tessier (General Manager at Canal+, then Chairman of *France Télévision* between 1999 and 2005), and Pierre Lescure (Chairman and CEO of Canal+ from 1994 to 2002) were commissioned to lead the negotiation of a digital cultural policy reform. Often with a background in senior civil service, these business leaders were close to the political elite and helped translate sectoral demands into policy proposals, playing a central role in defining policy mesures to fight piracy.

Yet, to limit the influence of private interests, expertise on digital issues was gradually captured by the administration. The internalization and

[13] FNAC is a French multinational retail chain specializing in the sale of creative works and consumer electronics.

translation of sectoral proposals followed two main paths: firstly, high-rank civil servants navigated from external expertise missions to offices of the executive government; secondly, new expert bodies were created in the periphery of the ministry department, to collect and accumulate technical resources on digital issues.

Regarding the first path, expertise missions enrolled young civil servants as rapporteurs who later joined the minister's cabinet or the Culture department. Thus, they participated in the implementation of political recommendations they had themselves expressed by "holding the pen" of the expert committee. For example, Jean-Baptiste Gourdin was rapporteur for the mission on "Music, creation and diversity" in 2010, then coordinator of the Lescure mission in 2012, before becoming chief of staff to the media regulatory authority's chairman, Olivier Schrameck in 2013, and then, deputy director of media and cultural industries at the Ministry of Culture in 2015. Olivier Henrard, rapporteur for a mission on private copying levy in 2006, became legal advisor to the Minister of Culture Christine Albanel in 2007, and then head of the National Center for Cinema (CNC). These high-ranking civil servants played a significant role in bridging the gap between legal scholars, technical experts and the Culture department, between the sectorial claims for innovative solutions and policymaking within the administration.

Secondly, the Ministry created new institutions to tackle the issues of copyright protection in the digital environment. The principle of a dedicated organization, depending from the Ministry of Culture was advocated by several senior civil servant as early as the 1990s, and more specifically mentioned in the public report on "France's soft power in the information society", submitted by *Parti socialiste* Deputy Patrick Bloche to Prime Minister Lionel Jospin in 1999. The Higher Council of Literary and Artistic Property (CSPLA) was created by decree in 2000. At first, the objective and spirit of the CSPLA resembled that of the Internet Rights Forum (see Chapter 4): to encourage discussions and coordination between key Internet and cultural players under the auspices of the State. The CSPLA was thus one of the first places where open licenses and the expansion of private copying exception on the Internet were discussed. Yet the CSPLA followed an institutional trajectory quite different from the Internet Rights Forum. First, contrary to the cross-sectoral ambition of the Forum, the CSPLA was firmly embedded in the cultural field. The number of representatives of the creative industries and artists quickly outweighed that of Internet users and Digital companies. According to one of its former members, the institution "gradually disconnected from the public" [Interview 43, September 2016] and became a powerful relay for sectoral interests. Furthermore, far from being an independent "administrative start-up", or even a competitor to the ministry department, as the Internet Forum had been at some point, the CSPLA remained closely linked to the cultural administration. The minister sets the work program and appoints the president and vice president of the CSPLA. By decree, the director of cabinet, the secretary general and several directors of the ministry are official members of the CSPLA, and since its inception, successive presidents have been appointed after a long career in the field of cultural public administrations. The most recent president is Olivier Japiot, whose career displays a movement from digital to cultural policies: in charge of technology and state reform at the beginning of his career, he then became a key player in defending the Dadvsi law (supra). He took over the CSPLA in 2018 and was renewed in 2021.

Beyond the creation of the CSPLA, the prominence of digital issues in cultural policy prompted a profound restructuring of the ministerial organization. After the Dadvsi and Hadopi debates, the reorganization of the ministry was justified by the revealed challenges posed by the Internet to cultural policy. This transformation of the administration was notably pushed by Olivier Henrard, policy advisor at the Ministry of Culture and the Presidency between 2008 and 2012. In an article written for the *Cahiers de l'administration et de la fonction publique*, he blamed "the inadequacy of organizational structures and skills [at the ministry] to address the challenge of the century: the massive dissemination and reproduction of creative works on digital networks".[14] According to him, intellectual and artistic property law was poised to become a strategic instrument for cultural action in the information economy. Hence, the digital revolution presented as much a challenge as an opportunity to reaffirm the role of the cultural administration vis-à-vis other ministries. He argued for a shift of the ministry's center toward creative industries, which he believed could strengthen the position of the department within the French government. Such an argument, which was very common among high-ranking cultural officials, was supposed to continue the

[14] Article retrieved and translated from https://www.linkedin.com/pulse/vers-un-ministre%C3%A8re-des-industries-culturellesolivier-henrard/.

strong position enjoyed by the cultural Ministry in France, with a vast administration, wide prerogatives and substantial means of intervention, compared to other European Countries (Dubois, 2013).

As a significant consequence of these bureaucratic mobilizations, a new division was created within the Ministry: in 2009, the Directorate for Media Development, formerly attached to the Prime Minister's office, was merged into a new General Directorate at the Ministry of Culture, dedicated to media and cultural industries, the DGMIC. Responsible for the development of creative industries at large, the DGMIC was more specifically endowed with expertise in the evolution of digital technologies. Agents of this new department also had to support the digital transition of creative industries, especially those whose position had been weakened by the development the web.

The ministry's reorganization marked the formal integration of digital issues into the organizational map of the executive government, not so much as a new policy domain, but as a set of policies to defend existing industries in the digital environment. This reorganization was also part of a more global reform of cultural policy that underpinned a new way of conceiving key elements of the national culture and linking them to the emerging digital economy, as shown by Philip Schlesinger in the UK (Schlesinger, 2019). It ultimately signaled the increasing hybridization of economic and cultural issues in the framing and implementation of IP laws and content regulation.

3.2 *Law Against Code*

During the ten years of heated copyright policy debates in France, high-ranking civil servants of the administration tried to assert their expertise against technological concerns and demands from digital activists. In particular, members of the *Conseil d'État* defended the primacy of legal code, over technological "code" (Lessig, 2006), in drafting digital policies. As a tradition of French ministerial offices, the appointment of members of the *Conseil d'État* (CE) as legal advisors is indeed presented as a bureaucratic rule to ensure the smooth proceedings of lawmaking at the government. In doing so, members of the CE assert an exclusive expertise in the "art of drafting legislation effectively", as notified by sociologist Bruno Latour in its study of the institution and its members (Latour, 2010).

In contrast to digital activists who lamented the lack of technological literacy on behalf of the state elite, members of the *Conseil d'État* were prompt to blame the improper legal interpretations made by activists during the Dadvsi and Hadopi debates. Olivier Henrard, legal advisor to Minister Christine Albanel during the Hadopi parliamentary debate, underlined the importance of technocratic expertise in the face of digital knowledge. As a legal advisor, he played a central role in drafting the Hadopi law and monitoring its passage through the French Assembly. In interview, he criticized the then "obsession" of politicians and activists with technology as a ruling force on the Internet: against the idea that "code is law", he considered that law is a code rarely understood by those who discussed it. He even estimated that the direction taken by the debate resulted from a general lack of legal competence on behalf of activists and politicians alike, criticizing a member of Parliament "who was a lawyer just as much as I was a ballet dancer", or the intervention in the debates of "gum lawyers, self-proclaimed specialists in pseudo-digital law":

> When you're drafting a bill, especially in this field where people, and I'm not just talking about politicians, but also cultural players and activists, where they have quite weak expertise, legally speaking (...), that is to say, people don't know how to draft bills and decrees, so they develop what I call a paranoid reading of legal texts, which consists of saying, 'yes, but what if, when you write this, someone enforces it in such a way'. And indeed, if there was a crazy judge, crazy cops, and a crazy administration, indeed they could apply the text that way. But in normal life, we don't apply texts in a crazy manner. (...) And you can't write the law while thinking of all the crazy ways the rule could be diverted from its initial goal, you can't state 'here is the rule and we should not apply it in such or such or such way'. This is simply not how you write the law. You fix the rule, not how it should be applied. [Interview 17, member of the Conseil d'Etat, Legal and digital advisor to the government (2008-2012), March 2016]

Olivier Henrard did not dismiss the political stakes of the text, but for him, the drafting of a bill was above all a matter for legal specialists, which should be left to members of the *Conseil d'État* as experts of lawmaking. In interview, he disqualified the criticisms leveled at the Hadopi Law by digital activists, considered as "paranoid readings" disrupting a highly qualified and codified exercise. For him, the effectiveness of the law had nothing to do with technical feasibility. On the subject of the Constitutional Council's censure, Olivier Henrard even got carried away:

> Honestly, the draft passed through the General Assembly of the *Conseil d'Etat*, where you have pretty much the best legal experts in France on administrative issues. I'll tell you more, President Bruno Genevois, whom you may have heard of if you've ever studied law, well, he's one of the high priests of civil liberties, he was the government commissioner for the Gisti Ruling in 1978! He really is one of most liberal representatives of the *Conseil d'Etat* regarding civil rights. These are truly incredible people, not only great lawyers but also great defenders of the institution as a safeguard of civil liberties. So, when President Genevois, who is a member of the General Assembly, was presented with the graduated response system, you know what he said? He said, "But I don't understand. These people have committed an offence, why are we warning them before punishing them?" The basic reaction of people who had nothing to do with political considerations was thus to wonder why we were warning them before punishing them! That's the extent to which there was no serious lawyer that could have been against the whole system!" [Interview 17]

In this excerpt of the interview, Olivier Henrard attempts to play down the Constitutional Council's censure, and more generally the vision of the "graduated response" as a repressive measure. He recalls members of the CE's astonishment at the precautions taken by the Hadopi. The reference to the 1978 Gisti ruling—a progressive decision regarding immigrants' rights in France—underlines their attachment to the protection of citizens' rights, sometimes even against the government. These references are intended to demonstrate the neutrality and progressivism of the *Conseil d'État*, an institution whose role in his eyes is to guarantee the rule of law and civil liberties. As a consequence, for him, the ruling against the Hadopi law by the *Conseil Constitutionnel*, which censured the graduated response system on the grounds of "protecting freedom of communication and expression", was merely an opportunistic political strategy to reassert the power of the institution in shaping social debates. Two visions of constitutional and legal authority, specific to France, were indeed opposed during the Hadopi debate. The *Conseil d'État* gathers top-ranking students that graduated from the National School of Administration, independent from political appointment. They play a key advisory role reviewing all draft legislations proposed by the government *prior* to being introduced before Parliament. On the contrary the *Conseil*

Constitutionnel gathers a handful of political members, appointed by governement, most of them former politicians (President, Prime Ministers of Heads of one of the two Assembly). They rule over the constitutional conformity of a legislation *after* it has been adopted by the Parliament.

In fact, both institutions claimed neutrality during the Hadopi debate. Legal expertise was instrumentalized in the internal struggles of the bureaucratic field. Yet, what is particularly interesting, is that legal expertise was also used as a weapon to distance the "stupefaction" effect provoked by the "digital revolution". Therefore, Olivier Henrard, among other members of the bureaucratic elite, blamed the State of "excessive reverence" provoked by the Internet at the time, a state where we "imagine that the most elementary opinions, even before talking about law and common sense, no longer apply in the digital sphere" [Interview 17]. While the novelty of Internet-related issues had given momentarily considerable weight to Internet activists and digital experts, the Hadopi debate marked a turning point from which senior civil servants rehabilitated their role and expertise in policymaking. It paved the way for Internet regulation to be taken back into the hands of the government staff and the bureaucratic elite, as we would witness in the 2010 decade. It also exhibited specific features of copyright policy debates in France, where, contrary to the US, the alliances between digital activists and prominent legal figures outside the government proved weaker, and the recognition of legal expertise remained favorable to the assertion of bureaucratic hold on Internet policymaking.

3.3 Taming Criticisms: Digital Activists at the Ministry of Culture

As a final dimension of bureaucratic integration of digital issues, the contribution of activists to cultural policies was gradually reduced and "domesticated" within administrative departments. Of course, the Hadopi debate did not eliminate all dissent and experimentation within the Ministry of Culture. Against the fallacy of a homogeneous department institution, some room must be made in the analysis for digital activists who joined the Minister during and after Hadopi, and tried to defend principles and causes inspired by the Internet communities from within the cultural administration. Following the trajectory and endeavors of these cause-bearers, this last section identifies the mechanisms through which the administration took on and reframed proposals coming from the digital world.

After the dead-ends of the Dadvsi and Hadopi laws, a reform of copyright policies was called for by several ministerial agents [Interviews 34, 43, 52]. All the more so as the reorganization of 2010 and the political changeover of 2012 brought new individuals within the cultural administration. Among them, Camille Domange, a young lawyer previously in charge of policy advocacy at Creative Commons France, became head of a new department dedicated to digital programs within the Ministry in 2012. In this capacity, he was entrusted with a report on "opening up and sharing cultural data", submitted to the Minister in December 2013. The report advocated a "digital (r)evolution in the cultural sector", introduced the idea of "hackability" for cultural institutions and opened up the possibility of "crowdfunding" as a legitimate form of public funding.[15] This vocabulary was until then quite unheard of in cultural expert missions and displayed a genuine attempt at mixing digital culture with cultural policy goals. At the same time, Juliette Mant, former political staff member to socialist MPs who took an active part in the Hadopi battle, became rapporteur for a new committee on reforming digital cultural policies.[16] She joined the ministerial cabinet as digital advisor in May 2013. Together with Camille Domange and other advisors and agents, Juliette Mant developed a "digital team" within the ministry, seeking to subvert traditional hierarchies and institutional ties with the industry in favor of a strong collaboration with digital associations. Together they launched a "Digital Autumn" festival in October 2013, conceived as a series of events dedicated to online creative practices, with a "dataculture hackathon" and a mashup workshop organized in partnership with free culture organizations such as Wikimédia France and the Open Knowledge Foundation.

Yet these proposals and the discourses underpinning them often felt out of place in the Ministry of Culture, and were sometimes criticized by other advisors, who, more in line with the position of O. Henrard described earlier, would rather close the Hadopi chapter and defend

[15] Public report available online at https://www.vie-publique.fr/rapport/33777-ouverture-et-partage-des-donnees-publiques-culturelles-pour-une-revol.

[16] The Comitee was led by Pierre Lescure, former leader of French channel Canal Plus. The mission was entitled "Acte 2 de l'exception Culturelle" (Acte II of Cultural Exceptionalism". It consisted of a large consultation of creative and digital players and several policy recommendations gathered in a public report handed to the President and the cultural Minister in May 2013. https://www.vie-publique.fr/rapport/33151-mission-acte-ii-de-lexception-culturelle-contribution-aux-politiq.

the protection of national creative industries. Therefore, as a way of circumventing the weight of this sectoral bureaucracy, the "digital team" sought to "cross-sectoralize" Internet policies by working with other departments and non-ministerial institutions, forging links with digital advisors of other ministerial cabinets—such as Education or Research—or members of open data services of public administration. By doing that, their strategy echoed the efforts of previous "evangelists"—the members of this "digital team" also spontaneously used this term in interviews—in order to develop a broader vision of digital policies, attentive to the Internet culture and specificities. In continuation with the claims made by activists during the Hadopi battle, they offered for example to introduce the legal protection of the online "public domain" and creative commons, or study the possibility of introducing collective licensing for the public funding of creation, a concept that would have totally transformed the action of the anti-piracy regulatory authority, the Hadopi.

But their efforts came up against bureaucratic hierarchies and installed routines at the Ministry. During the 2010's decade, pro-digital agents were gradually relegated at the margins of the institutions, while core technocrats confirmed their hold over digital policymaking. In a few months, the recognition of the online public domain and the development of public collective licensing was abandoned in favor of new anti-piracy mechanisms targeting technical intermediaries, such as advertisement companies or search engine. In the main time, the influence of industry representative was reinforced in the context of the upcoming arrival of new OTT US players in the sector, such as Netflix, who launched its service in France in September 2014 (Bellon, 2016). While memories of the tensions raised by Hadopi remained vivid within the ministry, the government chose to strengthen his support of creative industries, at the cost of giving up measures inspired by digital activism. For policy advisers that remained linked to Internet communities, the political costs of deviating from the sectoral doctrine became too high, especially in a difficult context for the cultural department, marked by strong budget restriction and increased pressure from the industries [Interview 67, female, digital advisor at the Ministry of Culture (2013–2014), April 2014]. From then on, the ministers' digital agents redirected their actions toward other issues, such as online media training, education and open data. And the regulation of Internet from the French cultural administration became strongly oriented toward the protection of national creative industries against the expanding market power of platfoms and content aggregators.

* * *

The example of copyright at the French Ministry of Culture illustrates the gradual bureaucratization of digital policies and a tendency toward the reaffirmation of the State's prerogatives to organize economic sectors in various silos. Admittedly, the digital revolution has created uncertainties and contributed to shifting the usual political boundaries: but administrative structures also resisted and framed new digital issues according to their own logics. Notably, sector-based intervention remained the norm, with the gradual integration of Internet-related issues within pre-existing ministry department. In many policy domains like culture, the sectoral elite has continued to defend objectives, clienteles and ways of seeing that remained partly unchanged with the digital revolution. The bureaucratic politics thus contributed to the "sectorization" of digital policymaking, which refers to the division of digital issues along traditional categories of public action. While Internet policy was first conceived as a global project for the reinvention of State intervention at the end of the 1990s, the following decades saw greater sectoral divisions of digital policies. In the cultural domain, we have observed a digitization of cultural policies, a process through which sector-specific digital issues are incorporated without subverting ministerial divisions and administrative hierarchies. The example of the Ministry of Culture can be generalized to other sectors of public intervention. In other ministry departments, the digitization of public policies has displayed similar features: a shift from external commissions to sector-specific expertise, the creation of dedicated bodies within the public administration, the mobilization of sectoral elites around specific issues. This was the case for example with the digitization of security policies at the Ministry of Interior: despite the many debates raised by the development of online surveillance, the ministry has extended its stronghold on the Internet, pursuing traditional policy goals such as the fight against terrorism and organized crime. While, in the opinion of many agents of the ministry, the Interior department was largely unprepared at the end of the 1990s, the administration has gradually developed new capacity for action: sector-specific expertise has been produced (a proliferation of reports and the development of a "doctrine" for cybersecurity), sector-specific institutions were created (*Office central de lutte contre la criminalité liée aux technologies de l'information* in 2000, Prefect in charge of fighting cyberthreats in 2014) and new systems and processes have been developed to surveil communications and report dangerous activities online.

The bureaucratization of digital policies leaves institutional entrepreneurs of large-encompassing Internet policies in a paradoxical position: on the one hand, digital technologies have become pervasive and Internet-related issues more salient, but, on the other, the cause and principles they defended have been relegated to the background of State action. In the next chapter, we will therefore study how digital activism within the State has shifted, seeking out gaps and opportunities in technocratic and political games that are far from definitely closed.

References

Aigrain, P. (2012). *Sharing: Culture and the economy in the internet age* (p. 244). Amsterdam University Press.

Allison, G. T., & Halperin, M. H. (1972). Bureaucratic politics: A paradigm and some policy implications. *World Politics, 24*(S1), 40–79.

Barthe, Y. (2003). Le recours au politique ou la problématisation politique 'par défaut'. *La politisation, Paris, Belin*, 475–492.

Bellon, A. (2016). La politique de concurrence au secours de l'exception culturelle: L'arrivée de Netflix en France depuis le ministère de la Culture. *Gouvernement & action publique, 4*, 119–140.

Benkler, Y. (2006). *The wealth of networks: How social production transforms markets and freedom*. Yale University Press.

Benkler, Y., Roberts, H., Faris, R., Solow-Niederman, A., & Etling, B. (2015). Social mobilization and the networked public sphere: Mapping the SOPA-PIPA debate. *Political Communication, 32*(4), 594–624.

Breindl, Y., & Briatte, F. (2013). Digital protest skills and online activism against copyright reform in France and the European Union. *Policy & Internet, 5*(1), 27–55.

Coleman, G. (2004). The political agnosticism of free and open source software and the inadvertent politics of contrast. *Anthropological Quarterly, 77*(3), 507–519.

Dubois, V. (1999). *La politique culturelle. Genèse d'une catégorie d'intervention publique*, Belin.

Dubois, V. (2013). Cultural policy regimes in Western Europe. *International Encyclopedia of the Social & Behavioral Sciences, 2nd edition.*, xx.

Fredriksson, M. (2015). The pirate party and the politics of communication. *International Journal of Communication, 9*, 909–924.

Latour, B. (2010). *The making of law: An ethnography of the Conseil d'Etat*. Polity.
Lessig, L. (2001). *The future of ideas: The fate of the commons in a connected world*. Random House.
Lessig, L. (2004). *Free culture: How big media uses technology and the law to lock down culture and control creativity*. Penguin Press.
Lessig, L. (2006). *Code* and *other laws* of *cyberspace*, Version 2.0. Basic Books.
Lessig, L. (2008). *Remix: Making art and commerce thrive in the hybrid economy*. Bloomsbury Academic.
Li, M. (2009). The pirate party and the pirate bay: How the pirate bay influences Sweden and international copyright relations. *Pace Int'l l. Rev., 21*, 281.
McAdam, D., Tarrow, S., & Tilly, C. (2001). *Dynamics of contention*. Cambridge University Press.
Menn, J. (2003). *All the rave: The rise and fall of Shawn Fanning's Napster*. Crown Business.
Olivennes, D. (2007). *La gratuité, c'est le, vol*. Grasset.
Ostrom, E. (1990). *Governing the commons: The evolution of institutions for collective action*. Cambridge University Press.
Peters, B. G. (2018, 7th Edition). *The politics of bureaucracy: An introduction to comparative public administration*. Routledge.
Schlesinger, P. (2019). The creative economy: Invention of a global orthodoxy. In *The Structural Change of Knowledge and the Future of the Social Sciences* (pp. 73–90). Routledge.
Sell, S. K. (2003). *Private power, public law: The globalization of intellectual property rights* (Vol. 88). Cambridge University Press.
Surel, Y. (1997). L'État et le livre: les politiques publiques du livre en France (1957–1993).

CHAPTER 7

Toward a Digital Mainstreaming

> There were two main ideas (...): that digital transformation was both a cultural and a technical transformation, and that the State's IT, in addition to a technological project, had to carry an organizational and managerial project and to promote cross-ministerial issues such as openness, transparency, consultation, contribution.
> Henri Verdier, Head of French Digital department, interviewed by *Acteurs Publics* magazine in November 2018.

In 2012, 85% of French households had access to the Internet, and 65% of individuals went online every day.[1] The Internet had become an integral part of French people's daily lives, and in many respects, the "digital revolution "seemed behind. With the dissemination of digital technologies throughout society, the Internet was no longer this confidential US network that had aroused suspicion among senior civil servants. The French administration itself was well on the way to digitization. All ministries had their own website, and citizens could access a wide range of online services: in 2012, a report by the Ministry of Economy and

[1] Eurostat, data compiled by the French National Institute of Statistics (INSEE).

A. Bellon, *A Socio-History of Internet Policies*, International Series on Public Policy, https://doi.org/10.1007/978-3-031-69099-0_7

the Prime Minister's office announced that 76% of administrative procedures had been dematerialized.[2] Within the State, Internet-related issues had been refracted into multiple sectoral policies: copyright protection at the Ministry of Culture, the fight against cybercrime at the Ministry of Interior, education in technologies at the Ministry of Education, etc.—no ministry had been spared from the digital transformation of its activities. But these digital policies seemed a far cry from the first revolutionary attempts to disrupt State intervention promoted by the pioneers. In many aspects, the State was still tiptoeing its way in cyberspace, leaving bigger-than-ever web companies in charge of norms and control of online activities. In 2012, digital policies failed to fully meet the challenges posed by the Internet to State intervention: contested by digital activists, they came up against the rapid transformation of technologies and the commercial hegemony of the Big Techs speci. At a time of global digitization of society, can we really speak of a complete institutionalization of government intervention on the Internet? What remains of the cross-cutting causes championed by the Internet administrative pioneers? And what challenges remained in regulating transnational markets under the hegemony of a handful of firms?

To address these shortcomings, some, like Henri Verdier at the head of a new cross-ministerial digital department created in 2015, thus continued to advocate a forthcoming revolution within the administration. Like him, many public servants are still encouraging the State's adaptation to the latest digital innovation and are calling for the endorsement of Internet principles in the conduct of public intervention. "Openness, transparency, consultation, contribution": more than ever, digital causes have become vague, consensual and yet still brandished by the bureaucratic entrepreneurs of a new digital age. The renewal of institutional entrepreneurship did not completely change the discourse of Internet pioneers, nor the obstacle they faced within the administration. Despite the ubiquity of digital issues and their media prominence, Internet policies remain for most of them a "second-rank policy".[3]

This paradoxical situation—the omnipresence of digital technology in the State combined with the marginality of some core principles of

[2] *France Numérique 2012–2020: bilan et perspective*, Public report handed over to the French Prime Minister, November 2011, available online: https://www.vie-publique.fr/sites/default/files/rapport/pdf/114000700.pdf.

[3] Interview 35, man, digital expert, June 20, 2016.

the Internet culture—invites us to reconsider the institutionalization of Internet as an object of government intervention in the light of concurrent changes in the bureaucratic and digital fields. In the second decade of the 2000s, the institutional enterprise of Internet policymakers is being transformed, and we observe a new ideal–typical step in the development of digital policies. This evolution of online public action is interwoven with the administrative history of State reform and the technical and social transformation of the Internet and the Web. On the one hand, during the Sarkozy presidency, under pressure from the EU (Hammerschmid et al., 2007), the modernization of the State has undergone an unprecedented politicization in France, affecting all sectors of public intervention. It has further increased the structural reform of administrative departments, as well as the centralization of decision-making processes around "strategic" poles such as the Prime Minister's and Presidents' offices, and the Ministry of Economy (Bezes & Le Lidec, 2016). On the other hand, the web economy has also reconfigured itself around the platform model (Helmond, 2015; Poell et al., 2019; Zittrain, 2008): the digital world is increasingly organized around a handful of major economic players, mostly from the United States, the so-called Big Techs or "GAFAM"—Google, Apple, Facebook, Amazon and Microsoft. Transformations within the bureaucratic and economic fields have impacted the stakes and the configurations of players involved in Internet policymaking, cracking former alliances between digital activists and companies, forging new cooperation between political and business actors. Policymakers no longer have so much to invent and legitimize a new field of intervention, as to bring coherence to dispersed digital policies, ensuring the State's capacity for action in the face of the new tech giants while extending the defense of increasingly fractured Internet activist's "causes".

The challenges faced by Internet policymakers are reminiscent of that faced by feminists or environmentalists in extending their activist perspective to various public policies. Studies on gender mainstreaming strategies (e.g. Caglar, 2013; Walby, 2005), for example, have highlighted the difficulties of dealing with other administrative departments and maintaining the coherence of feminist concepts underpinning various policies (Bruno et al., 2006). These works analyze what the spread of gender equality imperatives within public administrations does to the causes and institutions that defend them: they demonstrate that the standardization of policy objectives paradoxically reduces the role of those who promoted them in the first place (Jacquot, 2010). In the same vein, this chapter examines the forms and effects of a *digital mainstreaming*, defined as the global strategy of reinventing Internet policies underpinning the extension of digital issues to all areas of public action. It aims at capturing the many tensions and dilemmas that come with the spread of digital tools and digital perspectives within State bureaucracies. The chapter also draws on the pioneering study of national accounting tools diffusion by François Fourquet (1980): analyzing how these systems had been gradually "acclimatized" and "transplanted" into the administration, Fourquet dissected a process of "banalization" through which disruptive instruments lose their revolutionary features as they become new standards of policymaking.

This chapter analyzes the recent development of digital policies within the State and its relation to Internet politics and activists' causes. It looks at the places and agents that continue to support the latter, seeking in this way to pursue the revolutionary enterprise of Internet pioneers within the State, while the Internet Culture itself is increasingly under the influence of the Big tech companies that pretend to embody it. The marginal position of these agents in the government and administrative departments sheds light on the low degree of autonomy of Internet policymaking, caught up in a complex network of decision-making institutions (1). While these weaknesses somehow reactivate anti-bureaucratic discourses among Internet policymakers, they should not mask the profound reconfiguration of this institutional enterprise in transformed bureaucratic and political fields: as the digital revolution has left a strong mark on administrative practices and political discourses, Internet policymakers are left with the difficult task of ensuring the coherence of increasingly diverse strands of public intervention on the Internet, while defending their specific features as the vanguard of public policy and a model for State reinvention (2).

1 A Policy Defined by Its Shortcomings

Twenty years after the Hourtin speech and the emergence of the first Internet policies in France, despite the unprecedented spread of technologies in the administration and the importance of Internet-related issues in all policy domains, agents responsible for digital policies remain defensive and affected by the perception of their marginality within the government:

> Despite everything, it's still the digital guys against the rest of the world. [At the Prime Minister's office], I was absolutely alone. Well, I had some very good friends, very sympathetic, but for all that, if I hadn't had Axelle Lemaire and her cabinet [Secretary of State for Digital Affairs], I'd have been completely in a bind. I was all alone all day, talking about digital issues with people who, it's not that they didn't believe in it, but they didn't hold those values. If there had been a protocol at Matignon, out of 42 policy advisors, I would have been the 42nd. I had no legitimacy, I didn't have direct access to the Prime Minister". [Interview 62, man, Digital Advisor for the Prime Minister (2014–2017), December 1st, 2017]

Far from having always ensured the upward mobility of Internet policymakers, the development of digital issues has paradoxically contributed to the decline of their administrative importance. As seen in the previous chapter, in many sectorial departments, digital issues have been taken over by senior civil servants, reclaiming bureaucratic expertise on traditional domains of public intervention. The institutional weakness of Internet-specific policymaking must be understood in the light of the power relationship that binds the agents in charge of it to other policymakers, as well as to the various social groups with whom they interact. As regards traditional resources associated with the institutionalization of a new field of public intervention (Burstein, 1991; Dubois, 2008), Internet-related policies are rather defined by shortcomings: no ministry department, no specific professional body, and limited to no cooperation with sectoral players.

1.1 A Policy Without a Ministry

The sociogenesis of public policies has demonstrated the symbolic weight of having a specific government entity in the institutionalization of a new policy domain (Bereni & Revillard, 2018; Burstein, 1991; Lascoumes, 1994; Urfalino, 1997). The creation of a full ministry department makes it possible to unify skills and resources around a well-defined administrative territory. It fosters the accumulation of institutional memory, in the absence of which policies are constantly "reinvented" by those successively in charge of them. Last but not least, it provides key resources in the governmental decision-making process.

Yet, since their emergence at the end of the 1990s, Internet policies in France have never been grouped together within a specific administrative entity. Attached at times to the Prime Minister or the Ministry of

Economy, or Research, and increasingly split between different sectoral departments, digital issues have been partially handled since 2008 by a secondary governmental body, a deputy ministry. As interviewees recall, this kind of relegation has had important consequences for the making of Internet policies. It entails a smaller share of the global budget devoted to Internet-specific policies and contributes to the lesser consideration given to Internet-related issues in the government decision-making process. Besides, in France, deputy ministries are only invited to the weekly governmental meetings when a subject on the agenda directly concerns them; nor are they invited to the heads of office meetings that gather directors and vice-directors of the main ministries every Monday. Practically, it means that they cannot always defend their point of view against other ministries and often lose in cross-ministerial arbitrages.

Moreover, Internet decision-makers have been placed under the authority of their supervisory ministry, and over the last decades, conflicts have been frequent between the Ministry of Economy and the Deputy Ministry of Digital Affairs. During the 2012–2014 period, antagonistic visions opposed the two departments, as the director of cabinet from the Deputy Ministry of Digital Affairs recalled, explaining the "fundamental issues" pitting his team against the Ministry of Economy:

> Arnaud Montebourg's [*Ministry of Economy*] vision of digital technology was essentially defensive. Basically, for him, digital technology was a danger, it was destroying jobs and it was the ugly Americans, the neo-colonization of our industry, and so on. His main concern was digital sovereignty. While we were defending a completely different vision, advocating that digital technology was an opportunity, that we had to develop it, that we needed to become more digitally-savvy, otherwise France would always lag behind. But on the very morning of the [governmental] seminar [dedicated to digital technology], Arnaud Montebourg preempted the whole thing by giving an interview to *20 Minutes*, making the entire article a claim against the neo-colonization of net giants. A total counter-signal. That gives you an idea of the type of conflicts that existed within the government on this subject. [Interview 60, Director of Cabinet of the Deputy Ministry of Digital Affairs (2012–2014), October 2nd, 2017]

The blatant differences in vision and problematization became part of competing strategies, contributing to the "blurring" of political signals regarding Internet-related issues. They remained even during the 2014–2017 period, with a new Ministry of Economy far more favorable to digital companies. Indeed, when Emmanuel Macron was appointed "Minister for Industry, the Economy and the Digital Economy", he tried to monopolize digital issues to the detriment of the new Deputy Ministry. While the latter was preparing a law for a Digital Republic, defending new rights for Internet users and a bold open data policy, Emmanuel Macron and his ministerial office presented a new legislative initiative in favor of the French Digital Economy:

> To tell you the whole the story, we had at the same time [Prime Minister] Valls saying that he accepted the law for a Digital Republic, and Macron demanding to present a second law on digital issues. And in July 2015, President Hollande declared that there would be indeed two different laws. So, at that point, [Macron] picked up on some of the things we'd done, like innovation measures and patent issues, and partially emptied out our first draft." [Interview 64, Director of Cabinet of the Deputy Ministry of Digital Affairs (2014–2017), October 8th, 2019]

As shown in the previous interview's extract, the growing prominence of Internet-related issues tended to exacerbate competition within the government. While some administrations succeeded in maintaining an exclusive prerogative on specific issues, as shown in Chapter 5 with online copyright protection at the Ministry of Culture, the deputy ministry in charge of Digital Affairs became less and less able to build an ambitious and coherent Internet policy. A similar phenomenon of sectoral capture can be observed, for example, for education-related digital issues. In 2015, the Ministry of Education announced its own "Digital Education Strategy" defined without any consultation with other ministries. "They kept the best announcements for themselves, and we had to pick up the scraps" deplored a former member of the Digital Affairs Cabinet [Interview 59, policy advisor at the cabinet of the Deputy Ministry for Digital Affairs (2012–2017), September 14, 2017].

Defending the Internet causes such as the "anti-filtering culture" or "the protection of civil rights and liberties on the Internet" became a renewed strategy for Internet policymakers to circumvent sectorial capture of other digital issues. Even if this position means to oppose other ministries in their pro-regulatory attempt at controlling the Internet. Digital advisors of the government were seeking to put forward "the Internet's point of view" against sectorial concerns in the making of digital policies. Prime Minister advisor George-Etienne Faure recounted how he systematically scanned all draft laws for "digital" content, to check that "they weren't talking nonsense" about the Internet. In doing so, he often came up against sectoral standards, administrative routines and objectives developed by other ministry departments. This was particularly the case with the 2015 Law on Security. The bill, introduced by the Ministry of Interior, authorized the development of algorithmic surveillance systems on the Internet.[4] This provision was contested by activists and institutions, both inside and outside government. They denounced the ineffectiveness of the measures and the lack of respect for Internet users' privacy. But when confronted with the three "big" ministries responsible for the project—Ministries of Interior, Justice and Defense—digital policy advisors felt unable to exercise a digital "vigilance" and to influence government negotiations: "We tried to establish personal links with the Interior cabinet, (...) we gave them examples that proved it wasn't working (...) but on this subject, without a solid ministerial department on our side, we didn't often win the arbitrations" [Interview 62, Digital Advisor to the Prime Minister (2014–2017), December 1st, 2017].

In an increasingly competitive governmental space, the lower rank of "digital" policymakers thus contributes to the relegation of Internet causes to the background. The Deputy Ministry for Digital affairs tends to lose out on a number of arbitration decisions to the Ministry of Culture, the Ministry of Interior and the Ministry of Economy. These challenges also testify to the lack of recognition of the technological expertise put forward by digital policy agents to defend their point of view in inter-ministerial discussions.

1.2 A Policy Without Professionals

The institutionalization of a new policy domain is often supported by the professionalization of agents in charge of it, as shown by Vincent Dubois in the case of culture (2015). The recognition of specific jurisdictions, the assertion of know-how and expertise, accompany the autonomization

[4] Article 2 of the *Loi relative au renseignement* authorizes the automatic processing of Internet individual data to detect possible terrorist threats. The implementation of these systems, referred as "black boxes", entails the systematic implementation of filtering algorithms by telecoms operators, which recalls which the systems developed in PRISM by the NSA.

of new areas of public intervention. However, the Internet, as a policy domain, failed to be exclusively claimed and recognized by a profession or a sole administrative "body"—a *grand corps* in French technocratic language—, nor did it lead to the labeling of a specific expertise in the bureaucratic field. The sociology of professions has extensively studied the emergence of new professional groups and the way in which they gain recognition: it can be used here to understand, conversely, the impossible construction of an autonomous field of action by the various entrepreneurs of Internet causes. In *Systems of Professions*, for example, Andrew Abbott (1988) invites us to analyze the foundations on which professional powers are exercised and to study competitive struggles between different groups of experts. He shows that the construction and stabilization of professional jurisdictions rely on the mastery of knowledge acquired, negotiated and defended in different arenas. Yet in the case of digital policies, their definition and implementation remain the subject of continuing struggles within the bureaucratic and political elite, whose members have antagonistic views regarding the aims and modalities of governement intervention on the Internet. On the one hand, we find institutional entrepreneurs within the State who see themselves as the "guardians" of Internet causes, and on the other, the agents of their bureaucratic normalization—state engineers and members of the *grand corps*—who claim greater responsibility over digital issues.

Whereas Telecoms engineers had been disqualified from supporting the Minitel against the Internet in the 1990s (see Chapter 3), the technical *grand corps* were gradually regaining a central role in the administration of technological innovations in France in the 2000s. This was partly due to the reform of the civil engineers' curriculum after the liberalization of Telecommunications. As shown by Julie Gervais (2010), from the 1990s onward, technical *grand corps* were merged in order to adapt and preserve the role of civil engineers in society. In the case of the former Telecom engineering body, the merger with Mining and Industry engineers came with a redefinition of their jurisdiction and expertise, now including managerial skills and economic knowledge, and encouraged them to regain control of technological policies. At the Directorate-General for Enterprise (DGE) in the Ministry of Economy, civil engineers still steer the development of the French network infrastructure. For example, they have monitored the "*France Très Haut Débit*" plan ("High-Speed Internet for France"), an investment program to guarantee broadband coverage for the entire country. Although it involved a colossal budget (over three and a half billion euros), the project was largely endorsed by the government, without giving rise to any difficulty. A digital advisor, who does not belong to any of the major technical bodies, recognized in an interview that the influence of top civil servants on this aspect of digital policy was no longer an issue: "the core of digital policies, which historically was Telecoms extended to town and country planning, and now encompasses the development of networks, is mainly driven by the DGE. It is run by people who feel they have the sole right to define and implement this type of policy". Largely depoliticized, the control of the network infrastructure has once again become the sole responsibility of technical directorates and their civil engineers' members in the Ministry of Industry and Economy.

Alongside the new figure of these "engineers-managers", other members of the major administrative bodies have also been increasingly involved in the definition of digital policies. As shown in the previous chapter, the *conseillers d'État* (state councilors) are claiming a central role in drafting digital laws, in the name of their legal expertise. They have first stabilized the principles of public action to protect copyright online and have ensured the continuity of public intervention, despite political changes. From the 2010s onward, the *Conseil d'État* published several reports on Internet regulation testifying to the institution's growing interest in the subject. In 2014, the annual study of the institution was dedicated to the "digital economy and fundamental rights". It aimed to define "new regulatory principles" to guide public action on the networks: the notions of "informational self-determination"[5] and "platform loyalty" marked the beginning of a pro-regulatory turn pushed by these top civil servants in France. In 2018, a new study was devoted to the theme of "Public power and digital platforms", confirming the Conseil's position in shaping a new regulatory framework to counter the hegemonic power of the Internet giants. In France, digital policies thus increasingly refer to a "technical magistracy", defined by Pierre Lascoumes as the "reconciliation of legal imperatives, technical possibilities, economic cost and political expediency" (1994, p. 153). The involvement of technical

[5] Defined as "the right of an individual to decide and control the uses made of personal data concerning him or her". *Le numérique et les droits fondamentaux*, Étude annuelle du Conseil d'État, September 9, 2014, p. 26. https://www.vie-publique.fr/sites/default/files/rapport/pdf/144000541.pdf

and generalist *grand corps* in the policy process thus contributed to the standardization and bureaucratization of Internet policies.

At the same time, however, the stranglehold of senior bureaucrats is lamented by digital activists within the State, who present themselves as defenders of Internet causes and Internet users' rights. They denounce the weight and inertia of digital policies that have become "too bureaucratic" and reaffirm their distrust toward an administrative elite "who knows nothing about technology". In an interview [60], the head of cabinet of the Deputy Ministry for Digital Affairs criticized a "techno-push"[6] vision, which he saw as characteristic of State engineers:

> – We had the *Comité numérique de filière*, an old institution run by a venerable gentleman, more of a telecom guy. He promoted the classic state-led industry stimulus. They also created a structure, the Digital Observatory, with another venerable gentleman, a former member of SOPRA-STERIA [an information system consulting company]. So, in terms of ecosystem, we had telecoms and IT companies, and it was an absolute catastrophe.
> – Why is that?
> – If you like, they were the wrong people for what we wanted digital policies to be.

The extract contrasts two conceptions of digital policies, one inspired by old industrial public intervention, driven by two "venerable" members of the administrative elite, the other disruptive, targeting new economic players. As many other digital policymakers, the interviewee disqualifies the former in the name of the necessary modernization of public policies. In another interview [59], a digital advisor for the Deputy Minister also regretted the narrow conception of digital policy promoted by the administrative elite, which reduces Internet issues to the sole support of major IT and Telecoms companies. He related how, when the new Deputy ministry took office in 2014, the Industry directorate of the Ministry presented its plans for digital policies, compiled in a vast "ministerial portfolio" that bore witness to "typical ministerial allegiances and administrative inertia": "Their vision was to support national champions: you create the companies, then you create the markets. Our approach was

[6] In business jargon, the "technology push" strategy consists of imposing a new technology on markets from above, by creating the conditions for its production, marketing and adoption by consumers. It is the opposite of bottom-up innovation or "market pull".

completely different: we defended the decentralized aspect of the digital ecosystem, at the heart of the Internet."

Most of all, digital advisors criticized the lack of technical expertise at the top of the administration. The same interviewee considered for example that state councilors tended to ignore technological constraints when drafting legislation, which could lead to inapplicable or ineffective laws: "There is still a deep-rooted culture among some magistrates of saying 'we write the law, the application follows'. But once you've said that, technical mastery remains important, otherwise you're writing the wrong stuff" [Interview 59, policy advisor at the cabinet of the Deputy Ministry for Digital Affairs (2012–2017), September 14, 2017].

In cross-ministerial discussions, technical arguments fail to stand up to the authority of legal expertise and those who embody it. It reflects the lack of recognition of IT as a valuable expertise in the field of power. Whereas a public report of 2000 recommended that "the reform of the competitive entrance examination [for the National School of Administration – the ENA] should introduce a test on the applicant's knowledge in information and communication technologies",[7] this recommendation was never implemented. Teaching how the Internet and computers work never really found a place in the training of future senior civil servants. A study of the past papers for the ENA competitive entrance examination (2003–2017) even reveals that digital questions were completely absent from the subjects on which the future administrative elites had to demonstrate their ability. Given the growing importance of economics and the fact that public law continued to play a key role in the recruitment of the administrative elite (Biland & Vanneuville, 2012), knowledge in IT never became a strategic field of expertise for applicants. The elite's low level of technological acculturation is matched by that of political leaders, most of whom were still very unfamiliar with IT and the digital world at the end of the 2010s. The digital advisor to the Prime Minister provided a striking example of this state of affairs: "I spent three years working for Prime ministers who did not have a computer on their desk. And it's not even because they had a laptop at home. They are people who still work on paper... Even though Valls and Cazeneuve weren't old politicians, when they had a question, when they wondered about something, they turned to the people on their right shoulder. I tend to google my question, and

[7] *L'État et les technologies de l'information et de la communication*, Public Report to the Prime Minister, Commissariat Général du Plan, December 2000, p. 83.

so do you. But, they asked their right shoulder. So inevitably, you have a disconnection with ordinary Internet users." [Interview 62, man, Digital Advisor for the Prime Minister (2014–2017), December 1st, 2017].

One realizes how much digital practices distinguish political leaders in a negative way: it is the weakness rather than the intensity of their use of IT that characterized successive Prime ministers, in the eyes of the advisor. This borderline example, as revealing as it is exceptional, reflects a certain disqualification of IT know-how in the hierarchy of government. The lack of recognition of digital advisors echoes the difficulty they have in converting practical skills—such as computer programming, data science, website design and the use of open-source software—into a "science of government" (Ihl et al., 2003), deemed essential to Internet policymaking.

In the end, these various extracts pointed to the same logic: digital advisors tried to demonstrate in interviews their marginal position within the State, as a reflection of their objective distance (in terms of trajectory) or subjective distance (in terms of points of view) from the bureaucratic elite. This result mirrors the position of government members in charge of digital issues, whose youth, gender, ethnicity and career path also make them marginal figures in government (Box 1). In interviews, digital advisors highlighted attributes that distinguished their careers from the bureaucratic *cursus honorum*: "professional experience in a start-up" [Interview 64, Director of Cabinet of the Deputy Ministry of Digital Affairs (2014–2017)], a background as a "systems engineer" [Interview 62, man, Digital Advisor for the Prime Minister (2014–2017)] or as a "simple digital communicant" [Interview 63, Digital Advisor to the President (2010–2012)]. The marginality perceived or even claimed by these digital activists is also due to the lack of validation of their expertise and specific organizational resources in the bureaucratic field, especially facing senior civil servants from the instituted *grand corps*. Conversely, they present themselves as the "guardians" of the digital revolution within the bureaucracy, and claim an unprecedented proximity to Internet communities and their "causes".

Box 1 Gendered Politics and the Sidelining of Internet Policies

From 2009 onwards, one can notice a surprising feminization of digital policy in France, which contrasts with the presence of men among the "net evangelists" and "net entrepreneurs". Between 2009 and 2017, the government's digital portfolio was successively entrusted to three women at the French government, Nathalie Kosciusko-Morizet, Fleur Pellerin and Axelle Lemaire, who share, beyond their gender, a number of common characteristics. They were relatively young when they took office—36, 39 and 39 y.o. respectively—whereas the average age of ministers is 52. Their political careers were short-termed and displayed what political scientist Mariette Sineau (2001) called a "feminization from above", to describe situations where the nomination of a woman is considered as a *fait du prince* and women thus tend to derive their political legitimacy from a political mentor. One must add that Fleur Pellerin was one of the very few non White members of the government at the time.

The political and media treatment of women in charge of digital policy reveals the stigmatizing effects of the feminization of the political government of the Internet. For example, on January 28, 2015, *Le Canard Enchaîné* reported an altercation between Prime Minister Manuel Valls and Secretary of State for Digital Affairs Axelle Lemaire during a government seminar. The latter reportedly intervened to underline the importance of digital issues but she was answered by Manuel Valls: "You're a nice girl, but we'll talk about the Internet another time; today, we're preparing an action plan for education and urban policy. We have well understood the Internet problem, but we're not here today to debate it". Le *Canard enchaîné* then reported that the Secretary of State "burst into tears", forcing the Prime Minister to soothe her: "People are going to say I'm too harsh, but we all love you, Axelle!" This story was picked up by numerous online publications in France, which ran headlines on the Secretary of State's "tears" as infallible signs of her femininity and "youth" – Axelle Lemaire was, after all, 40 years old! This gendered framing, contributed to the disqualification of both the minister's action and the issue she was defending. It makes passion and emotion the driving force behind the political action of these stateswomen, instead of political conviction or reflection. Unfortunately, it seems to be a recurring mode of dealing with women's political action, especially on digital issues. Between 2012 and 2014, for example, the "rivalry" between Fleur Pellerin (Ministry of Digital Economy) and Aurélie Filippetti (Ministry for Culture and Creative Industries) pushed gender stereotypes to the limit in French the press. This treatment was reminiscent of that adopted to describe the conflicts between Christine Albanel, then Minister of Culture, and Nathalie Kosciusko-Morizet (Secretary of Digital Affairs), at the time of the Hadopi law. The media framing tended to hide the differences regarding conception of digital policies behind a mere question of "jealousy".

1.3 A Policy Without a Public

In recent years, public policy analysis has seen a revival of interest in the concept of policy "publics", as a link between the greatly disconnected domains of policy and politics (Goodin et al., 2006). The "public" or "audience" refers both to targeted social groups and to those who participate in the production of public action, an electoral body that is mobilized as a political support for new policies (Borraz & Guiraudon, 2010). From this perspective, the construction of a new policy domain relies on the enrollment of specific political categories that could contribute to policy changes and their legitimatization. At the end of the 1990s, the emergence of Internet policies had relied on a heterogeneous coalition of actors participating in the development of the French Internet: activists, scientists, experts and digital entrepreneurs. Although the defense of the Internet had brought together these different social groups, the ecosystem they formed was still divided by numerous fault lines (see Chapter 3). The alliances that presided over its formation have gradually crumbled over the first decades of the twenty-first century. New divisions have notably emerged between entrepreneurial and activist figures, who were once put together under the all-encompassing category of "Internet pioneers". While the former turned out to be entrepreneurs like any others, defending their interests in increasingly competitive markets, the latter endeavored to fight both the State and the major digital multinationals, as two sides of a technocratic wave breaking over the Internet revolution.

What is more, a particular feature of the French administration, at least before Macron's presidency, was its relative distance from big tech companies. Whereas revolving doors between the administrative elite and the private sector are commonplace in France, they mostly concern large French companies, notably those with State shareholdings (Dudouet & Grémont, 2007). The director of cabinet of the Deputy Minister for Digital Affairs in 2012 recounted that "*in the portfolio established by the Industry directorate of the Ministry for the digital, we only found Alcatel, Bull, Orange (…) big groups that are used to talking to Bercy anyway*", with frequent circulation between the Ministry and IT national champions. The distance between Big Tech and the French administration is also due to the very structure of digital markets, dominated by a few large multinationals, mainly from the US. With the advent of the "Net giants", France's IT champions no longer truly constitute the heart of the digital economy, which presents Internet policymakers with the challenge of renewing and organizing the dialogue with these new players.

Regarding the now quite long history of the Internet, the advent of these multinational firms is relatively recent. The Facebook social network was only founded in 2004, the year Google went public. As for X (ex-Twitter) and Airbnb, they only appeared two years later, in 2006. At that time, the future giants of the net were still largely unknown to French politicians, and exchanges between the administration and these companies were limited to rare meetings about specific issues.[8] Until 2011, there were only four Google representatives in France,[9] and no Facebook office in the country. The relationship between the French government and these multinationals had to be established from scratch.

Building a dialogue with big tech companies became the work of the government's digital advisors in the 2010s. Nicolas Princen, President Sarkozy's digital advisor, recalled a laborious enterprise, based on regular exchanges with Google France team [Interview 63, Digital Advisor to the President (2010–2012), February 7, 2018]. At the time, the group's French executives were seeking to "open the doors of government" to the company, so that they could meet with heads of department and political advisors. Meanwhile, the digital advisor to the Presidency sought to champion the importance of digital issues in a presidential cabinet that took little interest in them. The strategies of Google France's executives and the digital advisor converged around the same objective: the political valuation of the web economy. Google France thus commissioned a study on the weight of the digital economy from McKinsey, which concluded that "in 2010, the Internet sector accounted for over 3% of French GDP and 1.15 million jobs".[10] The study was then used by the digital advisor to defend the political importance of digital issues in the presidential cabinet: "It was important to be able to say, 'My portfolio is worth 60 billion euros a year'. People take you seriously". For Google's French executives, the report was an opportunity to demonstrate the weight of the

[8] For example, there was a few meetings in the 200S between the French Minister of Culture and Google's local representatives to discuss the company's agreements with publishers to digitize their book heritage.

[9] The first Google office ever opened in Europe was established in Hamburg, Germany in 2001, the second one in Dublin in 2003.

[10] McKinsey&Company, *Impact d'internet sur l'économie française. Comment l'internet transforme notre pays*. Public Report, Paris, La documentation française, 2011.

French market in Europe and to promote French expertise to the group's US management. Informally dubbed "*Google France and the Élysée, in the same boat against the world*" by Nicolas Princen, the joint strategy proved successful. A first meeting between Larry Page and President Sarkozy was organized in May 2010 followed by an "e-G8" in May 2011, in Deauville, France. After the setbacks of the Hadopi law, the forum was supposed to mark the reconciliation between the government and the Internet world. It featured major figures of the global Internet economy, such as Eric Schmidt (Google), Sheryl Sandberg and Mark Zuckerberg (Facebook) or John Perry Barlow (EFF), for whom it was the first official visit in France. Behind a consensus on the economic potential of the web, largely orchestrated and staged by digital advisors, many tensions yet surfaced between technologists and policymakers on the prospect of future regulations. Whereas Sarkozy pushed for further government control of the Internet to protect minors and the creative industries, Zuckerberg and others spoke out during the event against tight regulatory control of the Internet, considered contrary to the "spirit of the web". The e-G8 also brought to light the distance between the pro-regulatory approach of the French government and the deregulatory push promoted by the Web economy (Fig. 1).

The links between French political actors and US Tech giants thus remained "weak ties" in the 2010s, marked by principled divisions. Digital advisors had to pass through the French office of these large companies to reach the distant decision-making centers, in London, Bruxelles, or California. In order to influence the orientation of digital policies, the net Giants were indeed mostly involved in EU arenas, as acknowledged by digital policymakers: "The important matters are decided in Brussels. The French and the European teams are not the same, it's not the same level. Only when they came to the cabinet with someone from Brussels, or even better, someone from the headquarters, we knew that we had finally raised something" [Interview 59, policy advisor at the cabinet of the Deputy Ministry for Digital Affairs (2012–2017), September 14, 2017].

In the 2010s, French digital policymakers still struggled to meet "the players who mattered" and to involve web multinationals in shaping digital markets and Internet regulation. This was notably the case in 2014, when Netflix opened its service in France: while French companies—access providers, TV channels and film distributors—were consulted to work out a common strategy to prevent disruptions in the audiovisual sector, there was only one meeting between French politicians and the

Fig. 1 Dialogue between Maurice Lévy (CEO of Publicis[11]) and Mark Zuckerberg at the close of e-G8

headquarters of Netflix. This inability to establish a high-level dialogue with major gatekeepers weakened the strategy of the Ministry of Culture (Bellon, 2016) to negotiate with Netlix and impose strong obligations on video-on-demand players. From 2010 onward, the French teams of some major groups—notably Google and Facebook—have been reinforced, but their members reckoned that the strategic decision-making still happened in the US: "When there's an important decision to be made, it always happens in Mountain View" conceded a member of the "institutional relations and public affairs" department at Google France [Interview 38, July 22, 2017].

At the same time, the rapprochement (albeit limited) between digital advisors and Net multinationals contributed to widening the gap between digital policy entrepreneurs and activists. While the former claimed to

[11] Publicis is a French multinational and the world's third largest advertising and communications group.

champion major Internet causes such as net neutrality and privacy protection, they were increasingly struggling to win the support of Internet user collectives. This estrangement also revealed changes in strategy on the side of French Internet activists, which were resolutely anchored in a protest positioning. In 2016, *La Quadrature du Net* announced in a press release the end of discussions with the government, following an internal debate within the association: "Faced with a wall, you have to know how to do something other than bang your head against it. After years of legal violence, defeats and rollbacks of fundamental freedoms, faced with a political representation whose only logic is security, the *Quadrature du Net* refuses to waste any more time trying to rationally influence those who won't listen, and chooses to reorient its actions".[12] This break-up followed several of digital activists' "defeats", regarding first the recognition of non-commercial sharing and the legal protection of the public domain (see previous chapter), then relative to the Surveillance Act of 2015, that introduced black box algorithms at ISP to detect terrorist content. Perceived as a severe setback for online freedoms, these legal initiatives during the Hollande Presidency left *La Quadrature*'s members with the feeling that it was increasingly difficult to make their voices heard by decision-makers, and even a sense of "betrayal" that followed on from alliances with socialist representatives during the Hadopi debate in 2009. Internet activists gradually turned to other public arenas, notably law courts and regulatory authorities, to express their views.

To speak of a "policy without a public" is not so much to say that there is no audience concerned by digital policies, but rather that it is difficult for decision-makers to rally representatives of the Internet, to organize the networking of various interest groups and to legitimize their action in front of the public. Digital issues are not politically constructed, as if they did not represent any "electoral pool": "in a political program, it just has zero value, it doesn't seem to speak to the French public at all, so no one is interested in promoting them" [Interview 60, Director of Cabinet of the Deputy Ministry of Digital Affairs (2012–2014), October 2nd, 2017]. Despite the growing weight of digital technology in the economy, the marginal position of Internet policymakers partly results from the weakness of their ties with economic players of the sector, as

[12] Press release, May 17, 2016, « La Quadrature du Net leaves the Emergency State» [our translation] https://www.laquadrature.net/2016/05/17/quadrature_du_net_hors_etat_urgence/

much as from their distance to digital activists, considered "too demanding", and "impossible to satisfy" [Interview 62, man, Digital Advisor for the Prime Minister (2014–2017), December 1st, 2017]. Ultimately, the situation reflects a double difficulty in constructing the category of the "digital world" in the face of the digitization of all sectors of activity, as well as in regulating Internet markets in the face of their growing internationalization and the weight of major US companies.

2 Promoting Digital Policies After 2010: Repetition or Reinvention?

Despite the relatively marginal position of digital institutions and digital agents in the government, as described in the previous section, State intervention on the Internet is no less real, multi-faceted, omnipresent and objectifiable through speeches, programs and legislations. Facing competition from sectorial departments, limited means of action and a weak institutional position, entrepreneurs of digital policies use every means at their disposal to "extend their policy area" (Interview 59, policy advisor at the cabinet of the Deputy Ministry for Digital Affairs (2012–2017), September 2017), that is to say to increase their scope of intervention. Using the metaphor of a policy domain "under permanent construction", they describe the development of digital policies as a succession of moves to advance their specific concerns: "We are obliged to push several things separately, to work on opportunities, to bring one thing after another to the fore, and then if we see that it's taking, hop, we combine a few other issues. We move forward like that" (Interview 62, man, Digital Advisor for the Prime Minister (2014–2017), December 1st, 2017).

The making of Internet policies is the result of small conquests, of investment of spaces neglected by other administrations, of sudden politicization of causes, the fruit of repeated negotiations—in short, an incessant tinkering with bureaucratic rules in search for new opportunities. While this approach is reminiscent of the net evangelists of the 1990s, it also bears witness to the reconfiguration of the State's digital intervention in the twenty-first century. Internet policies are now embedded in new bureaucratic and political constraints: some are specific to this field of intervention, such as the cross-sectorial approach, the weight of technological constraints or the weakness of dedicated institutions... Others apply to all public policies: competition from transnational actors and organizations, the process of "Europeanization" (Saurugger & Raedelli,

2008), the pressure of budgetary discipline (Blyth, 2013; Siné, 2006) and the displacement of partisan agendas and political cleavages (Ford & Jennings, 2020). The renewed strategies of digital policymakers are part of a more global transformation of public action, of which they see themselves as the leading edge. Borrowing from the "revolutionary" rhetoric of Internet policies' first promoters, they are also reinventing institutional strategies and they are renewing the political significance of what "digital" policies refer to, in a bureaucratic space that has been transformed. More than ever, they rely on regulatory agencies and use the model of successful web platforms to make digital technologies a cross-sectorial instrument rather than a specific domain of public action.

2.1 *The Agencification of Internet Policies*

While the absence of a ministry dedicated to the Internet appears to be a factor of marginalization within the State, it also testifies to a more general shift in the exercise of public intervention from administrative departments to state "agencies", sanctioning new forms of action based on incentive, regulation or consultation (Christensen & Lægreid, 2006; Pollitt et al., 2001; Sześciło, 2022). New agencies have been consolidated over the last twenty years, and their prerogatives with regard to digital issues have been greatly extended.

The development of Internet policies initially gave rise to institutions on the fringes of the bureaucratic field. Inspired by the global governance of the Internet, these organizations, such as the Internet Forum in France, embodied the principles of multistakeholderism and distributed decision-making. But most of these institutions were short-lived, bearing witness to the hesitations and setbacks inherent in the first Internet policies. Others, such as the Hadopi and the CSPLA, which were contested at the beginning, proved more resilient, at the cost of becoming more firmly embedded in the bureaucratic field (see previous chapter). In 2008, a National Digital Council (*Conseil National du numérique* or *CNNum*) was also created to organize the representation of Internet interests at the government. Highly "business-oriented" at its inception, it took a more activist turn in 2013, with the entry of Internet pioneers and representatives of associations who relayed the causes of a civil and open Internet to the government.

Through their activities of expertise, consultation and recommendation, these agencies provide administrative support for the government regarding digital issues. During the drafting of the Digital Republic Act, for example, the Deputy Ministry for Digital affaires relied on the CNNum to organize a large consultation with public and private players: they drew up a list of proposals for the government and, above all, involved Internet users in the revision of the law draft, via a dedicated platform offering an unprecedented form of online participation[13] (Bellon, 2021). In contrast to a Deputy Ministry constrained by bureaucratic rules and governmental hierarchies, the autonomy enjoyed by agencies' members created a competition between the two institutions:

> You know, a minister needs to exist. If the president of the CNNum starts doing all the shows, if he saturates the public sphere, he kills the department for Digital Affairs. If we want a strong agency, that means we no longer need a Minister for the Digital Sector. Some people think that's what we need to do. Today, there are a certain number of people who think that we no longer need a Minister for the Digital Sector. It's not necessarily my point of view, but it's an idea that's circulating. The idea behind is that digital issues now live their own life in sectorial administrative arenas... And indeed, if we set up a strong agency that bang everyone over the head and scold everyone, it might be more effective than a minister who has no power. In any case, it's a real administrative question. [Interview 60, Director of Cabinet of the Deputy Ministry of Digital Affairs (2012–2014), October 2nd, 2017]

In the extract, institutional competition is measured through a media presence deemed more favorable to the charismatic President of the CNNum—at the time Benoît Thieulin, ex-evangelist of the 2000s. On the contrary, the Depuy Ministry's low governmental rank and limited means of intervention restricted her ability to speak out in the public sphere. Here, the digital advisor presented himself as an "architect" of government reform, questioning the most effective organization for steering digital policies: in his view, the increased sectorization of intervention on the Internet could make way for an autonomous super-agency that would hold the capacity for critical control over various digital policy domains. However, for many other government members, the CNNum was not the best candidate for the role. Composed of academics, experts

[13] *République-numérique.fr* was a platform to edit the law, open to the public between September 26 and October 18. In three weeks, it received 8,500 contributions from 21,000 participants.

and representatives of digital interest groups, the agency certainly enjoyed greater proximity to digital organizations, it could more easily resort to professional expertise and rely on associative relays for Internet causes. Yet the distance of its members from the centers of political decision-making contributed to the disqualification of the institution within the government. This illegitimacy was expressed by the PM's digital advisor: "The CNNum is, excuse me, but it's a bit like academics seen by the private sector. They're a bit crazy, they're not wrong, they're idea-makers and all, but they are not operational" [Interview 62, December 1st, 2017].

Contrary to the CNNum, more formal regulatory authorities gradually regained institutional legitimacy and new prerogatives in controlling digital activities and markets in France. First, the Telecommunications Regulation Authority (*ARCEP* for *Autorité de régulation des communications et des postes*) oversaw the smooth operation of networks in the market of former telecoms operators that have become Internet service providers. Since the European regulation (2015/2120) on open Internet access and the French Digital Republic Act (2016), the ARCEP has also monitored compliance with net neutrality principles. Regarding the protection of privacy online, the French data protection authority, the *Commission national Informatique et Libertés* (CNIL), created in 1978, was given the power to impose sanctions on companies that failed to respect the protection of personal data, following the revision of the French Data Protection Act in 2004. This latter prerogative has even been greatly strengthened with the adoption of the GDPR (2016) at European Union level. Finally, the French regulator for audiovisual content, the Superior Audiovisual Council *(Conseil supérieur de l'audiovisuel—CSA),* though long removed from any responsibility for web publications, has gained new responsibility for combating information manipulation and online hate. In 2022, after the adoption of a bill relating to audiovisual communication and cultural sovereignty in the digital age, the CSA merged with the HADOPI to form the Regulatory Authority for Audiovisual and Digital Communication (*ARCOM*).

The role played by these agencies in the formulation and implementation of digital policies contributes to the ministry's weakness. This is all the truer given that the autonomy and means of intervention of regulatory authorities have been considerably strengthened in recent years. This evolution marks a strong shift in the socio-history of digital policies: public issues linked to the expansion of the network and the power of platforms—such as the protection of privacy or the fight against illegal content—are now escaping the purview of administrative departments in order to be handled by regulatory authorities. Long sidelined in favor of the unfettered development of digital markets, the power and scope of intervention of regulatory authorities have been steadily expanding in recent years. Composed of multiple authorities, the field of independent public regulation (Vauchez et al., 2019) is now the core center of a liberal governmentality that organizes fair competition and risk mitigation on digital markets. New tools of public intervention, forming a rapidly expanding regulatory arsenal, such as compliance obligation, risk assessments and standards definition, are being invented in this key locus of governmental power.

The consolidation of regulatory authorities has also offered attractive positions for digital policymakers and provided new spaces for advocacy, where renewed "evangelization" campaigns can be observed.

2.2 *Old and New Evangelists*

George-Etienne Faure, digital advisor for Prime Minister Manuel Valls, is a typical figure of the new digital policymakers of the twenty-first century. Aged 35 when he joined the PM office, he did not participate in the "revolutionary spirit" moment of the first Internet polices, at the end of the 1990s. He presents himself, however, as the heir and guarantor of this "revolutionary spirit". He testifies in interviews to the symbolic weight of the "Hourtin speech" (see Chapter 4), which he discovered in discussions with other advisors and Prime Minister Manuel Valls. Following in the footsteps of the pioneers, he continues to champion the Internet causes within the State—the fight against censorship, the protection of digital "commons" and the free flow of information—as do most of the digital policymakers we met during our survey. He even confided that he contributed to the funding of *La Quadrature du net*, as an ultimate sign of his attachment to Internet activism and digital civil rights. But far from the heroism of the first "evangelists", his discourse is marked by an inflection, even a routinization, of the digital transformation of State and society. As he emphasizes his "marginality"—as well as the marginality of other digital advisors within the government—one could believe that the socio-history of Internet policies in France is an eternal renewal. Like the pioneers of the 1990s, these new policymakers insist on their atypical backgrounds and the difficulties they face in gaining recognition from the rest of the administrative elite: "digital issues are something for young people in the corner, it's almost a something for the trainees" (Interview 63), "we were seen as weirdos, almost as punks" (Interview 60), "we're almost always outvoted in government discussions" (Interview 59), etc.

Yet in twenty years, the dynamics of the fields of power have changed. Firstly, the trajectories of some early evangelists bear witness to their upward mobility within the bureaucratic field and the central role they have come to play in the making of digital policies. For example, Isabelle Falque-Pierrotin, former head of the Internet Forum, became the head of the French Data Protection authority in 2011. Closer to the private sector, Benoît Thieulin, following his position as webmaster for the French Government Information Service, and after managing the digital campaign of Socialist candidate Ségolène Royal in the 2007 presidential election, founded a public communication agency, *La Netscouade*. In 2013, he was appointed Chairman of the CNNum, where he was joined by several Internet pioneers such as Valérie Peugeot (Vecam) and Daniel Kaplan (Fing) (see Chapter 3). Together, they put forward the defense of an open Internet, new policy instruments to favor digital inclusion, as well as the recognition of a public domain of information and the protection of digital commons.

Yet in the first decade of the 2000s, new figures emerged. Among them, Henri Verdier enjoyed a meteoric rise within the government. A web entrepreneur with close ties to the *Parti Socialiste*, he played an active role in Hollande's presidential campaign. With no previous experience in the administration, he was appointed director of *Etalab*, a public service for opening up administrative data, created in 2011. From this small service with fewer than ten agents, he became in 2015 director of the State's digital, information and communication systems, at the head of a large department that included *Etalab*, the Innovation pole of State Reform and IT services.[14] Henri Verdier defended a bold vision of the Government as a Platform, open to the multitude of connected citizens. Largely inspired by Tim O'reilly's "Government 2.0", he published a programmatic book in 2017 on the transformation of politics in the digital age: *L'Âge de la multitude. Entreprendre et gouvernement après la*

[14] After Macron's election in 2017, he was replaced by another net entrepreneur linked to the public sector Nadi Bou Hanna. Henri Verdier was appointed Digital Ambassador for the Ministry of Foreign Affairs, a position he still holds today.

révolution numérique[15] (Armand Colin). An eclectic synthesis of intellectual reflections on the digital revolution,[16] the book received considerable media and political attention in France. Explicitly quoted during interviews or appearing on interviewees' bookshelves, the field survey enabled us to measure its wide circulation in the political and governmental fields. While the book seems to follow in the footsteps of the 1990s net evangelists, using the digital revolution as an opportunity to change the State, the authors nevertheless call for a new model of reform that is no longer so much that of the "Internet" as that of the "platform". This model refers to the need for the government to rely more on collective intelligence, by creating "contributory commons" that can be appropriated by innovators inside and outside the public administration. The authors consistently used Facebook, Google, Amazon, Netflix and Apple as models for a new organization of the State:

> What would it mean to transpose such a model to the public sector? Let's imagine that 100 applications could provide taxpayers with various interfaces and innovative experiences for declaring their income and paying their taxes online. Let's imagine that another 100 applications could provide jobseekers with the possibility of reorganizing the offers proposed by the employment agency, according to the results of recommendation algorithms as powerful as those of Amazon or Netflix. That 100 applications could blend the resources of separate administrations to offer a single platform integrating several services (...). That these same services could be mixed with others that have nothing to do with administration (...). Let's imagine that all the services provided by the administration could be available in our Gmail account, on our Facebook page or on our Twitter feed. (pp. 238–239) [our translation]

As the model of "Government as a platform" spread over Europe,[17] references proliferated in political speeches as well as think tanks' reports and

[15] The Age of Multitude. Business and Government after the Digital Revolution.

[16] References to Silicon Valley essayists and digital entrepreneurs (Zuckerberg, Larry Page and Serge Brin, Pierre Bellanger, etc.) are juxtaposed with those of critical intellectuals (Toni Negri, Michael Hardt, Yann Moulier-Boutang) in a hybrid synthesis that seems typical of the general knowledge expected from top civil servants.

[17] The platform model and its ability to transform the processes by which public services are produced, and the value these services delivers to citizens, has gained a lot of attention in Administrative Science (e.g. Brown et al., 2017; Cordella & Paletti, 2013; Janssen & Estevez, 2013).

conferences where political, administrative and private players met. At the head of a new department for digital transformation between 2014 and 2017, Henri Verdier launched bold programs to implement this vision. For example, a series of "public start-ups" were created at *Etalab*. Based on public data, they associated young contractors outside the administration to develop new public services, such as a programming interface for tax calculation (openfisca), a platform for information on the various social benefits one could ask (mes-aides.gouv.fr) and a national register of cab availability (le.cab).[18]

Henri Verdier was emblematic of the reinvention of the digital policymaker as a start-up entrepreneur. The start-up was indeed quoted as an inspiration for institutional entrepreneurship, exemplifying both the need for innovative disruption within the State, as well as a positive appropriation of the limited resources allocated to digital projects. As "State start-uppers", digital policymakers considered that they have to innovate with small budgets in order to find their place in a competitive bureaucratic field. The PM's digital advisor explicitly and spontaneously endorsed the metaphor in an interview:

> The nicest compliment I've ever received, I mean outside the digital sphere, was from Véronique Bedague, the Prime Minister's director of cabinet. She called me up one day at a party and introduced me to the new environmental advisor, saying: "I want you to explain to him how you set up your own start-up". I didn't immediately understand, so she went on "Today, nobody disputes that the digital is a legitimate concern, everyone knows that you're a helper, that you work with everyone, that you're the one to talk to when we have a digital-related question". Knowing that the environment is more of an identified political issue than digital technology, I really took that as a compliment! [Interview 62, man, Digital Advisor for the Prime Minister (2014–2017), December 1st, 2017]

This concept of defending digital issues as you "set up a small business" entails a number of shifts in the approach to digital policymaking. Firstly, it is now part of a broader project to support innovative firms, identified as a potential target audience for digital intervention, halfway between

[18] For a detailed survey of platform-state administrations, see Marie Alauzen, *Plis et replis de l'État plateforme. Enquête sur la modernisation des services publics en France*. Thesis in sociology under the supervision of Fabian Muniesa, defended on October 18, 2019 at the École Nationale Supérieure des Mines.

impossible-to-please activists and "overly distant net giants": "With start-ups, we could find this historic, decentralized and innovative culture of the Internet. All this was very compatible with a fairly tough stance on the Tech Giants. It was a policy for the little guys against the big guys" [Interview 62, *Ibid*]. One could even hear in the discourse of digital advisors echoes in the distinction between these "small", "poorly identified" and "little listened-to" economic players, bearing the cardinal values of the Internet, and their own situation as bureaucratic entrepreneurs of digital policies. This echo plays with the ambivalence of "standing for" start-ups at the government: digital advisors meant that they defended the interests of these economic players, as well as embodied the "start-up" culture, by importing their visions and innovative methods into the administration.

For start-up policy also reflects new forms of public intervention, featuring policymakers with limited resources compared to the Ministry of Economy for example. In November 2013, members of the Deputy Ministry for Digital Affairs launched the "French Tech" program, a support system for French start-ups emblematic of a new way of doing economic policy. Indeed, "French Tech" relied almost solely on a "label" which the Deputy Ministry made available to companies or cities: it was a distributed policy, largely based on the initiative of local partners and economic players. The implementation relied simply on a series of events and international trips to promote the label in France and abroad. The models of Apple and Google directly inspired this strategy, where "brand-management" and "communication" were key elements to value the label. Criticizing traditional investment mechanisms as too cumbersome, too costly and not very effective, digital policymakers claimed the "lightness" and "flexibility" of this new policy instrument, "built with the economic players themselves" and developed by a small team of public agents. Because it circumvented long and tedious administrative processes, the "French Tech" initiative was presented by its agents as a "coup de force", a "radical innovation" directed against both "bureaucratic routine" and "political reluctance": "Nobody understood anything, we *bypassed*[19] all the institutional structures, we totally uberized them" [Interview 60, Director of Cabinet of the Deputy Ministry of Digital Affairs (2012–2014), October 2017].

[19] The interviewee used the English word.

Hence, digital policymakers tend to imitate digital entrepreneurs, bringing the imperative of "disruption" into the administrative field, using emblematic words ("bypass", "uberize") borrowed from the tech world in their discourse. As if digital policymaking were now a mere question of "disrupting" public action, overturning the way in which State's intervention had been conceived and modeled. As if the State should be considered not as a system of administrative departments, but more specifically as a tech enterprise business, inspired by the model of the platforms that have transformed the economy.

2.3 *The Digital Instrument*

State intervention on the Internet refers to a multiplicity of administrative institutions and initiatives, at the risk of blurring the category of "Internet policies". From open data to support for start-ups, from the fight against online hate to market governance and administrative modernization, Internet policies stand for a wide range of programs and modes of action. When asked about the delineation of these policies, agents offered this type of answer:

> – Digital is protean, it's everywhere. But, there is a global strategy. Everyone can see the direction in which we want to move. I mean, digital is exactly what I was telling you about the right-left divide for others: it structures us. Even Laure de la Raudière [a right-wing MP, expert on digital issues], if she were Secretary of State, she wouldn't be doing very differently from what we had been doing.
> – *But can you give me a formal indication of this direction? If everyone can see where you're going, is it more towards defending online rights? or transforming the economy?*
> – It's all of the above. And that's the problem. Digital doesn't have a heart.
>
> [Interview 62, man, Digital Advisor for the Prime Minister (2014–2017), December 1st,2017.]

The interviews indeed failed to provide a precise definition of what digital policies were or should be. Or rather, they defined digital policies by form rather than substance. The "absence of a heart" once again calls to mind the unique architecture of the Internet, the first major decentralized network, which fostered its global expansion and technical success.

In contrast to a definition in terms of objectives or content, digital policies would thus refer to a particular form of public intervention. Many of the agents we interviewed used this idea. For example, to explain the common ground between Internet policy at the Interior Ministry and at the Ministry of Economy, this advisor rather called for the digitization of security issues:

> For me, the real digital issue at the Ministry of Interior and Security is the transformation of the department through digital technologies. How they could develop a "Government as a Platform" approach, how they could use collaborative technologies, open source intelligence. We need to see digital policies in every sector as a transforming agent. [Interview 60, Director of Cabinet of the Deputy Ministry of Digital Affairs (2012-2014), October 2nd, 2017]

The advisor made an interesting shift in the interview: asked about the policies led by the Interior Ministry—notably the fight against online terrorism—and its link with other Internet-related issues, he reframed the question in other terms: how can digital technologies improve State action against terrorism? Suddenly, Internet policies appear less as a set of causes to be defended than as a vector for the general transformation of public policies, whatever the domain. The principle of "Government as a Platform" can become an umbrella for policies that may have opposing logics, scattered between different administrations.

Building coherence on digital action requires discursive strategies deployed in administrative reports, speeches and interviews that, while considerably blurring the perimeter of activities covered by the "digital" category, also promote its ubiquity. Behind the dispersal of Internet policies, the "digital strategy of the government" provides a common understanding of the multiple transformations of public action accomplished in its name. Such a vision of the digital is also promoted in the CNNum's 2016 report, which defines the digital "as the engine and instrument of the dynamics of change and modernization at work within public authorities" (p. 7)[20]. While the CNNum remains a forum for promoting the "causes" of the Internet within the State, shown for example in the institution's work on open data or encryption, it also

[20] https://cnnumerique.fr/files/uploads/2017/04/Rapport-dactivite-CNNum-2016.pdf.

fully participates in the standardization and trivialization of digital issues, around the principle of disruption. The "defense of the Internet" now rests less on the promotion of a technology with emancipatory potential than on the engineering of change that imports the models of digital entrepreneurship into public administration: the deployment of algorithms in public regulation, the opening up of public data for the public/private construction of new services, the establishment of platforms to encourage participation and legitimize public action, etc. The many references to the "culture of the Internet", that digital policymakers keep on embracing, subordinate the politics of "causes" to a politics of change, driven by the now conventional rhetoric of the necessary "distribution" of IT services, the "transparency" of political organizations, the online participation of citizens and the "free circulation" of information in and out of government. This discourse enables digital policymakers to assert their cross-sectorial role, opening up prospects for administrative reconversion in an increasingly competitive space for the production of public policies.

Above all, these discourses reveal an important shift in terms of understanding what the digital is and stands for in the administration, from a set of causes to defend to a new way of doing things and delivering public services. The digital has thus become a key "instrument" in the global reform of public policies and the neo-liberalization of governmentality (Lascoumes & Le Galès, 2007). The idea of "digital mainstreaming" should therefore be understood less as the dissemination of Internet causes within the State, than as their dilution into a program of digital transformation extended to all public policies. It makes it possible to circumvent the limitations of a weak domain of intervention, as shown earlier, by asserting "digital technology" as a powerful instrument of action, for all public policy domains.

* * *

From 2010 onward, the development of Internet policies in France has been characterized by a paradoxical institutionalization of the "digital" within the State. When we look at the institutions or the people in charge of these policies, we observe scattered entities with limited resources faced with large ministerial departments such as the Economy, the Interior or the Culture ministries, whose agents have successfully claimed control over specific areas of digital intervention, where Internet issues are subsumed under traditional policy goals. This state of affairs marks the defeat of the "revolutionary" enterprise of the 1990s: digital policymaking has remained distant from the core organizations of the government, specific expertise in IT has not been recognized and policymakers still struggle to mobilize economic players and activists from the Internet world. Developing new digital policies relies on opportunistic strategies: policymakers attempt to position themselves in areas that inter-ministerial competition has left vacant or to modify at the margins political projects defined by others.

However, this seeming defeat must be tempered with the incredible spread of digital instruments and platform models directly inspired by Internet communities, and the web economy in particular, within the State. The convergence of State reform and the Internet revolution has indeed become a permanent feature of the neoliberal transformation of governmentality, marked by a trivialization of the "revolutionary" rhetoric within the administration: the "platform State", the "administrative start-ups", the "uberization" of public action are the patterns through which State action is thought through. This development marks the victory of a technocratic reformism that is neoliberal (Mudge, 2008) rather than libertarian in its endorsement of the "digital revolution ". In 2017, the election of Emmanuel Macron as president of a French "Start-up Nation" also demonstrated political appropriation of this digital mainstreaming. The support of numerous public and private digital entrepreneurs for his candidacy marked the convergence of social, political and economic interests around a rhetoric of "disruptive change", weakening the administrative structure of social action. The model of the digital markets has now become a policy in itself, both as a political orientation and a global program for the neoliberal transformation of the government.

References

Abbott, A. (1988). *The system of professions: An essay on the division of expert labor*. University of Chicago Press.

Alauzen, M. (2019). *Plis et replis de l'État plateforme. Enquête sur la modernisation des services publics en France* (Doctoral dissertation). Université Paris sciences et lettres.

Bellon, A. (2016). La politique de concurrence au secours de l'exception culturelle: L'arrivée de Netflix en France depuis le ministère de la Culture. *Gouvernement & action publique*, (4), 119–140.

Bellon, A. (2021). L'élaboration de la loi république numérique au gouvernement: sociologie du travail politique des réformateurs numériques. *Réseaux, 1*, 23–53.

Bereni, L., & Revillard, A. (2018). Movement institutions: The bureaucratic sources of feminist protest. *Politics & Gender, 14*(3), 407–432.

Bezes, P., & Le Lidec, P. (2016). The politics of organization. The new divisions of labor in state bureaucracies. *Revue française de science politique, 66*(3), 407–433.

Biland, É., & Vanneuville, R. (2012). Government lawyers and the training of senior civil servants. Maintaining law at the heart of the French state. *International Journal of the Legal profession, 19*(1), 29–54.

Blyth, M. (2013). *Austerity: The history of a dangerous idea*. Oxford University Press.

Borraz, O., & Guiraudon, V. (2010). Les publics des politiques.in *Politiques publiques 2. Changer la société*, 11–27.

Brown, A., Fishenden, J., Thompson, M., & Venters, W. (2017). Appraising the impact and role of platform models and Government as a Platform (GaaP) in UK Government public service reform: Towards a Platform Assessment Framework (PAF). *Government Information Quarterly, 34*(2), 167–182.

Bruno, I., Jacquot, S., & Mandin, L. (2006). Europeanization through its instrumentation: Benchmarking, mainstreaming and the open method of co-ordination... toolbox or Pandora's box? *Journal of European Public Policy, 13*(4), 519–536.

Burstein, P. (1991). Policy domains: Organization, culture, and policy outcomes. *Annual Review of Sociology, 17*(1), 327–350.

Caglar, G. (2013). Gender mainstreaming. *Politics & Gender, 9*(3), 336–344.

Christensen, T., & Lægreid, P. (2006). Agencification and regulatory reforms. *Autonomy and regulation. Coping with agencies in the modern state*, 8–49.

Cordella, A., & Paletti, A. (2019). Government as a platform, orchestration, and public value creation: The Italian case. *Government Information Quarterly, 36*(4), 101409.

Dubois, V. (2008). Cultural policy in France-Genesis of a public policy category. *Centre for European Political Sociology (GSPE)*, 1–33.

Dubois, V. (2015). *Culture as a vocation: Sociology of career choices in cultural management*. Routledge.

Dudouet, F. X., & Grémont, E. (2007). Les grands patrons et l'Etat en France: 1981–2007. *Sociétés contemporaines, 04*, 105–131.

Ford, R., & Jennings, W. (2020a). The changing cleavage politics of Western Europe. *Annual Review of Political Science, 23*(1), 295–314.

Fourquet, F. (1980). *Les Comptes de la Puissance*. Éditions Recherches.

Gervais, J. (2010). Merging to survive? Institutional legitimacy and material considerations in the light of the reorganization of corps within the French civil service. *International Review of Administrative Sciences, 76*(3), 425–441.

Goodin, R. E., Rein, M., & Moran, M. (2006). The public and its policies. *The Oxford Handbook of Public Policy, 6*, 1.

Hammerschmid, G., Meyer, R. E., & Demmke, C. (2007). Public administration modernization: Common reform trends or different paths and national understandings in the EU countries. In *Cultural aspects of public management reform* (Vol. 16, pp. 145–169). Emerald Group Publishing Limited.

Helmond, A. (2015). The platformization of the web: Making web data platform ready. *Social Media+ Society, 1*(2), 2056305115603080.

Ihl, O., Kaluszynski, M., & Pollet, G. (2003). *Les sciences de gouvernement* (pp. 218-p). Economica.

Jacquot, S. (2010). The paradox of gender mainstreaming: Unanticipated effects of new modes of governance in the gender equality domain. *West European Politics, 33*(1), 118–135.

Janssen, M., & Estevez, E. (2013). Lean government and platform-based governance—Doing more with less. *Government Information Quarterly, 30*, S1–S8.

Lascoumes, P. (1994). *L'Éco-pouvoir: environnements et politiques*. Paris, La découverte.

Lascoumes, P., & Le Galès, P. (2007). Introduction: Understanding public policy through its instruments—From the nature of instruments to the sociology of public policy instrumentation. *Governance, 20*(1), 1–21.

Mudge, S. L. (2008). What is neo-liberalism? *Socio-Economic Review, 6*(4), 703–731.

Poell, T., Nieborg, D., & Van Dijck, J. (2019). Platformisation. *Internet Policy Review, 8*(4), 1–13.

Pollitt, C., Bathgate, K., Caulfield, J., Smullen, A., & Talbot, C. (2001). Agency fever? Analysis of an international policy fashion. *Journal of Comparative Policy Analysis, 3*, 271–290.

Saurugger, S., & Radaelli, C. M. (2008). The Europeanization of public policies: Introduction. *Journal of Comparative Policy Analysis, 10*(3), 213–219.

Siné, A. (2006). *L'ordre budgétaire: l'économie politique des dépenses de l'État*. Economica.

Sineau, M. (2001). *Profession: femme politique: sexe et pouvoir sous la Cinquième République*. Presses de Sciences po.

Sześciło, D. (2022). Agencification revisited: Trends in consolidation of central government administration in Europe. *International Review of Administrative Sciences, 88*(4), 995–1012.

Urfalino, P. (1997). *L'invention de la politique culturelle*. Paris, La documentation française.

Vauchez, A., Boucobza, I., Bui-Xuan, O., Chahsiche, J. M., Lepina, T., Vargovčíková, J., & Vincensini, C. (2019). *Un champ de la régulation publique indépendante?* (Report for the Mission de recherche Droit et Justice, Paris, France).

Walby, S. (2005). Introduction: Comparative gender mainstreaming in a global era. *International Feminist Journal of Politics, 7*(4), 453–470.

Zittrain, J. (2008). *The future of the internet—And how to stop it*. Yale University Press & Penguin UK.

CHAPTER 8

Conclusion: A Multi-Faceted Digital Revolution

From the contested emergence of State intervention in "cyberspace" to the multiplication of digital regulations, Internet policies offer an original case to study the emergence of a new policy domain in contemporary bureaucracies. More broadly, they enable us to grasp the profound changes in government and economic organization that have accompanied the digital revolution. While public action in the digital world increasingly relies on well-established administrative institutions in Western countries—notably ministerial departments and regulatory authorities with expanded powers—the institutionalization of Internet policies remains largely unfinished. The actors, instruments and principles of digital government are still under construction, in line with current technological innovations, political dynamics and economic balances of power. In 2024 only, the implementation of new regulations regarding AI or regarding the spread of disinformation online shows the ever-developing role of public institutions in organizing digital markets and innovations.

Although incomplete and partially specific, the development of Internet policies in France, which has been analyzed in this book, provides a number of lessons about how nation States deal with technological change, and the part they have played in the advent of a multi-faceted "digital revolution ". This final chapter looks back at these results and suggests a number of avenues for future research.

A. Bellon, *A Socio-History of Internet Policies*, International Series on Public Policy, https://doi.org/10.1007/978-3-031-69099-0_8

1 From Pioneers to Platforms

A revolution did happen. Contrary to the preachers of bureaucratic inertia or patent libertarians who only saw nation States as the gravediggers of Internet revolutionary ideas, Western governments have made a major contribution to the digital revolution. While this revolution has often been presented as a spontaneous process, which took place without any public intervention, nation States, as we have seen, have played a central role in accompanying this phenomenon, in France as elsewhere: they have supported the development of new economic players by promoting soft-regulation on digital markets, they have urged the technological modernization of administrations and businesses alike, legitimized new models of entrepreneurship, spread a technological culture among the population, etc. The digital revolution has been imposed by the State, through the actions of a political-administrative elite anxious to preserve its role in the information society. Its contribution relied on multiple alliances with the Internet worlds, initially with Internet pioneers and activists, and now more often with major players of the digital economy. For public policies, more than simple vectors of the digital revolution , have also favored the transformation of information networks and the organization of online public spaces. Since the scientific project of a distributed architecture, the Internet has indeed been profoundly "centralized" (Zittrain, 2008), that is to say reorganized around powerful gatekeepers that accumulate the attention and the data of online users. While the Internet still allows the most expert users to circumvent or escape government control, States' capacities have paradoxically been increased with the concentration of communications and exchanges around a handful of digital firms. The latter have indeed become partners in the implementation of various public policies as well as major players in the global governance of networks. Exchanges between government bureaucracies and the management of these multinational firms, still limited until the end of the 2010s, have since gradually increased in Europe. They are reshaping public action in the twenty-first century, based on a dense configuration of interdependencies between the State and the Internet.

The political role of large tech companies calls into question the tradition of self-regulation of technical intermediaries that was in force since the end of the twentieth century. It favors a new neoliberal governmentality (Cohen, 2019) based on the principles of *compliance* and the required *transparency* of platforms as a condition of their new role in organizing and shaping online markets. These changes are epitomized by current regulatory initiatives such as the Digital Market Act and the Digital Services Act adopted in the European Union in 2022. These "new laws of the web" (Badouard, 2020) reveal the reshaping of government/ Internet relation. Without having lost its social consistency, the boundary between the Internet and the administrative worlds have thus shifted and appears more porous than ever, crossed by data exchanges or by new elites who navigate between the public affairs offices of tech companies and the expert departments of regulatory agencies. Rather than always opposing them, the ambition to embody the general interest, the imperative of transparency to the public, and the belief in digital solutions are becoming common features between State and Internet organizations.

2 From Internet to Digital Policies

Despite all these evolutions, the Internet has not been established as a separate and autonomous policy domain, marked by clear-cut institutions and the recognition of specific professional knowledge within the public administration. Rather, after twenty years of State digital action, we can observe the dilution of the category "Internet" in many sector-based digital policies. The development of Internet policies invites us to abandon the generic notion of a policy domain and to play with three closely related concepts: "causes", "sector" and "instrument". Their articulation, and their respective importance, make it possible to distinguish different configurations that characterized State action on the Internet. In the 1990s, it was common causes that cemented cross-sectorial alliances between advocates of public support for the Internet against the Minitel in France. Policies of the time reflected the influence of Internet activists and entrepreneurs in policymaking, fostering a preference for outside expertise and distributed modes of governance. Gradually, these causes were yet translated and subverted by the administrative elite to push for the modernization of the State. Digital technologies thus emerged as a core instrument of government action, designating both the technological tools through which policy are implemented and the representations associated with them (Lascoumes & Le Galès, 2007). Digital tools, from algorithms to platforms, have become the common feature of an increasingly disparate set of public policies, gathered under the banner of State modernization and improvement. From culture to security, the digitization of public policies refers to the deployment of a new governmentality based on technologically-mediated relations and the circulation of data between citizens, businesses and public institutions. Thus, digital policymakers in the State now intend to represent—that is to say stand for as well as defend—a new economic sector, that of start-ups, developers of artificial intelligence systems or content aggregators, broadly inspired by the platform model. As partners and targets of digital public intervention, they also contribute to the gradual privatization of State action (Jeannot & Cottin-Marx, 2022).

We could thus put forward the hypothesis that these hybrid forms of institutionalization, articulating political causes, instruments and sectors, more generally characterize contemporary public policies. Like digital policies, gender equality or the environment are policy domains whose institutionalization can be captured by the legitimation of activist causes and/ or the adoption of cross-cutting instruments. Facing global social and economic challenges, State agents are indeed seeking to elaborate new public action objectives (causes) by shaping relevant markets (sectors) and deploying far-reaching solutions (instruments).

3 From the Digital to the Bureaucratic Revolution

While governmental players have contributed to Internet development and the spread of technological culture throughout society, the book has shown above all the extent to which the digital revolution has been an opportunity to foster a "bureaucratic revolution" within the State. From the 2000s onward, digital technologies have become part of the modernization repertoire in administrative reform policies: with public service applications, online consultation platforms, or software to monitor the lawmaking process, State action has been profoundly *digitalized*. This concept refers as much to the use of digital technologies as to the dissemination of new modes of governance inspired by the Internet, such as the free flow of information, the networking of public services, the central role of data, the "distribution" of administrative task or the reliance on the multitude of citizens.

Of course, these transformations have been taking place unevenly across public bodies, sectors and level of government. While some public administrations are now entrusting decisions or the selection of citizens to AI—in the domains of education, social welfare or healthcare (Eubanks, 2018)—others are still using paper. Proponents of the only-digital approach and opponents of automation continue to coexist within the state bureaucracy. The latter, regarding this issue as so many others, has never been more plural, complex and divided. The bureaucratic reinterpretation of a cyberculture full of promises may well have disappointed or sidelined its most enthusiastic supporters, while other agents jumped on the bandwagon as an opportunity to maintain or establish their domination over some areas of government action. The conversion of technical expertise into bureaucratic capital was not always to the advantage of the pioneers, and old hierarchies have not disappeared in favor of a new "Internet meritocracy". Even today, developers, activists and other workers of digital policies still lament the lack of recognition they receive within large administrations and denounce the abandonment of the most disruptive projects (Alauzen, 2019).

Indeed, digital technologies are enrolled in power struggles that pit administrative agents against each other. In this sense, they do not simply reproduce intra-bureaucratic inequalities and antagonisms, but reshape them. Like the budgetary power, the digital power—which is not so much about IT expertise as about control over the development and use of technological tools in the administration—has in fact become a new means of bureaucratic control. The increased production and circulation of data within the administration have strengthened the possibilities for internal (of the State administration on itself) and external supervision (of the State on its constituents). In the bureaucratic field, the deployment of digital technologies has fostered the concentration of powers around central ministry departments, such as the Ministry of Economy, and reinforced the role of the *grand corps* in defining and implementing new rules for the regulation of digital platforms. While the digital dimension of many public policies is now widely accepted, the recognition of specific expertise or causes seems to have partly failed in favor of technocratic skills and bureaucratic capital.

4 From State to Society

The prominence of digital issues has thus favored the rise of reform-minded civil servants who obtained key positions at the head of regulatory agencies or digital departments. On the contrary, activist figures have been gradually marginalized, relegated to poorly endowed "movement institutions" (Bereni & Revillard, 2018). The latter keep on defending Internet causes within a policy process that is increasingly subject to economic or security logics. In the name of the Internet utopia, they struggle to bring a discordant, but little-heard voice to the governmental arena.

Consequently, apart from the fields of power, the digital revolution had a strong impact on the structuring of social movements. Even if Internet pioneers have expressed their disappointment and disenchantment regarding a digital revolution that neither truly democratized political participation nor decentralized the production of information, their demands have been durably inscribed in the social movement. The globalization of networks and the circulation of policy frameworks have also consolidated a vast transnational movement for the defense of rights and freedoms on the Internet, opposed to a digital technocracy represented as much by administrative bureaucracies as by Tech Giants. From scattered and short-lived organizations that characterized the 1990s, digital activism has become institutionalized and professionalized: in France, *La Quadrature du Net* appears as the figurehead of the fight against the extension of censorship and digital surveillance. Yet this professionalization also came with a more general transformation of Internet causes, which can be seen both in the motives behind mobilizations and in the alliances between Internet activists and other collectives. Defending the digital "commons", for example, has become a central motive for new coalitions between Internet activists and environmentalists, to the detriment of mobilizations on media independence and the right to communicate. The free flow of information, for its part, has recently been overshadowed by the denunciation of the privatization of information power, in the hand of hegemonic platforms. And finally, the fight against generalized surveillance is led in conjunction with civil rights associations of lawyers. Digital collectives have borrowed arguments and modes of action from these groups to legitimize their causes, increasingly taking their claims to court.[1] At the same time, the technological tools they have developed for coordination, advocacy and dissemination of

[1] For example, NOYB ("none of your business"), a European organization for digital rights created in 2017, has launched several strategic actions in front of European courts to enforce privacy regulation after the adoption of the GDPR.

information have spread beyond Internet activism, becoming a permanent feature of the repertoire of contention.

5 From France to Europe

Although based mainly on a French fieldwork, the results presented in this book should not be considered as merely specific to this country. A closer look at neighboring States shows similar trends regarding the digitization of public policies and its combination with the advent of a new governmentality in Europe.

Let's take the example of Germany. Its lead over France in terms of access to the Internet was rapidly eroded in the 2000s. In 2010, Internet use in the two countries was quite similar (roughly 80% of the population).[2] Regarding e-government activities, France, Germany and the United Kingdom, displayed similar levels of use in 2014, below Nordic countries where the digitization of the administration has been particularly rapid—more than 70% of the population of Sweden, Iceland, Denmark and Finland used the Internet to obtain information from public authorities in 2014.[3] If bureaucratic opposition to the Internet in France was partly based on the success of the Minitel at the end of the 1990s, other factors, such as the low distribution of IT knowledge in the administration, the heavy cost of e-government programs and/or the lack of coordination between administrations have also contributed to slowing down the spread of technology in Europe's large bureaucracies (Klumpp, 2002; Nixon et al., 2010). Yet, pushed by international organizations and the European Commission, the modernization of administration through digital technologies has become a common rule among member-states, fostering a global agenda for neoliberal reform. Indeed, in Western democracies, the development of the information society was largely based on the liberalization of telecommunication markets and a "soft-regulation" approach for digital markets. Besides, the digitization of public policies has been accompanied by a reconfiguration of the role of

[2] https://ec.europa.eu/eurostat/web/products-data-in-focus/-/KS-QA-10-050.

[3] Source Eurostat. The situation is a little more mixed in southern and eastern Europe. For example, some countries such as Slovenia and Slovakia are particularly advanced when it comes to deploying their public services on the Internet, while others such as Italy and Croatia are lagging behind. For a broader account of e-government policies in Europe see Nixon et al. (2010).

the State in society and the economy: a State that spends less, is more transparent, and whose intervention is based on the market. Fostered by European "better regulation" agenda and the 2001 European White Paper on Governance, this approach was more particularly chosen for the Internet, and codes of conducts or multistakeholder organizations were adopted for online content regulation.

Yet, from the 2010s onward, this approach was met with new efforts from European governments to implement a stricter control of the Internet. In the UK, the Cameron-Clegg coalition pushed for filtering systems at the ISPs level to block domains and URLs hosting copyrighted material as well as terrorism or child pornography. A few years later, Germany was the first EU member-state to implement a new regulation that directly proscribed how large platform moderated harmful content: the Network Enforcement Act or *NetzDG* (Gorwa, 2021). This initiative was quickly followed by a series of legislative initiatives in France, adopting a similar approach for the regulation of speech online, increasing the liability of platforms and establishing mandatory levels of transparency and enforcement (Badouard, 2020). These developments, anticipating the shift in platform regulation at the EU level, show the importance of studying domestic politics to understand global changes in Internet governance.

Despite these common trends, there are still some national specificities, notably regarding the functioning of domestic bureaucracies, that could explain the relative influence of some departments and professions, or the various rhythms of digital change in European countries. The main differences lie in the definition of administrative boundaries and the role devoted to specific professions within the State. In European Union countries, the Internet almost never benefited from a separate ministry department. On the contrary, digital issues have often been grouped in secondary institutions (under-secretariats or deputy ministers) and/or attached to various policy sectors, with their own logic and priorities. In countries like Germany and Sweden, digital issues are handled by the ministries of transport or energy, with an emphasis on network infrastructure development as an industrial issue. In the UK, digital development has long been the responsibility of the Department for Creative Industries and Communications, focusing on intellectual property and the content industry, as it has in France.

What the book does demonstrate, however, is the heuristic interest of a sociological approach attentive to bureaucratic politics and institutional structures, in order to understand the mechanisms of digital transformation in the State, its main obstacles and the conditions for its success. Far from having been simply imposed from above or from the outside, the digitization of public policies is underpinned by institutional enterprises, embedded in power relationships between actors and organizations that shed light on how digital instruments are appropriated, interpreted and subverted, and how the State continues to act in the digital society.

* * *

In the end, this book has aimed to offer a new perspective on the digital revolution, even if one that is circumscribed historically, geographically and sociologically. A multiple, complex and ambiguous phenomenon, the digital revolution has been the subject of numerous political, activist and academic appropriations as a category for thinking about social transformations linked to the spread of information and communication technologies. These sometimes-conflicting appropriations tend to blur its understanding as a social phenomenon inscribed in recent history: its dating—is the revolution underway or over? When did it really begin?—and above all its effects—on the economy and political life—are still under question. Instead, this book shows that the digital revolution could be understood first and foremost as the cultural and social product of those who promoted digital transformation in their own sector, field or country. We can only stress the importance of a sociological study of these entrepreneurs of the digital revolution, attentive to their beliefs, their resources and their social trajectories through various social spaces, both inside and outside national bureaucracies. This book has also made a case for reintegrating the study of the digital revolution into a set of interlocking processes. The links between the "digital revolution " and the "neo-liberal turn", already suggested by works on the intellectual history of the Internet, have been illuminated here by the articulations between State reform and the production of Internet policies. These combined dynamics reveal the political ambiguities of this revolution, which the elites of public and private bureaucracies, against whom it was initially directed, were ultimately able to seize and adapt to their own interest and logics, while remaining convinced of the need to pursue its original emancipatory ambition.

While we must continue the analysis of administrative digital transformations and the appropriation of technology within the State, this history has been stripped of its revolutionary trappings. The trivialization of Internet causes and the omnipresence of digital references in the field of government should not, however, blind us to the major reorganizations taking place in the shadow of the digitization of public action. The automation of public services, the growing use of surveillance technologies and the deployment of new regulatory tools signal a deepening of the logics uncovered in this book. The democratic stakes of government intervention in the digital world have never been higher. Far from closing a page in the history of the State and the Internet, this book hopes to open new avenues for research. It calls for the development of a sociology of digital government that is attentive to the interweaving of these technologies with the economic and social power relations they contribute to produce and modify.

References

Alauzen, M. (2019). *Plis et replis de l'État plateforme. Enquête sur la modernisation des services publics en France* (Doctoral dissertation). Université Paris sciences et lettres).

Badouard, R. (2020). *Les nouvelles lois du Web: modération et censure*. Seuil.

Bereni, L., & Revillard, A. (2018). Movement institutions: The bureaucratic sources of feminist protest. *Politics & Gender, 14*(3), 407–432.

Cohen, J. E. (2019). *Between truth and power. The Legal construction of information capitalism*. Oxford University Press.

Eubanks, V. (2018). *Automating inequality: How high-tech tools profile, police, and punish the poor*. Martin's Press.

Gorwa, R. (2021). Elections, institutions, and the regulatory politics of platform governance: The case of the German NetzDG. *Telecommunications Policy, 45*(6), 102145.

Jeannot, G., & Cottin-Marx, S. (2022). *La privatisation numérique. Déstabilisation et réinvention du service public*. Paris, Raisons d'agir.

Klumpp, D. (2002, September). From websites to e-government in Germany. In *International Conference on Electronic Government* (pp. 18–25). Springer Berlin Heidelberg.

Lascoumes, P., & Le Galès, P. (2007). Introduction: Understanding public policy through its instruments—From the nature of instruments to the sociology of public policy instrumentation. *Governance, 20*(1), 1–21.

Nixon, P. G., Koutrakou, V. N., & Rawal, R. (Eds.). (2010). *Understanding e-government in Europe: Issues and challenges*. Routledge.

Zittrain, J. R. (2008). *The future of internet—And how to stop it* (p. 352). Yale University Press.

Index

A. Bellon, *A Socio-History of Internet Policies*, International Series on Public Policy, https://doi.org/10.1007/978-3-031-69099-0

V

W

The manufacturer's authorised representative in the EU is Springer Nature Customer Service Centre GmbH, Europaplatz 3, 69115 Heidelberg, Germany. If you have any concerns regarding our products, please contact ProductSafety@springernature.com

Printed and bound by CPI Group (UK) Ltd, Croydon, CR0 4YY

01/10/2026

02225953-0005